for
Saenvih,
a journey both spiritual
& political.
Enjoy!
Mai Aunty

the LIVES *of* FREDA

The Political, Spiritual
and Personal Journeys
of Freda Bedi

ANDREW WHITEHEAD

SPEAKING
TIGER

SPEAKING TIGER PUBLISHING PVT. LTD
4381/4, Ansari Road, Daryaganj
New Delhi 110002

Published in paperback by Speaking Tiger 2019

ISBN: 978-93-88070-75-1
eISBN: 978-93-88070-76-8

10 9 8 7 6 5 4 3 2 1

Typeset in Adobe Caslon Pro

Printed at Shree Maitrey Printech Pvt. Ltd., Noida

For Anu, who crossed cultures and countries

Contents

Introduction

When Freda Houlston confided that she was going to marry the handsome Sikh student she'd been seeing, her best friend, Barbara Castle, replied: 'Well, thank goodness. Now at least you won't become a suburban housewife!' Freda's mother was exactly that—a housewife in the suburbs of Derby in the English Midlands. It would have been natural, expected indeed, for her daughter to fall into that same groove. In fact, Freda refused to fit into any groove. She broke the mould—not once, but repeatedly through the decades. In a world where issues of identity—bound up in race, gender, religion and nationality—loom so large, the manner in which she crossed these boundaries speaks directly to us today.

'It was my destiny to go to India,' Freda declared. And from the moment of her marriage to B.P.L. Bedi at a registry office in Oxford in the summer of 1933, she regarded herself as Indian and adopted Indian dress. It would be another year or more before she set foot on Indian soil. By the time she disembarked at Bombay (now Mumbai), twenty-three years old and with her baby son in her arms, she had already co-edited with her husband four volumes about the country she was to make her home.

She lived for two-thirds of her life in India, adopted its national cause and customs, and took an Indian passport. She served a prison sentence in Lahore as part of Gandhi's protests against an Imperial power which happened to be her motherland. She was an English champion of Indian nationalism. Freda Bedi delighted in confounding accepted definitions of identity. She could not easily be categorised and saw no reason why she should be. 'One day she was standing in the Lahore Post Office buying stamps,' said her publishers. 'An American looked at her blue eyes and Punjabi dress, and his curiosity broke the bonds of formality. Walking up to her, he asked: "Excuse me, are you English?" She smiled and said: "I am—and I am not."'

Her spiritual journey was as profound and remarkable. She was church-going as a youngster but by the time she enrolled at St Hugh's College, Oxford, in 1929, she no longer regarded herself as a Christian and never returned to the faith she was born into. She encountered Buddhism in Burma in her early forties, and a few years later her endeavours to help Tibetan refugees marked her most intense moment of illumination. The solace she found in Tibetan Buddhism emboldened her to enrol, in the mid-1960s when such adventures in eastern religions were rare for western women, as a novice nun. A few years later, she took full ordination—the first western woman to do so in Tibetan Buddhism, and quite possibly the first woman in the Tibetan tradition ever to receive this higher level of initiation. She went on to perform two remarkable services which helped Tibetan Buddhists adapt to exile—recognising and meeting the need to educate young incarnate lamas, giving them the skills and confidence to find new audiences; and persuading her guru, the 16th Karmapa Lama, one of the highest Tibetan lamas, to make a pioneering rock star-style tour of the west in 1974 to spread Buddhist teachings and accompanying him on this five-month peregrination across North America and Europe.

Freda challenged barriers of gender as well as of nation and religion. When she was born women did not have the vote in British Parliamentary elections; Oxford University's first woman professor

(Agnes Headlam-Morley, who had been one of Freda's tutors) was appointed fully fifteen years after Freda graduated; the Church of England, the church into which she was confirmed, ordained no women priests or deacons in England in her lifetime. Her own prominence in politics and religion, and her pioneering role in women's education and journalism, is made more exceptional by the exclusion of women for much of the twentieth century from large areas of public endeavour.

Throughout her life, Freda constantly reinvented herself. There was a restless, questing, aspect to her alongside the discipline and compassion. She was a woman of faith—but one who was an active leftist before alighting on the religion which came to define her. She must have been rare among nuns in once having drilled, rifle on her shoulder, in a people's militia. Yet the three big ruptures of her life—from a provincial town to a women's college at Oxford University, from England to India, and from welfare work to ordination as a nun—were not a repudiation of her past. Thirty years after she left Derby, girls at her old school were collecting money for a new school Freda was setting up in the Himalayan foothills for young Tibetan lamas. Her best friends at Oxford remained in touch all her life, even once she was in holy orders. While wearing the maroon robes of a nun and with her head shaved, visitors sometimes commented how quintessentially English she still seemed.

Her life was shaped by two tragic deaths—that of her father on the First World War battlefields, and of her second child while still a baby when Freda had lived less than two years in India. There was an emotional vulnerability evident from her childhood onwards. And a steely determination too—once she had decided on a course of action, she saw it through.

Freda and Bedi's marriage was a heart-warming, insurgent romance, a defiance of convention, and an intellectual and political collaboration. The couple were, in Freda's life-affirming words, 'two students in love, refusing to recognise the barriers of race and colour, dissolving their religious differences into a belief in a common Good, united in their love of justice and freedom ... a marriage based on everything that was good in us.' But it wasn't always an easy marriage. Her husband was, in the arresting phrase of their US-resident daughter, 'a chick magnet'—and the issues within Freda's marriage must have had some influence on her pursuit of a spiritual life, taking vows which required celibacy as well as meditation and renunciation.

This is not an official biography. The initiative to write this book rested with me; I had come across mention of Freda Bedi while delving into the story of Kashmiri nationalism and had met a handful of people with vivid memories of her. As I found out more about her, the parallels with my own life captured my attention: from a northern grammar school to Oxford; on the left; married to an Indian; with India-born children; and deeply engaged with Kashmir and its troubled politics. There are plenty of points of contrast too—in particular, I am not a Buddhist—but the manner in which Freda moved comfortably across those frosted barriers of race and nation, and identified herself so completely with her adopted country and culture, galvanised my interest. This is not simply a story of how Freda Bedi became a Buddhist nun, and what she did while wearing those maroon robes; her earlier life is not recounted here simply as a prelude to a pre-ordained vocation. This is a life story which explores the personal, the political and the immersion in India, as well as that last spiritual arc of her life.

This would be a much lesser book without the encouragement of the Bedi family—their willingness to talk openly about their parents, and to allow access to their remarkable archive of letters, documents and photographs. All three of Freda's surviving children—Ranga, Kabir and Gulhima—are fiercely proud of their mother. Ranga Bedi, the oldest by more than a decade, kept in touch with many of his parents' old friends. Kabir Bedi, a big figure in cinema and TV, at one time intended to make a film about his mother. So they have been purposeful in assembling a family archive—much more than a biographer has any reason to expect. A collection of letters received is always helpful—a series of letters sent is a rare and invaluable bonus. Towards the close of her life, Olive Chandler, one of Freda's Oxford friends, gave to the Bedi family a lovingly kept file of letters, postcards, and Bedi family newsletters received over almost half-a-century—an extraordinary window on a remarkable life.

'You do know about the recordings?' Kabir Bedi asked as I was taking my leave after my initial interview with him about his parents. I didn't. A year or two before she died, Sister Palmo—as she was then known—came to visit Ranga and his family in Calcutta. She had bought a cassette recorder and used this to make a series of recordings reflecting particularly on the first thirty years of her life. She made extensive notes, which the family still has, and then talked directly into the microphone—haltingly at first, and then with increasing fluency and intimacy as she got into her stride. These tapes were made, no doubt, for her family—to satisfy their curiosity about her personal story. As you might expect of a nun in her sixties looking back over her life with her grandchildren in mind, her recorded memories tended to privilege the spiritual over the political and to gloss over the episodes of personal anguish. Nevertheless, these tapes stretching over several hours have informed this biography more than any other source of information. They provide an intimacy, a closeness of contact, which would otherwise be inconceivable. They also offer an answer to questions that inevitably worry the biographer: did Freda keep a regional accent, for instance? (She didn't.)

While two of Freda's closest Oxford friends became household names in Britain—Olive Shapley as a much loved broadcaster and Barbara Castle as the most successful woman politician of her era—she is not as widely celebrated. Indeed in the country of her birth, she remains an unfamiliar name. In India, she was a friend and colleague of such towering figures as Jawaharlal Nehru and Kashmir's Sheikh Abdullah and a confidante of Nehru's daughter,

Indira Gandhi. She features in a group photograph taken in 1945 which includes three future prime ministers of India and two of Indian Kashmir. But here too, the range of her endeavour and influence is largely unacknowledged.

Freda Bedi demands a biography not so much because of her fame, or the big jobs she held, or her political impact or institutional legacy, but because of the way she lived her life. She was no saint and never pretended to be, and at times she made difficult decisions which hurt those around her. She constantly crossed borders—not simply national borders, but also those less tangible lines which divide on the basis of faith, ethnicity and sex. In Freda's lifetime, these lines were more deeply etched than they are today—but they remain deep social and political fault lines, and for those who wish to bridge them, Freda's life and achievements are astonishing, indeed inspiring.

Timeline

1909 Dec 2   Freda's parents, Nellie Harrison and Frank Houlston, marry in Derby

1911 Feb 2   Freda is born at home at Monk Street in Derby

1918 Apr 14   Frank Houlston dies in northern France during the First World War

1920 Sept 18   Nellie Houlston marries again, to Frank Swan

1929 Oct   Freda enrols at St Hugh's College, Oxford

1933 June 21   She marries a fellow student, B.P.L. Bedi, at Oxford Registry Office

1934 May 13   Their first child, Ranga Bedi, is born in Berlin

1935 Nov 28   Tilak Zaheer Bedi is born in Lahore—he dies the following summer

1940 Dec 4   B.P.L. Bedi is detained indefinitely for anti-war activities

1941 Feb 21   Freda is jailed after courting arrest as a protest against the war effort

1946 Jan 16   Kabir Bedi is born in Lahore

1949 Sept 15   Gulhima Bedi, the Bedis' only daughter, is born in Srinagar

1953   Freda encounters Buddhism on a UN assignment in Burma

1958	Aug	Freda's mother-in-law, Bhabooji, dies
1961	Oct	She establishes the Young Lamas' Home School in Delhi
1966	July 14	Her mother, Nellie Swan, dies
1966	Aug 1	Freda is ordained as a Buddhist nun by the 16th Karmapa Lama
1968	Nov 17	Her brother Jack Houlston dies aged 56
1972	July	Freda, now Sister Palmo, takes full bhiksuni ordination in Hong Kong
1977	Mar 26	She dies in Delhi aged 66
1989	Dec 10	Berinder Dewan, the Bedis' adopted son, dies aged 57
1993	Mar 31	B.P.L. 'Baba' Bedi dies in Italy aged 84

Tibetan Buddhist Terms

Freda Bedi, when a Buddhist, often bestowed the 'blessings of the Triple Gem'—a reference to the three jewels or refuges of Buddhism: the 'Buddha', meaning both the historical founder of the faith and the full enlightenment he achieved; the 'Dharma', the teachings of the Buddha; and the 'Sangha', the community of lamas, monks and nuns pursuing the Dharma, or sometimes more broadly all those following the Buddhist path.

A 'lama' is a spiritual teacher or senior religious practitioner; a 'guru' is a personal spiritual guide—the relationship between student and guru is central to Tibetan Buddhism; a 'tulku' is a recognised incarnation of a high lama; and 'rinpoche' is an honorific term indicating reverence and spiritual authority. While monastic practice is central to Tibetan Buddhism, many tulkus and rinpoches choose not to pursue a monastic life.

A Tibetan Buddhist nun would normally be addressed as 'anila' or 'ani'; 'getsulma' signifies a novice nun and 'bhiksuni' or 'gelongma' denotes full ordination.

Prologue

Putting on the Robes

It was the biggest decision of her life, the one for which she is most remembered, but Freda Bedi didn't tell her children that she was being ordained as a Buddhist nun. There was no family council, no private conversation, not even, it seems, a letter to announce her intention.

She may have been thinking back thirty years or more to the time she made the journey from Oxford to the family home in Derby in the English Midlands. Her mission then was to tell her mother that she intended to marry her Punjabi boyfriend. It hadn't gone well. The strain of persisting with that romance in the face of disapproval from her family and college had precipitated a breakdown. Nellie was quickly reconciled to her daughter's marriage—though less so to the thousands of miles that came to separate her from her family in India. Freda could well have had all that churning in her mind as she prepared to take her vows, laden with a profound sense of loss: her mother died just two weeks before the ordination.

So at this second crucial juncture of her life, Freda decided to act first—and to let her children know simply by appearing in her nun's robes and with her head shaved. It didn't go well.

'There was this terrible feeling of betrayal,' Kabir Bedi recalls. It was 1966 and the height of the Delhi summer. Kabir was twenty, a student at one of India's most prestigious university colleges, St Stephen's, and still recovering from a broken back. Handsome and

confident, he was dabbling in modelling and broadcasting which were
to be his entry points to a successful career in film. He understood
that Buddhism loomed increasingly large in his mother's life, but
hadn't been prepared for her ordination as a nun.

'I was living in a hostel and I was told that Mummy's come in to
town and would I go and see her.' She was staying in Nizamuddin, a
middle-class corner of Delhi, with a close family member who Kabir
regarded as an uncle. 'I went there and I suddenly saw her and she
had shaved her hair and she was in Tibetan Buddhist robes. Firstly,
there was the shock of seeing her like that, and secondly was this
feeling of betrayal that she hadn't told me before she did it. I had
been so close to her in her journey to Buddhism, everything she went
through, that for her to do something like that without telling me
was incomprehensible to me.'

He was angry and said so. Why? he demanded of his mother;
why now? He still remembers her response. '"It is something I felt
I had to do and I knew if I started discussing it with everybody,
God knows what might have happened."' Kabir was seven when
his mother found Buddhism while on a United Nations mission
to Burma (now Myanmar). He had accompanied her back there
when she studied meditation, and had himself enrolled briefly as a
novitiate. He had worn the robes and shaved off his hair—in much
the same manner as his mother had now done. He had spent time
with his mother at the camps in Assam set up for the Tibetans who
fled across the mountains to escape Chinese rule—that's where she
first became immersed in Tibetan belief and culture. He had taught
at the Young Lamas' Home School she established. It had felt like
a shared journey. Now Freda, Sister Palmo as she became known,
had decided to press on alone. 'I raised all the silly arguments I
could think of: your daughter's still in college, she's not married,
how's she going to manage? All silly things. But basically, I was
angry because I felt betrayed. There was a terrible sense of loss. It's
like, you've lost your mother.'

Gulhima, Kabir's sister, was a tempestuous sixteen-year-old. She had just finished boarding school in the north Indian hills—a Tibetan girl, one of those Freda had taken under her wing, was among her fellow pupils there. Guli was close to both her parents—but her mother and father no longer lived together. Freda spent much of her time at the lamas' school in Dalhousie, a day or more's travel north of Delhi; Bedi, an exuberant and increasingly outlandish character, had a new household. Guli regarded Kabir, and her oldest brother Ranga and his wife Umi, as her 'rocks'—she stayed with them during school holidays.

She found out about her mother's ordination from Kabir. 'I came to his place at the weekends, and it was a funny way that he broke the news to me. He said: "one thing you will never have to worry about again is to buy Mummy a comb." I said: "what on earth do you mean?" He said: "she couldn't tell you herself—she wanted me to tell you."' Gulhima was furious—both about her mother's decision and about how she was told of it. 'I had no problem about her becoming a Buddhist but when she became a nun I felt abandoned. I didn't like that she had become a nun and didn't have the guts to tell me—she didn't want a scene and knew that there would be one.'

Ranga, then in his early thirties and living with his family on a tea estate in Assam, was more understanding. 'There wasn't any warning,' he says, 'and yet I think there were signs on the horizon.' Freda had told her husband of her intention to become a nun. According to the family, he wept—but gave his blessing. She had taken informal vows from her teacher, the 16th Karmapa Lama, three years earlier and had lived a celibate life for still longer. The romance of the marriage had faded as had the political comradeship, and Freda and Bedi took strikingly divergent spiritual paths in middle age—but the bonds forged in Oxford, Lahore and Srinagar remained strong, and her husband's understanding and support was important to her.

Freda received her ordination from the 16th Karmapa Lama on 1st August 1966 amid the splendour of Rumtek monastery in

Sikkim, five-thousand-feet up in the foothills of the Himalayas.
The religious centre dated from the eighteenth century, but was in
ruins when the Karmapa Lama—having fled across the mountains
to escape China's occupation of Tibet—chose it as his new base.
It was officially inaugurated as his seat on the Tibetan New Year
in 1966. Sikkim was a small princely state bordering Tibet under
Indian suzerainty, and was fully integrated into India—much to
China's indignation—only in 1975.

A few days after the ceremony, still at Rumtek, Freda received
what was clearly an anguished letter from Kabir. Manorma Dewan
was part of the extended family—her husband's flat was the venue
of Kabir's meeting with his newly-robed mother—and remembers
the central message of that letter: 'you have become very selfish'.
Manorma agreed with that view. 'I personally thought: Guli is still
very young; she should have thought about her. I told my husband.
I personally thought it is OK to become a nun but you have to take
care of your children.'

Freda replied immediately by telegram, and followed that up with
a three-page handwritten missive to her 'darling son'. Kabir still has
that letter. 'I have been in a maze of pain, feeling your and Guli's,'
she wrote. 'You all knew one day this step would be taken; we even
joked about my losing my hair! Somehow, now had to be the time.
The inner renunciation was complete long ago.' It was a deeply
personal and impassioned plea to her son for acceptance. 'I did not
want to dramatise it, write + tell you. I can't write about things so
deep inside—they are beyond words. Speaking is a little easier (I
told Papa) but paper does not really convey the necessity—not just
for me, but for all of you too. But I did feel—still feel—that you
would understand.'

The newly-ordained nun's shock and bewilderment in the face
of Kabir's broadside was unmistakable. She sought to reassure him
that she was still there for her children.

Things are the same, at least outwardly, except for my dress. We will meet + spend holidays together as usual. Mother love doesn't just dry up. I can still see your little face as it was when you drank my milk + Guli on her first birthday, with that full moon face of hers. You needed me then; you need me now. I am still there. If Papa at any time needs me in advancing age, I am also still there…

I thought that, with that special understanding we all have for one another, the birth could be painless. But I had not realised that the cutting of the birth cord <u>must</u> cause pain. It heals. The link between the baby and the Mother does not cease. It continues. Nothing ceases. In a way, this time I am The baby. And I <u>need</u> you all, your love + protection, even physical help, even if in another way.

She wrote of the loss of her mother—the English grandmother her children hardly knew. 'I am sure all the prayers are helping her … I saw her in my dream.' And she assured Kabir and Gulhima, 'you are both near, like the blood in my veins.' Freda had ample emotional intelligence. It was not on best display in the method by which she revealed her new vocation to her children. This letter was an attempt to make amends.

If there was a quality which Freda Bedi possessed in still greater abundance, it was determination. She had thought hard about her decision to become a nun, and there was no hint in her letter to Kabir of doubt or regret. 'To take an ordination in direct line from the Buddha is an inexpressibly sacred thing. In a way an ordination is not only a renunciation: it is a protection, + way.' It was the way she had chosen for herself, shaped by her immersion in Buddhist teaching and in the lives of the young Tibetan incarnate lamas she had helped to mould. She wanted her family on board—but the decision was not open to negotiation or reconsideration.

For a woman who had earlier been an advocate of communism, it's tempting to suggest that she replaced one faith with another. Tempting, but wrong. As with so many of those won over to the communist cause during the dark decade of the 1930s and the world war that followed, Freda's impulse was moral and ethical rather than ideological. Bedi was a much more committed communist, a party man who enjoyed the intrigue and bravado that went along with allegiance to a semi-clandestine movement, and for a few years she joined in largely out of loyalty to her husband. Her embrace of India's national cause, again born out of a keen sense of justice and equity, was much deeper rooted—and more abiding. She was furiously busy and much celebrated as an apostle of Indian nationalism. Once independence was achieved, the absence of that sense of purpose must have left a void, as would the waning of her marriage and the increasing self-reliance of her children. Freda's decision to become a nun was a spiritual one, a resolution of a quest evident since her childhood, but the public and personal rhythms of her life made that act of renunciation easier.

Kabir says he came to terms with his mother's decision within a matter of weeks. Guli took a little longer to come round. The anger and hurt was replaced by respect and pride. Freda was as good as her word, she was still there for her children: counselling Kabir through his at times turbulent love life; being at Guli's side as she gave birth; and coming back from religious trips abroad with what Ranga describes as 'frilly-fancy' clothes and Marks and Spencer underwear for his young daughters.

Her renunciation was also an abdication of the financial support to her family—not that she had been able to help them all that much in the previous few years. Towards the end of her deeply emotional letter to her son, Freda turned to the pedestrian matter of money. 'Kabir, I don't forget all your financial worries too. Your bravery in facing them, + your determination not to worry me with them are something very special. Thank you from the bottom of my heart.'

When Freda had given up her job with the Indian government to work with Tibetan refugees, she also forsook her government salary. Her husband had never had a regular income apart from his five years working in Kashmir. The family were skint and Freda had to call on favours from friends in high places to help her younger children through college. 'Has Guli's scholarship come through from Auntie Indu?' she enquired of Kabir in that same letter. Auntie Indu was Indira Gandhi.

Two years after her ordination, Freda went on a year-long retreat at Rumtek. There she was visited by her old Oxford friend, Olive Shapley, who had become a much-loved voice of BBC radio. Olive brought with her a portable tape recorder, and recorded an interview—apparently never broadcast—about Freda's spiritual journey and all she had given up when she became ordained.

'You see, I have no regrets at all,' the nun insisted, 'because what had to be given up is given up. It fell off naturally—as I say, like an apple falling off a tree. And we don't have to give up loving those who are near and dear to us. We have to give up attachment, which is a different thing. To be attached is a great burden not only for you personally but for the people to whom you are attached. Love is the great thing—and that doesn't change ... So if I have caused any suffering to my children I'm very sorry about it. And I think they understand that. But by the blessings of the Triple Gem'—a reference to the three key aspects of Buddhist belief—'everything has gone on ever so well since I left and the older brothers take more interest in their sister and things like that. But I think there's no loss, in fact I think there's a gain. It's impossible to explain this to anybody but I think when you go around India and you see my family, I think you will understand.'

Olive did understand and was supportive of her friend's decision—she would hardly have made the long journey to Rumtek, with her sons in tow, if it had been otherwise. She had known B.P.L. Bedi at Oxford and hadn't been too impressed by him, so may not have been surprised that Freda was ploughing her own furrow. Olive's own allegiances had in some ways echoed her friend's—a much fiercer though transient commitment to communism, and a more distant interest in the East and its belief systems. Sitting in a small room at the monastery, Olive asked with deceptive innocence: now what has brought you here? Sister Palmo began at the beginning. 'Well, I was born in Derby,' she replied. 'And funnily enough in a place called Monk Street.'

That's where we should now head.

1

The Suicide Club

Freda Houlston's childhood was suffused with a sense of absence and loss. She was happy, cared for and loved. The household was, if not at all prosperous, then comfortable. She liked its semi-rural location on what was then the outskirts of Derby in the East Midlands. But she missed her Dad. When she was five, her father, Frank, went to war. He never came back. He ended up serving in the Machine Gun Corps, where the rate of attrition was exceptionally high. Frank Houlston was killed on active service in the spring of 1918 and is buried in one of the war cemeteries in northern France where so many of his generation lie.

Freda had only the haziest recollections of her father—what she called flash memories of seeing him digging in the garden, or playing with her in the sitting room; she both could and couldn't remember him. The family photo collection has a fine portrait of Frank Houlston in military uniform. This can't be too long before his death as his cap bears the crossed-machine guns badge of the Corps. Alongside the posed childhood photos of Freda and her younger brother, there's a particularly striking family shot, professionally taken, of Nellie in a long black dress, probably in mourning. Freda is wearing an elaborate white summer dress, a large ribbon in her hair, and is reading a book; her brother, perched on a plinth, is in a sailor's suit. There are no photos of Freda with her father.

'This death shadowed my whole childhood,' Freda reminisced many years later. She came to regard the concept of fatherhood as 'somehow very sacred'. As a girl, she found the annual Poppy Day memorials for the war dead harrowing because they would 'open the wound again and again, so that I almost fainted many times at school when this service was being held.'[1] Frank Houlston's name is inscribed on the war memorial in the grounds of St Peter's parish church in Littleover. He worshipped there and was a 'staunch' member of the congregation. His death turned his wife against religion. Nellie Houlston was left a widow while still in her twenties, with two young children to bring up. She stopped going to church and abandoned any belief in the God that she believed had abandoned her. But in deference to what she knew would have been her husband's wishes, she sent her children to church and to Sunday School. The void that the absence of her father created pushed Freda towards what was the defining aspect of her life, a restless personal quest which culminated almost fifty years later in her ordination as a Buddhist nun. And her childhood involvement in the parish church offered her an initial glimpse of the spiritual—of saints' lives, valour and suffering, and the power of prayer and meditation.

Freda recalled that her childhood home had on the wall a large copy of the popular painting by the Victorian-era artist, W.F. Yeames, harking back to the English Civil War of the 1640s: 'And when did you last see your father?' In the canvas a young boy from an imaginary Royalist family is being questioned by a panel of soldiers from Cromwell's army. The viewer's sympathy rests with the upright young child, faced by the enemies of his absent father, and troubled about competing loyalties to family and to truth. Freda remembered being taught the boy's supposed response to his interrogators: 'I saw him last night in my dream.' The choice of living room artwork might seem insensitive but was clearly an attempt to honour a missing father.

Freda's mother's rejection of religion was more striking because she met her husband at church. They were both at that time Methodists, and married at the Primitive Methodists' Bourne Chapel in Derby, now demolished but then a spacious and imposing place of worship. Freda's paternal grandparents were members of the congregation there. Primitive Methodism was an austere and unadorned form of non-conformist religious practice which appealed particularly to the respectable and aspiring working class. It preached discipline and thrift and encouraged a radical outlook on life. It was the faith into which Freda was born, and some at least of her social and political attitudes must have been imbibed from this tradition which challenged both political deference and social injustice.

The Houlston family was part of an artisan tradition—skilled workers who sometimes ran their own distinctly modest businesses—which stretched back to before the large engineering, rail and printing plants that came to define Derby's economy. Freda's grandfather John Houlston—a determined teetotaller who lived until almost eighty—was a watchmaker and jeweller. He was both craftsman and shopkeeper, repairing and selling watches. Freda believed that he had been a migrant from continental Europe—though the census records suggest, more prosaically, that he was born in Birmingham. In the audio recordings Freda made when in her sixties, she suggested that both her parents' families had their origins in, or links to, Europe: to Germany, France, perhaps Italy. She suggested the family name may have been a corruption of Holstein, a region in northern Germany. It's as if she was fashioning a narrative of border crossings which helped to set the scene for her own repeated crossing of boundaries—geographic, racial, religious.

A photograph still in the family shows John Houlston with workman's apron, jacket and cloth cap at the door of his premises in King Street, a short walk from the centre of Derby. By his side, conspicuously smartly dressed and ill-at-ease in front of the camera, is a boy of perhaps nine or ten. This is Frank, Freda's father; the picture appears to date from the 1890s. The shop is strikingly basic: the watches are displayed not in a shop window but what is little more than a front parlour window of an ordinary terraced house; the cramped signboard above the window bears the shopkeeper's surname and nothing more. 'It was a tiny place, a little jeweller's and watchmaker's shop, as attractive to us'—Freda commented, looking back on her childhood—'as the Old Curiosity Shop.'[2]

Frank and his brother both followed in their father's footsteps, earning a livelihood as watch repairers and jewellers. Frank was twenty-four when he married Nellie Harrison, the daughter of a local coal merchant. She was still a teenager and described on the marriage certificate as a photographer. Frank seems initially to have set up a shop in a mining village outside Nottingham, but it didn't fare well and he moved back to Derby and established a watch and jeweller's business on Monk Street. This was an altogether grander shop than his father's. While John had worn working clothes to be photographed at the shop doorway, Frank posed in tie and waistcoat; his name was painted on the glass; the windows were well stocked. This gave every impression of being the shop-front of a substantial business. In social terms, the Houlston family appeared to be making its way. Frank was renting the shop, but in the census returns he insisted on recording that he was an employer as well as a shopkeeper and craftsman. By the time Freda was born—on 5th February 1911— Frank and Nellie had moved to a bigger shop a few doors away at 28 Monk Street. This offered better accommodation for a young family in a sharply angled corner property with an unconventional layout. It was two houses as one, with two front doors on different streets, a double shop-front and living space above.

Freda Marie Houlston was born at home in that 'tiny shop in the heart of old Derby', as she remembered it. It's still there, now a tanning salon looking out on the barren vista of a car park and dual carriageway which have cut Monk Street in two. The far section of Monk Street and adjoining terraces have survived largely unscathed in what is now, and was then, a working-class locality. The corner shops and pubs, the back alleys, the workshop yards, are all still evident, if some way from flourishing. Walking those streets is the closest you can get to communing with the Derby into which Freda was born. By the time her brother Jack came along the following year, the family had moved to Littleover, a neat Derby suburb—and another step up in the world. During the First World War, they were living on Wade Avenue, in a home distinctly grander than the city centre terraced streets. It was also a safer place to live during the war. There was just one Zeppelin bombing raid on Derby which caused casualties, but the rail and engineering works were obvious potential targets, and Freda had distant childhood memories of hearing a wartime bomb drop on the city. By the time they moved, Frank had also changed his religious allegiance from Methodism to the Church of England—whether this was convenience, or religious conviction or a sense that the established church was better suited to his rising social status is unclear.

Frank Houlston didn't enlist immediately but was called up towards the end of 1916. He served initially in the locally-recruited Sherwood Foresters and later as a private in the Machine Gun Corps. When the war started, each infantry battalion had a couple of machine gun teams attached to it. The sickening slaughter on the Western Front persuaded the British army that they needed to deploy machine guns in larger units and with more expert soldiers. The Corps was established in October 1915 and gained a reputation for heroism—the guns were often placed well in advance of the front line—and for heavy casualties. So heavy that the Corps became known as the Suicide Club. Of the 170,500 officers and men who served in the Corps during the war, more than 12,000 were killed and another 50,000 wounded. Frank died on 14th April 1918 and is buried along with almost a thousand other combatants at the Aire Communal Cemetery neat St Omer. He left behind children aged seven and five.

War had brought a profound rupture to the Houlston family. Frank's enlistment and death prompted his widow, reluctantly, to take a more active role in the business and her mother was brought in to help look after the children. Eventually Freda's uncle took on the Monk Street shop—it remained in family ownership for another half-a-century. Still more unsettling for Freda and Jack, two years after her husband's death, Nellie Houlston married again. The Swan family were neighbours in Wade Avenue. Frank Swan, a railway clerk, lived with three older unmarried sisters. He was in his mid-thirties and clearly cossetted and set in his ways. 'It was not a marriage of two young lovers,' Freda commented. 'Only when he saw my mother as a young widow with two children did it occur to him that it would perhaps be a good idea for him [to marry] and somehow the marriage was arranged.'[3] Freda described her stepfather as good natured and affectionate, but he seems not to have been much involved in her and her brother's upbringing and was preoccupied with country walks and amateur opera and dramatics. Nellie took her new husband's name; her children did not.

There were no children of Nellie's second marriage. And the family's upwards social mobility continued—eased, it seems, by family money. Nellie took up golf, with notable success, getting to and from the course by motorbike—which in the inter-war years must have marked her out as daring. That independence of spirit was passed on to her daughter, who also at one point in her life travelled to work in Delhi on a scooter. The family eventually moved to a newly-built detached house on one of Derby's most desirable streets, Keats Avenue in Mickleover. The big attraction for Nellie, who took a particular interest in the design of the house, was its location—overlooking the golf course.

For Freda, Wade Avenue was the childhood home which stayed in her memories. Unlikely as it seems now, she says that Littleover provided a country childhood. She remembered the laburnum, lilac and pear trees in the garden, and the rural walks with her brother over to Mickleover. Her mother was a good cook and inventive seamstress, and she and her brother felt well looked after. 'I was dressed up in white needlework dresses threaded with blue ribbons,' she related; 'one of her accomplishments was that she was an extremely clever tailor in a domestic setting and especially good at making clothes for small children.' These memories—recorded at the close of her life, when she was at peace spiritually—may be a little rose tinted. But alongside the devastation at the loss of her father, she clearly had happy recollections of home, family and locality. The only other big cloud over her childhood was a bout of diptheria which she was fortunate to survive.

At school, Freda shone brightly. She went to a small fee-paying school, Hargrave House, then on to Derby's leading girls' school, Parkfields Cedars, and in this small pond—there were fewer than five hundred pupils—she excelled. The school magazine is a roll call of Freda's achievements. She routinely was joint winner of her form prize; she contributed poems and articles; she won a municipal prize for an essay on health; she was one of three girls who got honours in her School Certificate exams; she was on the committee responsible for the magazine; she was an additional prefect; and in her final year at school, she was head prefect.

She loved the school, which she described as 'in an old colonial building, whitewashed, and it had two cedar trees outside just above the tennis courts.' (It no longer survives—burnt down in an arson attack.) The teachers were kind and dedicated, and her French teacher in particular was nurturing and encouraging. She played golf occasionally and learned ballroom dancing, but she was above all a studious pupil. Every year, a handful of girls from Parkfields Cedars went on to university, but admissions to Oxford and Cambridge were rare. Freda hadn't intended to apply. She was persuaded by a school friend to keep her company in studying for and sitting the Oxford entrance exams. Freda was called for interview; her friend wasn't. She didn't get a place, but was told that if she spent some time in France she had a good chance of being admitted to study modern languages the following year.

It would have been no small matter for a seventeen-year-old schoolgirl to live abroad without any family at hand, but Freda's mother was supportive, and Freda herself showed the courage and initiative evident throughout her life. With the help of a pen friend, she managed to get a place, at no cost, at a high school in the cathedral city of Reims. It was close enough to the First World War battlefields to be able to visit her father's grave, 'overgrown with cat mint and Dorothy Perkins roses'.[4] She stayed with her friend's family and for a while in a boarders' hostel, and in spite of being homesick and deciding that her love of the French language didn't extend to its spoken form ('I couldn't stand the noise, the sound of French voices'), the confidence and experience she gained served its purpose; she secured admission to Oxford at the second attempt. Indeed, she left Parkfields Cedars with a clarion call of academic distinction: a state scholarship, a county major scholarship in which she was placed third in the county as well as a place at Oxford—awards which bore prestige and more importantly ensured the Freda had sufficient money to take up the place she had secured. Two Oxford women's colleges competed for her favour. She 'has been offered admission to Somerville College, and an exhibition [minor scholarship] at St Hugh's College,' reported the *Derby Daily Telegraph*. 'She has chosen the latter.'[5]

There are only a few straws from Freda's school-going years which point to her later involvement in politics. In February 1929, she spoke on behalf of France at a model assembly of the League of Nations held at Derby Central Hall. Parkfields Cedars had a flourishing school branch of the League of Nations Union, an organisation which often proved to be a stepping stone towards the organised left. What she saw of deprivation in the poorer parts of the city left its mark on her. 'I can still remember the days when children in our slums in Derby used to run around with bare feet because they had no shoes,' she recalled almost half-a-century later. 'Incredibly undernourished babies used to be seen in the hands of utterly incompetent mothers.'[6]

Her spiritual interests were more evident. She was confirmed at St Peter's—though she had no great liking for the minister there, nicknamed Brown Owl because of his hooked nose and spectacles. She read Anglo-Catholic literature as well as lives of the saints and enjoyed taking Holy Communion: 'a direct communication, a sense of awe in the face of the divine.' Many years later, she recalled to her fellow Buddhist Sheila Fugard that she visited a local Anglican church for solitary contemplation—often St Peter's, but perhaps also on occasions the more timeworn St Edmund's at Allestree or maybe the elegant All Saints in the heart of the city which had gained cathedral status in 1927.[7] 'The only thing I could think of was to get away into the church when no one was there, when it was quiet,' she told a radio interviewer several decades later. 'So I tipped away from home in the early morning before school hours, and during the last two years at school I used to sit in church at home and just wait. There was a prayer in my heart certainly.'[8] But she was repelled by the humdrum life of the local parish church in Littleover with its 'obsession with church fetes and meetings and services and an utter lack of understanding of anything connected with the spiritual life in its deeper sense ... I realised that Brown Owl's sermons and all the things that went on in the church had just no meaning for me at all.' By the time she headed to Oxford she regarded herself as a free thinker—not in the sense of rejecting religious faith, but simply that she would not be pigeonholed into a particular religion or denomination.

'The story of my childhood'—Freda recalled with perhaps more candour than she intended—'is really the story of building up whatever talents I had to the stage of being able to enter Oxford University, which was a highly competitive thing.' She looked back on Derby as a prelude to her life. Once she had headed out to university,

Freda's links with her home city became slender. Her mother was of course a continuing reference point. Both mother and stepfather came to her wedding at Oxford, in spite of any reservations they may have harboured about a Punjabi son-in-law. Nellie went out to Lahore to visit, and to see her oldest grandchild, Ranga. But once Freda had settled in India it was thirteen years before she took the long journey back to England, bringing her one-year-old son, Kabir, with her. Freda was not at hand to visit her mother in her old age—she died in 1966, four years after her husband—and felt some guilt at her absence.

Jack didn't share his sister's academic ability and chose a very different path in life. 'We are all rather in a turmoil at home at present—my brother has just joined the Navy!' Freda wrote in September 1931 to her Oxford friend Olive Chandler. 'He did it on his own—and never told any of us until he was all through but for the final medical exam. Dad was rather incensed—but Mother managed to calm him down ... She says next November, when we are both away, doesn't bear thinking about. But there was no sense, anyhow, keeping him in Derby where trade is so bad, and there was no prospect of being able to keep himself for years to come.'[9] Jack was coming up to nineteen. He managed to disguise that he was colour blind, passed the medical examination and spent more than twenty years in the navy, attaining the rank of Chief Petty Officer. Freda and Jack had been close as children, but saw little of each other as adults—he missed her wedding because he was at sea and although he travelled widely he seems not to have come out to India to visit. The close-knit Derby family which had endured the shared grief of Frank Houlston's death dispersed and the skeins of affinity, though real, became stretched.

2

The Gates of the World

'It was a very quiet little student that came up to St Hugh's College and wore the long exhibitioner's gown to lectures,' Freda Houlston recalled, but for a 'provincial girl ... it was really the opening of the gates of the world.'[1] If there was a timidity about Freda when she enrolled at Oxford, it had been banished by the time she emerged from her years as a student. Her horizons broadened immeasurably and she gained greatly in confidence. Freda made life-long friends at Oxford, engaged in politics for the first time, became absorbed in India and its claim to independence, and within days of finishing her final exams, was married in the city's registry office to a fellow student. It was a romance which broke rules and crossed boundaries and conventions. At the close of her Oxford years, rather than returning to Derby, she headed out with her Indian husband to Berlin, and from there to Lahore, the capital of the still undivided Indian province of Punjab. Oxford was the last chapter of her life in England, and of her English identity. From here on, she was Indian.

Freda arrived at Oxford in the autumn of 1929. Her college was, like her school, all girls—all the Oxford colleges at that time were single sex. Women's colleges had been established from 1879 but women had been able to receive degrees only as recently as 1920. Women students were outnumbered and marginalised, sometimes described patronisingly as 'undergraduettes' and in colleges which tended to be on the fringes of the university district. St Hugh's was the outlier. It's a little over half-a-mile north of the Bodleian Library, but 'Oxford undergraduates cocooned in city-centre colleges generally consider it to be situated somewhere in the vicinity of Dundee.'[2] The college was modern by Oxford standards. It had been established in the 1880s with a handful of students and began moving to its present location off Banbury Road in 1913. It would have still felt new at the time Freda matriculated. St Hugh's was also small, cosy even, at that time admitting fewer than sixty undergraduates a year. And it was 'not so snotty' as other women's colleges and cheaper too, making it 'the college of choice for those who could only just afford to come to Oxford.'[3]

At St Hugh's, Freda promptly became firm friends with two other young women who had also just arrived at the college, both of whom attained considerable fame. Olive Shapley, from a radical and Unitarian middle-class home in south London, went on to be a pioneering broadcaster and presenter of BBC radio's 'Woman's Hour'; 'a great human,' Freda recalled, 'whose tremendous spirit and humanity and whose love of art endeared her to me.' Barbara Betts, who became better known as Barbara Castle, was born in Chesterfield, not far from Derby, and brought up in the textile city of Bradford in West Yorkshire. Her family were socialists and she went on to be the most prominent British woman politician of her time, a formidable Labour cabinet minister who took on portfolios including employment and industrial relations. Barbara 'brought with her the flavour of the north of England that I was brought up in,' said Freda. All three engaged in left-wing politics while at Oxford, though in different fashion and degree—but the strongest bond between them was that they stood out from the conventional, public school-educated girls who then constituted a large part of the college intake. Although the women's colleges were not quite as upper crust as the men's, it was still a forbidding atmosphere for middle-class youngsters from the provinces. 'Many grammar school girls recall feeling like outsiders at St Hugh's,' according to a historian of the college. 'They lacked the manners, conventions and sense of entitlement exhibited by a small but influential group of students from the top public schools.'[4]

All these friendships stood the test of time and of Freda's personal and spiritual journeys. Forty years after their Oxford days, Barbara Castle entertained her old friend to lunch at Westminster. 'She sailed into the House of Commons dining room in her flowing Buddhist robe, serenely indifferent to the covert stares at her shaven head.'[5] Olive Shapley took her two sons with her to visit Freda at a monastery in Sikkim. There were other St Hugh's friendships that persisted over the decades. Pam Bourne was in the next room to Freda at college, and gained renown as an ocean-going sailor—she later moved to South Africa, and Freda met her again when visiting the country as a Buddhist nun. Olive Chandler was, said Freda, 'my good conscience'—they wrote to each other over almost half-a-century, and it was Olive, a civil servant, who wrote her obituary for the college magazine. Freda certainly had the gift of making and keeping friends.

She had another gift, her good looks—tall and slim, her fair hair often done up in twin buns over the ears, with a round and innocent-looking face and blue-grey eyes. 'She was strikingly beautiful,' Olive Shapley recalled, 'and was sometimes referred to by the other undergraduates as "the Mona Lisa".'[6] Barbara Castle also found Freda to be 'strikingly attractive' while adding that she 'was not as light-hearted as Olive and I were, alternating between bursts of gaiety and moods of deep and almost sombre seriousness.'[7] Freda was not a natural rebel in the way that Olive and Barbara were, but she too chafed at the restrictions endured by St Hugh's students which were, even by the standards of the day, petty and onerous—especially when it came to men. 'There was not much to distinguish the social life of women undergraduates at that time from that of the pupils of the genteel boarding schools which a lot of them had just left,' Olive

Shapley commented waspishly—she said that 'chaperone rules' meant that the only way a St Hugh's student could meet a man alone was to have tea very publicly in a tea shop.

> A walk in a park, a punting expedition, a ride in a car or a meal in a restaurant were all regarded as highly suspect activities, and heavily penalised. You could go to a men's college for afternoon tea, but only in pairs. You could entertain a gentleman yourself for tea in your room, but also of course with a college friend there. For this you also had to drag your bed out into the corridor, a task which often required the help of your male guest and was guaranteed to cause hilarity if not acute embarrassment![8]

All three women on occasions flouted the rules, though only Freda—probably the least habitual transgressor—got into serious trouble as a result.

'I think what first attracted Olive and Freda to me when I arrived at St Hugh's was my campaign for sexual enlightenment,' Barbara Castle recorded with customary mischief. Her own and fellow students' knowledge of what was coyly termed the facts-of-life was limited. By Barbara's own account, she organised a whip round in the students' common room, raising the six shillings to send off for a book entitled *Planned Parenthood*. 'Explicit and illustrated with diagrams, it became one of the most thumbed books in the college, but the revelations did not immediately precipitate me into a life of sin. My knowledge of sex remained second-hand.'[9] One of Barbara Castle's biographers has suggested that in her first few terms at Oxford, her passions may have been directed (probably in a fairly chaste manner) towards other women, Freda among them.[10] Crushes of this sort were not unusual. Castle included in her autobiography a rather grainy photograph of her and Freda in a punt on the river at Oxford, reclining and gazing into each other's eyes—as much a pose as a statement of attachment but an indication of their closeness all the same. Olive Shapley got a little more of the action. She visited

Barbara in the summer and discretely spent the night with Barbara's brother. The following day she travelled on the train to London with Barbara. 'Somewhere just before Stockport I suddenly thought, "I am no longer a virgin!" Barbara leaned across the railway carriage, tapped my knee and said, "And you can take that silly smile off your face."'[11]

As a fresher, Freda was determined to make the most of Oxford. She became her year's representative on *The Imp*, the college magazine, and both wrote for it and featured in it—

When Socrates bore / Down upon F--- H---,
  She vanquished him clean / With 'what *quite* do you mean?'

—a snatch of student doggerel which suggests that her college contemporaries found her both bold and questioning.[12] 'I joined just about every society one could imagine, from the League of Nations society to the ornithological club,' she recalled. 'I listened to Bach in the college chapels; I went to Holy Communion; I went to Manchester College, a Unitarian college; I listened to Tagore; and to Dr Radhakrishnan when he first came with his magnificent lectures on Eastern philosophy.'[13] These recordings made towards the end of her life also demonstrate another legacy of her college years: if she ever had a Derby accent then, by accident or design, it disappeared; her precise and clipped voice bore an Oxford cadence. The same can be said of Olive Shapley—a manicured Oxford accent with no echo at all of south London. Only Barbara Castle retained a regional accent, perhaps because she reaped a political dividend from it.

Both Freda's close friends at St Hugh's remembered her as having a spiritual aspect. Olive Shapley described her as 'a romantic and an Anglo-Catholic and very interested in religion; I can remember her reading the lives of the saints and the mystics.'[14] She also had a telling memory of an early encounter of all three women:

During the first walk that the three of us took together in the University Parks, we were passing some poplars and Freda said. 'How lovely they are without their leaves. The boughs look like the hair of some Botticelli angel.' Barbara stopped dead in her tracks, looked at her and said, 'My God, what a damnably silly thing to say. I hope you're not going to go on like this all the time!'[15]

But the spiritual and the aesthetic was not the defining aspect of Freda's time at Oxford. By her own account, she regarded herself as a seeker but no longer a Christian. She never returned to the religion of her birth. As a student, she was more absorbed by politics and above all by India and the man who introduced her to the country and its cause.

Freda relished the camaraderie of college life. 'We talked endlessly, mainly between nine and midnight over large cups of cocoa or Bourneville made in the College pantries. Everything from socialism to Karl Marx, Proust, D.H. Lawrence, the family, to the new fields of Birth Control and travel were the subjects of conversation.'[16] Initially, she worked hard—the 'first year was one of study,' she recounted. But her enthusiasm for the course waned. 'Suddenly, I couldn't be bothered … I could speak French fluently already. I wanted to learn other languages, to understand the world.' She was also concerned about what a modern languages degree would point her towards: 'It was the flash of understanding which showed me French could only lead me to becoming a teacher or lecturer. And I passionately did not want to go back into the world of childhood that being a teacher meant.' She was closing in on what she did wish to pursue as a career. 'My eyes were on journalism, writing [and] interpreting that incredible international adult world that poured into magazine and newspaper.' She even met the editor of the *Derby Daily Telegraph* who promised her an opening once she had her degree, but she never went back to her home city. She did eventually carve out a reputation as a journalist, and demonstrated curiosity and social concern as well as the ability to communicate, but only after several years in the line of work she had been so keen to avoid: teaching and lecturing.

Freda followed her friend Barbara Castle's example and switched from French to Philosophy, Politics and Economics (PPE), also known at that time as 'Modern Greats'. It may have been more congenial but she didn't shine academically. Freda's tutors' reports paint a picture of a diligent student, but one who found the transition from being the outstanding pupil in a small secondary school to the more exacting environment of Oxford rather daunting. There were a few positive remarks about her work, particularly in her optional subject of international relations. Some dons commented on her accomplished writing style, and one found her essays 'always stimulating and intelligent'. The chorus of misgivings, however, swelled towards the end of her university career: 'Still rather weak and slow'; 'has hardly found her feet in the subject'; 'still finding difficulty in marshalling her facts'; and most woundingly, 'she has great difficulty recognising the relevant parts of an argument'. Freda emerged from St Hugh's with third-class honours, not quite as damning a statement of mediocrity then as it would be now, but clearly not the degree she hoped for. Neither Barbara nor Olive fared any better; all three women got thirds.[17]

The only substantial published account that Freda has left of the University, written during her last year for the *Calcutta Review*, pointed to what must have been a personal grievance, the disparity between wealthy and entitled students and those with much more limited resources. 'The undergraduate of little or no money of his own has entered into the preserves of the rich and fortunate. Quite a considerable number of the men now—even a larger portion of the women (about 75%) who have stiffer competition for entrance—are students only because of State, School or College scholarships. There is bound to be a change of outlook: a more practical view of education.' She made clear that such a practical perspective needed

to take account of the increasingly threatening international situation
and the political and economic turbulence at home:

> Oxford—any university—is a community of young people, not
> a beehive of book students. The Oxford of today which refuses
> to be lured by the calm of mellow buildings is going to be of far
> greater use to the future than the scholastically inclined students
> of the past. When Gandhi fasts in India, when Manchuria is a
> scene of conflict, when disarmament is having a hard struggle to
> survive, and the unemployed, reaching alarming proportion, march
> footsore and hungry into the town—is it any wonder that the
> 'dreaming spires' are of minor importance? The problems facing
> the world today are so great that there is little time for dreaming
> even in Oxford.[18]

This was not simply an observation; it was the quiet declaration of
a personal agenda.

Freda relished Oxford's internationalism, reflected above all in
the students who gathered in the home of Alfred Zimmern, the
University's first professor of international relations who played a
part in the founding of the League of Nations (and also, though
Freda doesn't mention this, an active supporter of the Labour Party).
'A Pole argues with a German—Madame Zimmern who gathers
the circle together is herself a Frenchwoman. Indians talk with
Americans, a Chinese butts in, an English girl and an Italian pick
up the thread of conversation ... A Chinese educationalist, a Jugo-
Slav, and a Pole are among the latest speakers. Everyone criticises,
suggests, tries to understand and appreciate. The informal circle round
the fireplace is never still.' The gates of the world had not simply
opened for Freda; she had ventured through enthusiastically. By the
time she wrote this account, she had embarked on a relationship
which also crossed boundaries—of religion, race and nationality—and
which was to change her life utterly.

Baba Pyare Lal Bedi was the love of Freda's life. The romance was strengthened by the common causes they championed and their intellectual collaboration, but it was above all a love story. There is nothing to suggest that Freda had any other boyfriend. Her own account of how she met her husband is both poetic and charming. It may well be not so much as she remembered it as how she wanted their relationship to be remembered. 'My destiny was to go to India,' she confided. 'How it happened that I married an Indian, how it happened that I began to meet Indians, I really don't know. They were just part of the Oxford scene.' In the recordings made in her son's home in Calcutta the year before she died, Freda spoke lyrically about how she first met B.P.L. Bedi, outside one of the University's main lecture halls:

> I was always known for being a little late. But one morning—for some reason known only to the cosmos—I was twenty minutes early. And that morning too, for some reason, B.P.L. was also twenty minutes early. And I thought to myself, well, I think I'd better say good morning to him or say something inconsequential because, after all, he'll think that I'm snubbing him because he's an Indian student and I shouldn't do that. So I said 'good morning' and made some remark about the day's news—and he said 'good morning' and also made some remark or said yes or no or something like that. And that was all.[19]

Bedi realised that he had been boorish, and to make amends he sent Freda a note asking her to tea in his college room.

> I was quite surprised to receive the invitation. And college rules were such in those days that I had to take with me a chaperone—you were not allowed to go alone to the room of the men students. ... But we found him warm and interesting, a very interesting mind, and of course knowing each other over a cup of tea made us friendly and we used to meet at the Majlis, the Indian club,

and we used to meet at lectures and so on, so I got to know him quite well.

After a while, they started sharing a simple lunch in Bedi's room. He was at this time a vegetarian, and they would eat fruit and bread or whatever he cooked up on his stove.

We became very good friends, very good companions, and slowly I didn't bring with me any chaperone; I used to go to his room without a chaperone. Now this was done by practically all the students in the university because this chaperone rule was obviously nonsense, and people just didn't take chaperones. But in my case, because I was a white English student and he was a brown Indian student, the gatekeeper of the college reported against us, that I was going to his room without a chaperone. And I had to suffer the indignity of being sent down from Oxford for a week or two at the end of term. Nothing very serious but it brought me up against the question of racial discrimination.

This first-hand experience of racism was a defining moment. She could either back off, and accept that this was a border better not traversed, or she could make a point of challenging the prejudice she encountered.

St Hugh's college records for 1932 confirm that Freda was disciplined, though with no details of her alleged offence. 'Miss Houlston had been rusticated for the last week of the Hilary [spring] term for a breach of University and College discipline,' the Tutorial Committee recorded; 'this had been reported to the Derbyshire Education Committee.' The punishment was not severe but it must have been deeply humiliating. Rather than derailing the relationship, Freda recalled that it strengthened the bond between them. 'It was really the suffering that I had to undergo, going down early, and that he had to undergo, realising that he'd been the cause of it, that brought us closer together.' Barbara Castle set down her own account of how Freda and Baba became a couple. 'They decided to write a book together ... and most afternoons she went openly to his room in Hertford [College] to work on it with him. An officious porter reported them. She had committed a heinous offence and was rusticated [suspended] ... as a punishment. But she was a girl of spirit and was not going to be brow-beaten. On her return she resumed her visits to Bedi, in the digs outside college to which he had been moved, only this time she decided to give the disciplinarians their money's worth and started an affair with him.'[20]

The greater interruption to Freda's studies at Oxford was caused by a collapse in her health. College records show that she 'went down due to illness' in March 1931 (that's before she met Bedi)—though it's not clear for how long. The recollection of her friends is that she later had to take time out from her studies as a direct consequence of her relationship with Bedi, or more particularly the disapproving reaction that ensued. 'Her mother, her friends and her college were all opposed to the match,' Olive Shapley wrote. 'She became ill and had a nervous breakdown, and was later admitted to a mental hospital. Barbara and I, still flouting the bigotries of the period, stuck by Freda and did all we could to see her through her illness.'[21] Often in her life, Freda took the road less travelled—indeed there was almost a contrariness about her—but it was at a considerable personal cost.

B.P.L. Bedi was a Sikh, though he didn't wear a turban, and two years older than Freda. He was handsome and well-built, jovial and outgoing. He had been all-India champion at throwing the hammer and a wrestler, and he continued to be a sportsman at Oxford. Bedi was, by his own account, from a well-off, feudal-style family and bore the distinction of being a direct descendant of the religion's first guru. His home village of Dera Baba Nanak, on the banks of the river Ravi and now just yards on India's side of the international boundary that Partition drove through Punjab, has a particularly honoured place in the annals of Sikhism. His father, who had died in his mid-thirties a few years before his younger son went to study overseas, was a magistrate and had land in the village. Bedi studied at Government College, Lahore, and while not then particularly active in politics, he read Gandhi's newspaper *Young India* regularly and absorbed the increased nationalist and anti-British sentiment evident at that time. After getting a degree in Punjab, Bedi enrolled at Hertford College, Oxford, in October 1931 to study Philosophy, Politics and Economics. He was following in the footsteps of his older brother in preparing for the hugely competitive Indian Civil Service exams. While his brother was successful, B.P.L. quickly decided that he had no intention of becoming part of India's administrative elite, a decision which disappointed his family and marked a decisive break with the bulk of India's England-returned establishment.

By the time Freda reached St Hugh's, there were approaching 2,000 Indian students in Britain—but only forty-two were at Oxford. 'There were very few of them,' Olive Shapley remarked, and 'mostly rich.'[22] In spite of the modest numbers, Indian students were prominent, not least in the elite Oxford Union debating society, at this time a male preserve. Dosoo Karaka, a Parsee from Bombay, was elected the first Indian president of the Oxford Union in November 1933. Indian students may have been largely from their country's elite, but they were not immune from discrimination. Karaka made his career in journalism, and in what he called his first newspaper article of any consequence, he wrote that 'even Oxford is not free from the Colour Bar. No doubt there is a generation of Englishmen now "up" at Oxford which realises the unfairness of such prejudices. Yet there are still some among them, brought up in the old school of thought, who cannot regard their fellow-undergraduates from among the coloured races as their equals. Somehow they are instinctively aware of colour in a man.'[23]

The temper of Indian politics in the early 1930s, and the three unsuccessful Round Table conferences in London intended to shape India's constitutional future, kept news of and from India on the front pages. Gandhi attended one of these conferences to argue for responsible government, but the other two were boycotted by the Indian National Congress, the main nationalist party. Indian nationalism and the means of achieving that ambition was one of the burning issues of the day. Among those on the left, there was a great deal of sympathy for India's goal of self-rule and disquiet about the manner in which Britain governed and policed its Empire. Indian students—Bedi among them—often came to Britain with little more than vague sympathy with the independence movement, and while studying became determined nationalists and sometimes were also won over to a form of internationalism, communism. Those British students they mixed with often shared these political allegiances.

The Majlis, established in 1896, was the main forum for Indian students at Oxford. It was not overtly political, to the extent of being at times bewilderingly naive. In January 1934, the *Oxford Mail* ran an eye-catching headline: 'FASCISM NO SOLUTION TO INDIAN PROBLEM—Oxford Majlis' Decision in Debate With Fascists'.[24] There were other complaints of a lack of nationalist resolve. A student at left-leaning Ruskin College, Terence McCarthy, attended the Majlis's annual dinner at the Randolph Hotel in 1932 and was surprised to discover that a former viceroy of India was the chief guest. He was even more shocked when the peer broke Majlis convention by proposing a toast to the King-Emperor. 'Communist and Nationalist Indians rose to pledge loyalty. Despite all their revolutionary talk, they lacked the guts to brave the eye of Imperial England's hireling. I, a British worker, alone remained seated.'[25]

The Majlis had a chequered existence, with frequent complaints of lack of activity, paucity of membership and close-to-unmanageable debts. It staggered on from one crisis to another. 'What is the good of the Oxford Majlis?' one Indian student asked aloud in 1931. 'Most members are dissatisfied with it most of the time.'[26] Nevertheless, Dosoo Karaka, at one time president of the Majlis, insisted that it exercised considerable influence.

The little rectory of St Aldate's in Pembroke Street where it meets every Sunday provides an opportunity for the sixty or seventy Indians who come from various parts of that great continent, and who are scattered all over the university, to keep in touch with each other and with the latest developments in India, which the daily newspapers do not fully or accurately report. It is primarily a social body … Although its membership is restricted to Indians it does not close its doors to others. In fact, its meetings are always attended by outsiders, who come as guests of the members of the club to get something of the Indian environment.[27]

Among the well-wishers and the curious was a regular contingent from St Hugh's. Barbara Castle recounted that Freda 'used to come with us occasionally to meetings of the Majlis, the mock parliament where Indian undergraduates threw themselves into rowdy and often disorderly debates.'[28] That's where bonds of affinity between Freda and her boyfriend developed. Freda's sense of social justice was outraged by the manner in which Indian nationalism was suppressed, and her sense of the spiritual was intrigued by the culture and philosophy of the East.

Freda wasn't the only one of the group to fall in love with an Indian fellow student. Olive Shapley, in her remarkably candid memoirs, recounted that her 'first real lover was a Muslim':

He was about seven years older than me and had already taken a degree somewhere in India. He was a lovely gentle man and he knew a great deal about life and love and politics. Later on he spent some years in prison for his beliefs. The eastern people put a great value on love making. I thought I was very lucky to be initiated by somebody like that … but I did not think of marrying him.[29]

Olive didn't name her lover—but provided enough clues to allow for a confident identification. Sajjad 'Banney' Zaheer was at that time a student at New College—he graduated in 1931 with a third-class degree in history. He went on to become a renowned Urdu writer and a founder of India's Progressive Writers' Association; he was also a communist of long standing. They went their own ways after Oxford but kept in touch—Olive's son recalls accompanying his mother to visit Zaheer and his family in Delhi.[30] Zaheer and Bedi knew each other well, and Olive's adventurous romance may have emboldened Freda—and indeed her boyfriend—in turning a friendship into a more intimate relationship.

Olive Shapley mentioned that her Indian lover 'pointed the way' for her in politics—in the direction of communism. While Barbara became a stalwart of the Labour Club, which was itself not immune to Soviet sympathisers, Olive devoted herself energetically to Oxford's newly established, communist-aligned October Club—indeed, a student newspaper passed comment on her zeal in selling the *Daily Worker*.[31] Freda also came along to their weekly gatherings, though she was not as determined in her pursuit of communism as either Olive or indeed Bedi. All the same, when her relationship with Bedi became public, it was described as an October Club romance. 'We had meetings and other events,' Olive Shapley recalled of her days as a student communist, 'read a lot of Marx and Engels and discussed them endlessly. ... [We] were anti-empire, which was a radical stance at that time.' Olive's involvement in student communism left what she called 'an enduring blot on the secret files.' Decades later, she was still 'visited regularly by a gentleman from MI5 who quizzed me about my activities over a pot of tea. This did not really worry me and I always looked forward to his visits. It was one of the few occasions that I ever got news of my old friends.'[32]

The vigilance, albeit belated, of the British security service provides a window on the membership and activities of the October Club. Cambridge student communism in the 1930s spawned a celebrated cluster of Soviet agents at the heart of the British establishment. When this became apparent twenty years later with the defection to

Moscow of two senior figures in British intelligence, Guy Burgess and Donald Maclean, MI5 became alarmed about how little they knew about Oxford communists at that time. They resolved to find out—and were assiduous in approaching one-time members of the October Club who might be happy to share information about their former comrades. They were fortunate that the club's founder—an American, Frank Strauss Meyer—had recanted of his student communism and was happy to cooperate.[33] And still more valuable for MI5, another onetime member of the October Club, Francois Lafitte, divulged the names of all the Oxford student communists he could recall. Freda and Bedi were both on the list—'Seemed to me both to be close fellow-travellers. They married and went to Lahore ...'—and so too was Sajjad Zaheer, a 'very capable Indian and close friend of Olive Shapley.'[34]

Meyer and others established the October Club at the close of 1931, as a left-wing breakaway from the Labour Club. 'We decided to organize the October Club quite on our own, with the idea of using it to attract those interested in Communism and forming a guiding group inside it,' Meyer told MI5. 'At the beginning we had considerable contempt for the official Communist Party'—a suspicion which was reciprocated. The Communist Party of Great Britain was at the time a small, workerist and distinctly sectarian force of a few thousand members.[35] By the spring of 1932, the October Club's core of ten or twelve activists had joined the party, and after its first year of activity that number had doubled and the club's membership was in the hundreds. In its early months, the October Club achieved attention with a string of big name speakers, one of whom, H.G. Wells, was subject to barracking for being critical of Moscow. Escapades such as singing the communist anthem 'The Internationale' at an Armistice Day service to honour the war dead and street fights with fascist students earned the club a certain notoriety. The political atmosphere at the time was highly charged, and the Oxford Union's resounding endorsement in

February 1933 of a motion 'that this House will in no circumstances fight for its King and Country' caught global attention; the *Daily Express* lamented that 'the woozy-minded Communists, the practical jokers, and the sexual indeterminates of Oxford have scored a great success with the publicity that has followed this victory.' In the wake of that controversy, a book on *Young Oxford and War* was rushed out, edited by V.K. Krishna Menon and with contributions from students of various political loyalties. Dick Freeman, a founder of the October Club, wrote about the radicalisation of Oxford students, and the emotional and political impact of the reception and support given in October 1932 to unemployed hunger marchers from the north—for many students the first direct experience of the poverty and misery of those without work.[36] The October Club made a political impact out of all proportion to its numbers. Michael Foot, an Oxford student (and a Liberal) at the time and later a leader of the Labour Party, commended it as 'the most lively and enthusiastic club in Oxford.'[37]

Freda, along with many October Club stalwarts, had started out as a member of the Labour Club and then gravitated towards the breakaway group. 'The idealism of our generation was the idealism of helping the underprivileged,' she recalled. 'If the Labour Club to which I belonged ... had any meaning, it was showing that we cared if people hadn't got enough food when they took the government dole, and we did care if the hunger marchers went all the way from Reading to London, we cared if there were children in the slums with no shoes and that children hadn't got enough food.' Her years in Oxford, she said, were 'radical years ... we used to attend all the clubs like the Labour Club and later on the more extreme October Club ... The whole atmosphere was electric with social demands and social change. We were, as it were, the Depression generation.'[38] Both Freda and Bedi attended the socialist G.D.H. Cole's lectures and Harold Laski's seminars on Marx and—in a joint activity which served to demonstrate both their intellectual and personal compatibility—they scoured the British Library to track down Marx's journalism about India.

Many years later Sajjad Zaheer argued, with a touch of self-importance, that Indian students were the seed corn of the student communist movement at Oxford. 'I must record this,' he stated, 'that at Oxford, during this period, the first communists in the whole university were Indians—one or two others and myself.' He and B.P.L. Bedi reflected a trend among privileged Indians who came to study in Britain and became so attracted to communism that it shaped their lives. For Bedi, the October Club was the induction to an involvement with communism which stretched over twenty years. Minoo Masani, another Indian from an elite background who was on the periphery of the communist movement when a student in England, declared that it was not an accident that the 'aristocracy' of the Indian Communist Party came in large part 'from the class of people whose parents could afford an expensive foreign education.'[39]

Bedi was prone to bragging and placed himself in retrospect more at the centre of events than he appeared to his contemporaries. He was not among the most high profile Oxford communists, and perhaps lacked the discipline and intellectual drive which marked out the most effective student political organisers. But he had one very valuable trait at a time of political turbulence, when rival groups often sought to disrupt each other's meetings—his physique:

So then, as a University tough, my duty used to be to stand at the gate so that any persons coming to break up [the meeting] would know that I was standing at the gate. ... This reputation had been spread. Thus my place became just at the gate, listening inside, and watching what was happening while somebody was addressing the meetings.[40]

When the playwright George Bernard Shaw came to address the October Club, Sajjad Zaheer recalled, there were fears of an attempt to stop him speaking. 'So we decided to defend that meeting and among the chief defenders of the meeting was my dear friend, B.P.L. Bedi, who was at that time physically the strongest man at Oxford.'[41] Over time, Bedi's commitment to Marxism deepened to something more than simply muscular:

> I became more and more drawn to it, not in just a vague leftist form, but Marxism as a way of life and a philosophy. ... As I delved deeply into it, naturally I was drawn into friendships with people who had similar convictions. ... I almost became a Lenin idolator and I had no hesitation whatsoever in getting a very big picture of his and just plopping it in my room and hanging it up.[42]

Bedi became convinced that India would not become free without a more assertive and militant approach than Gandhi and the Congress leadership were willing to countenance. His repudiation of Gandhi's advocacy of civil disobedience and non-violence also brought an end to his vegetarianism.

That didn't stop Bedi and others venerating Gandhi when he visited Oxford while attending the Round Table Conference. 'Yes, we had him over at Oxford,' Bedi recalled many years later, probably speaking of Gandhi's address to the Oxford Majlis in October 1931. 'My heart was so overflowing with love and devotion that I just got out from the crowd and went low and touched his feet. Now, it was this demonstration ... done by an Indian student and that too a communist student which absolutely shocked the hall ... Though our paths differed our ideology did not stand in our way of adoring him.'[43]

Freda also heard Gandhi speak and admired his single-minded—if idiosyncratic—pursuit of India's independence. Together with Bedi, she set up the Gandhi Study Group, from which stemmed one of their most ambitious publishing ventures, though Bedi recalled that there was also a personal agenda. 'The first thing which Freda and myself decided ... was that we must do something which would draw us closer. So, we founded the Gandhi group in order to examine and expound the teachings of Gandhi.' The name was also chosen, he added, because it was safe and less likely to attract the attention of the university authorities. The speakers it attracted were not so safe, and included Shapurji Saklatvala, a Bombay-born Parsee who for much of the 1920s was the Communist MP for Battersea, as well as Muhammad Ali Jinnah, later the founding father of Pakistan. Along with the October Club, this Gandhi Group affiliated to the communist-led Federation of Student Societies—though several of Gandhi's followers in Oxford resented this left-wing act of appropriation. 'They regretted we had called it the Gandhi group but it was founded only to criticise Gandhiji from the communist angle.'[44]

Faction-fighting and name-calling was intense amid the loose network of groups which recruited among the Indian student community and equally tiny nationalist-inclined diaspora. 'The multiplicity of organisations in London devoted to propaganda for Indian freedom has been a source of endless confusion to the comparatively small colony of Indian residents and students,' one commentator complained.[45] The most substantial journal and the one that caused most concern to the British authorities was *Bharat*, the word increasingly used by nationalists for India. Initially published by the Oxford Majlis, by early 1931 Sajjad Zaheer had become the editor of the journal, which was viewed by the British authorities as 'definitely revolutionary and communistic and ... likely to have an unwholesome effect upon the minds of any Indian Students who may happen to get hold of it.'[46] The other main nationalist publication in Britain was *United India*, published by an oddball figure, G.S. Dara. His tone was anti-communist but sympathetic to both the Indian National Congress and to Britain's Independent Labour Party, which was to the left of the Labour Party and had a greater focus on colonial issues. Bedi wrote a brief, and hot-blooded, article for

United India to mark India's 'independence day' in 1932 (Congress had made a largely rhetorical declaration of independence on 26th January 1930). He thundered against 'the insolent alien Government' ruling India and offered homage to 'those men, women and children who fell under the British bullet, bayonet and baton; while fighting non violently for the freedom of our dear Motherland.'[47]

The following issue of *United India* was described as 'the Oxford number' with brief pieces by twenty-six students, including prominent political figures such as Tony Greenwood and Michael Foot and at least ten Indian students. Freda Houlston was also among the contributors. This appears to have been her first published article about India. It was very brief and insubstantial but confirmed her increasing identification with Indian nationalism. She praised the 'conviction and courage' of Indian women activists—including a young Calcutta woman who had fired five shots at the British governor of Bengal—and likened them to Mrs Pankhurst and the suffragettes.[48] Olive Shapley was also among the contributors, with a distinctly more militant attitude towards women's activism—reflecting the class-against-class outlook then dominant in the communist movement and its disdain for achieving piecemeal reforms:

> If the woman's movement in India is to be used to prop-up the capitalist system for a few more years before its inevitable collapse, then purdah and child-marriage would be lesser evils. The women of Russia did not achieve their emancipation through the media of welfare centres, baby clinics, and women's institutes, and it is greatly to be hoped that the women of India will not be deceived by these sops to their awakening consciousness.[49]

B.P.L. Bedi wrote about India's 'determined youth'—'the youth recognises no *via media*; it is either freedom or death.' Sajjad Zaheer also contributed, and the two moving forces in the October Club, Frank Meyer and Dick Freeman, sent in a paragraph of revolutionary agitprop which while of little merit as political analysis offers a telling reflection of the political mood among student militants:

> Imperialism is as much of a curse for the British working class as for India. We further believe that the interests of the British workers and the Indian masses are identical—and just as the British worker has to fight against treacherous leaders ... so the Indian worker has to fight its Ghandi [sic], its Jawaharlal [Nehru] and its Bose. It is just as essential for India's revolutionary youth to get rid of its worthless nationalist illusions, as it is for England to eradicate the 'Rule Britannia' mentality.

The paragraph concluded, predictably, with the slogan: 'Workers of the World Unite'—which jarred with Bedi's style of signing off with the words 'Bande Mataram', the title of the hymn to the motherland which had become the anthem of Indian nationalism.

In the summer of 1932, perhaps while recuperating from her ill health, Freda travelled in northern Germany. She wrote articles for the *Derby Evening Telegraph* about German family life and about the merits of German men, their cheerfulness, domesticity and love of order.[50] If this was also an interlude to allow both Freda and Bedi to consider whether they were certain about marrying, it didn't disturb their intentions.

> I remember him saying to me at that time: 'I've nothing to offer you because I'm only just a member of the Indian national movement, a follower of Gandhi, and for all I know you might have to wait for me outside jail walls. I've really nothing to offer you—except my love and this companionship that I feel we have.' And to me it seemed the only thing—I never thought about it twice. I just said: 'Yes, well whatever it is, let's share it together.' And that's how we became engaged.

She now had the 'traumatic' task of telling her mother. That day, she recalled, she had to go to the dentist but was so tense that the tooth couldn't be taken out. 'So I went back home with the tooth still in—and the thought now I must tell my mother. And at that time I remember she was washing the dishes—in Derbyshire we call it washing the pots—at the sink in the kitchen, and I told her that I had decided to marry B.P.L. She was very quiet and then she said: Well, I trust you and your judgement and I know you wouldn't marry a bad man, and you do as you wish, but I'm only sorry that you'll leave England.'[51]

Freda is being less than candid about her family's response to the relationship. She would not have been so anxious about breaking the news if she expected her mother to receive it tolerably well. She was losing a daughter. Freda never had any doubt that marrying Bedi meant making a life in India. In middle-class Derby, the idea of a daughter marrying out of her race, religion and nationality was at that time almost unthinkable and vanishingly rare. Freda's eldest child believes there was a threat to disinherit Freda—and indeed she didn't inherit her mother's house (though as a Buddhist nun she had little need of it). But however great the anguish, a lasting breach was avoided and in the Easter holidays, Bedi came up to Derby and met his wife-to-be's brother and mother—and judging by photographic evidence, succeeded in allaying their fears.

3

Everything That Was Good in Us

Freda and Bedi made public their engagement early in 1933, in their penultimate term at Oxford. 'This was'—she said—'a minor sensation'. It was certainly front-page news for the *Oxford Mail*, which published a photograph of the couple, apparently taken in the parks with both wearing scarves to keep out the winter cold.[1] Word also reached the student journal *Isis*. Its 'Dovecotes' gossip column, with its ear to the ground at the women's colleges, reported that both Freda and Bedi 'are, of course, prominent members of the October Club. Miss Houlston, who wears a very lovely acquamarine solitaire on her ring finger, told me ... that they will be married soon after Schools [final exams] and that they will live in India, where she hopes to carve out for herself a career in the writing of books about that land of mystery and promise, henceforth her own.'[2] Even at this early date, long before she had ever set foot there, Freda was coming to regard India as her country.

The couple had friends and allies among the academic community in Oxford—notably Professor Alfred Zimmern and his wife, Lucie, of whom Freda had written so fondly in her article for the *Calcutta Review*. That affection was clearly reciprocated. Among the Zimmern papers at the Bodleian Library, amid letters from the prime minister, arrangements for summer schools in Switzerland and a mass of academic correspondence, is a postcard sent from 'Freda and Bedi' to Madame Zimmern in May 1933. 'Your "naughty children" want

to see you. When could we come during this week?' The Zimmerns
were away, so Freda followed up with a longer missive:

> This is just a small note literally on the eve of Schools to tell you
> that our marriage has been fixed for June 21st at 11.30 A.M.
> My mother and father are coming up for it, but unfortunately
> my brother will be on the sea 'somewhere off Scotland.' We are
> both of us very disappointed that he can't come.
>
> We are dividing our time at present between the last revision
> for Schools, and a search for a flat as we intend remaining a few
> weeks here until the Viva is over …
>
> We shall remember you both on the 21st—and hope you will
> remember us.[3]

Both Freda and Bedi signed the note.

'Barely a week after finishing Final Schools,' Freda wrote a decade
later, 'we were married in the dark and poky little Oxford Registry
Office. The registrar looked sour and pointedly omitted to shake
hands with us. We came out, with my parents and a cousin from
India, into a drenching downpour of rain … "Don't worry," said my
husband. "Rain is auspicious for an Indian bride."'[4] A photograph on
the front page of the *Oxford Mail* showed Baba Bedi, wearing jacket
and tie and pugri-style turban, holding an umbrella over his new
wife. 'The bride, a tall slim girl, looked charming in blue and white,
the dress having the merest suggestion of white epaulettes. She wore
a small white cap at a fashionable angle and had a buttonhole of
carnations.'[5] The *Derby Evening Telegraph* reported that the couple
were planning to honeymoon in Italy before moving to Berlin and
eventually settling in Lahore. 'They refused to discuss their plans
and shunned publicity.'[6] As well as Freda's mother and stepfather,
the other family member in attendance was Kuldip Chand Bedi, the
groom's cousin, who later also married an English woman; few if
any of their Oxford friends were present. There was a 'very simple'
wedding breakfast—'we both decided that we were not going to

have a big party or make a fuss'—and then the newlyweds went
back to Bedi's lodgings.

Freda believed that she was the first Oxford woman undergraduate
to marry an Indian fellow student. Plenty of Indians had married
British women, but not fellow students. The India Office in London
had a file of unhappy letters from British women, often from a
working class background, complaining that they had been deserted
by their Indian husbands, who had returned home at the end of
their studies promising to arrange for their brides to join them since
when there had been silence.[7] Both Hindus and Muslims in India
were at this time covered by a code of personal law which meant
that they could marry in England even if they already had a wife
in India, and could return with their English wife and take another
wife. Seeking to annul a marriage in these circumstances was not
straightforward. The Lord Chancellor's office proposed to set-up
what was insensitively referred to as 'the Polygamy Committee' to
address the issue, but all that was done was to urge registrars to warn
would-be brides of the potential legal peril.

Tucked away in an India Office file is a cutting from a tabloid-style
news magazine warning of the consequences of falling for a suave
Indian student. It bore the headline: 'The Lure of the Coloured Man:
terrible dangers of bogus romance exposed'.[8] Scores of 'handsome'
Indian students at British universities married British girls every
year, the article suggested. 'In the majority of cases these men are
already married to Hindu girls.' There was a parallel, if less alarmist,
discussion of mixed marriages in Indian student publications. 'Not
in bitterness against English women, but just as a statement of fact,
it is fair to record that Indian students leaving India are warned
by their parents and relatives to keep away from the women of
this country,' wrote an Indian student at Oxford. 'This warning is
based on the consequences of marriage between Indians of social
position and English women who are not equal to the situation in
education, wisdom and culture—to put it as mildly and politely as

one can.'[9] On both sides, attitudes to an inter-racial romance were hardly encouraging.

'By all social laws and canons,' Freda wrote, 'it was a marriage doomed to failure'—

> two students in love, refusing to recognise the barriers of race and colour, dissolving their religious differences into a belief in a common Good, united in their love of justice and freedom for the least and poorest.
>
> … In the eyes of the world, a wild marriage without financial foundations, without social foundations, or orthodox religious foundations. In our eyes, the only marriage we could either of us bear to think about, a marriage based on everything that was good in us.[10]

As she wrote those lines ten years or so after her marriage, Freda must have been thinking back to the hostility that she and Bedi faced, and the personal crisis it provoked. However 'wild' her marriage, she was determined to make it work. Having breached the barriers of race and religion, she would not allow any of her detractors to say: I told you so.

While the racial and cultural differences between the couple were the most obvious, they also had contrasting temperaments. Bedi was large, loud, gregarious and a natural raconteur; Freda was quieter, more contained, with a personal warmth but—at this stage of her life—not as outgoing. They both had an impulsive streak; of the two, Freda was the more disciplined and determined. There was a class difference too. While Bedi was not as privileged by background as some Indian students at Oxford, he had grown up knowing and expecting deference. However much he may have sought to disavow this sense of inherited entitlement, traces of it remained. Bedi was also, at their marriage, much the more cosmopolitan of the two. He had been taught by Britishers in Lahore. He had travelled widely on his way to Oxford. Freda hadn't got to know any Indians, probably hadn't rubbed shoulders with any, prior to coming to Oxford, and at the end of her years there had not travelled beyond western Europe. One had seen something of the world; the other was yearning to do so.

Freda and Bedi began their married life in his room at Summertown in north Oxford. They had to wait and see if they had a viva, an oral exam sometimes required if the written papers left some uncertainty about the class of degree to be awarded. Both would have been disappointed by their degrees. Freda's 'third' was at least one step up from Bedi's fourth class honours, a classification which no longer exists and suggests a bare sufficiency of the requirements for an honours degree.

This academic setback didn't dampen Bedi's ambition to study for a doctorate. He secured a research scholarship—in Berlin. By the summer of 1933, Hitler was already Germany's Chancellor and the Nazis were consolidating their hold on power. In July, they became the only legal political party. The communists, a mass party in Germany which attracted millions of votes, were an early target of the Nazis. They were forced underground—their leadership, and many of their elected representatives, were arrested. The German capital was not a comfortable prospect for a mixed race couple with a record of communist activity. 'The great question was: should we go?—because the menace of fascism was then becoming very real,' Freda recalled. Her new husband thought it was worth the risk.

They decided to make their way to Germany in a leisurely manner, and to have a honeymoon holidaying across Europe with Berlin the final destination. It was a honeymoon with a difference—Freda and Bedi travelled with a friend, an Indian from East Africa who had a car and was a keen driver. 'So we three, with a couple of tents, wandered around Europe—in France and Belgium and Germany, Czechoslovakia, Austria, Hungary, Italy. We had a really beautiful car-and-tent tour.' One striking photo in the family album shows the couple on the beach in bathing suits. In mid-August, Freda sent a postcard from Italy to her college friend Olive Chandler. 'Tour all OK. Very brown + well. I like Venice but it's xxxx hot. Am leaving later for Dolomites + Austria (Vienna). Thence to Germany.' Her forwarding address was the Thomas Cook's office in the heart of Berlin.[11]

The newlyweds arrived in the German capital a few weeks later and Bedi formally enrolled at university in October. By then, Freda was pregnant. They managed to get a quiet place to live a little out of the centre towards Potsdam, bordering the Wannsee lakes. 'It was a really lovely place—a charming German cottage with a lovely garden, and we had some very very happy months there preparing for the child.' This was their focus—getting ready for the start of a family so early in their married life. Politics took a back seat, though as Hitler tightened his grip on power, the signs of racial intolerance were evident all around.

> We led a very simple life. Sometimes we used to go to the big markets on Alexanderplatz to buy cheap fruit and vegetables and I remember one day coming back triumphantly with some beautiful Jaffa oranges and presented a plate-full to my landlady. But she turned up her nose and said: I don't eat Jewish oranges. So then I found out that the landlady was also a Nazi, which I didn't know before. It was all around us.[12]

She ventured to the university for her first lessons in Hindi from a Punjabi professor. 'In our class there were just three people—two elderly ladies, one a representative of the German aristocracy, and one, although I didn't know, the wife of a Nazi. But both charming women. Politics never entered into our lives, we were just learning Hindi and we were trying to understand something at the same time of Indian philosophy.'

Another pressing priority was establishing a relationship, albeit at a distance, with her widowed mother-in-law, who spoke no English. Freda was clear from the start that with an Indian husband, she was now Indian too. After her wedding day, she made a point of dressing in Indian clothes—often a sari, not the simplest of garments to wear. Her letters to Bhabooji, the family's name for Bedi's mother, display the charm and emotional intelligence which served her so well throughout her life. Writing in early October 1933, when Berlin must have been arrestingly new, Freda told her mother-in-law that 'our life seems to be taking on a more solid + peaceful complexion again. I will write to you as regularly as I can. It is a very great pleasure to me that you want me to write and if it gives my dear Mother pleasure I shall be delighted to do so.' She wrote of the regret in having to wait another year before meeting her Indian family, her love for her husband, and their plans for 'a quiet and studious life' in Berlin as a preparation for their work in India.[13]

What Bedi's mother would have been seeking is some sense of whether her new daughter-in-law would fit in with her Indian family or would lead her son away from it. She will have found Freda's letters reassuring:

you will want to know the little details of our life. They mean so much to a woman, I know. I am like it myself. I wear my Saree as often as I can, and only when we are leading a particularly strenuous life, as in camping or househunting, do I leave it off. I have some amusing experiences. I wore it on all the frontiers and received an undue amount of deference from Customs officials; I wore it in towns and every waiter in the restaurant came to my feet ... I am very fond of wearing the Saree. Pyare tried to teach me himself, but being a man, he did not at all understand how women do it (bless him!) and so I was taught both by an Indian girl student at Oxford, + particularly by a very nice Indian lady, Mrs Haji ... who was visiting London

And as a further affectionate touch, Freda signed her name in Punjabi script.

A month later, the dutiful daughter-in-law was writing again—

about the warm underwear that she made sure Bedi wore to guard
against the chilly Berlin winter and the sweater that her mother was
knitting him for Christmas.

> Now about the most important thing. You will have read in PL's
> letter about the baby. I am very, very happy about it, as is natural,
> because I love PL so much. So you will have a small grandchild
> to spoil when we come back to India. There is a great deal of
> preparation to be made, and this is all the heavier because I am
> alone in Berlin, separated from both you and my own mother.
> But it will be a labour of love.

'This is a very long letter', she concluded, 'and whoever translates
it to you will have a lot of trouble. But I expect you like letters as
long as possible.'[14]

Alongside Freda's personal and emotional ties to India was a
political and intellectual commitment. She saw her marriage to
Bedi as in part a shared collaboration; their purpose was to support
India's freedom movement by personal advocacy and by creating
wider awareness of the nationalist case. This joint endeavour took
firm root in Oxford and persisted in Berlin and by the time the
couple left the German capital they had served as the originators and
editors of an impressive series of books about contemporary India,
an achievement the more remarkable given that both editors were in
their early twenties and one had never stepped on Indian soil.

Their first title was a selection of Gandhi's writings published in
1933 as a slim volume of eighty pages. It was in German and with
a preface by a renowned Protestant theologian Rudolf Otto. The
book bore the title *Gandhi: Der Heilige und der Staatsmann*, (Gandhi:
the saint and the statesman). Freda and Bedi selected the items,
which were variously spiritual and campaigning in tone, and wrote
an introduction dated November 1932, early in their final academic
year in Oxford. How it came about, and how it was received, is
unclear—it could well have been at Alfred Zimmern's initiative. Of

all their writings, this is the title most easily available in the original edition—so it seems to have sold well.

Emboldened perhaps by this initial venture into print, the couple moved on to a much more ambitious project: *India Analysed*. 'At that time the Round Table Conference was on and I felt that something on India must be projected,' Bedi recalled; 'by that time I had met Freda my future wife and we were collaborating intellectually. It was a joy working with her and we planned together.'[15] They approached Victor Gollancz, London's leading left-wing publisher, who agreed to a series of volumes about India. Freda and Bedi were the joint editors and enlisted renowned academics and experts in Britain and India to provide rigorous articles about India's place in international institutions, its economy, trade and fiscal situation. Four volumes were planned, each containing five essays—though the final volume on constitutional issues never appeared.

Gollancz had an impressive list, and at this time was publishing books of such renown as J.B. Priestley's *English Journey* and Vera Brittain's *Testament of Youth* as well as a wide range of current affairs titles. In all, they published upwards of a hundred books a year. India did not greatly feature, so *India Analysed* filled a gap. The editors dedicated all three volumes to 'the Oxford University Gandhi Group in whose discussions the need for this series was realised'. The goal, they explained, was to offer a picture of present-day India:

> We have attempted to provide an interesting and detailed account of the Indian situation to-day, and the forces that have gone to make it up, but an account that is neither too technical nor lacking in general interest. It is intended first and foremost for the man with an intelligent interest in Indian affairs who is not satisfied with the scrappy and often biased accounts he finds in the newspapers; and secondly for the student who will only find such material by spending time he can ill afford among a pile of Indian journals.[16]

They certainly aimed high in the contributors they enlisted. Their friend and mentor Alfred Zimmern, Oxford's first professor of international relations, had pole position in the first volume, writing on 'India and the world situation'. His counterpart at the London School of Economics, C.A.W. Manning, examined 'India and the League of Nations'. Both were big names but not—as they conceded—specialists on India. Only one of the five contributors was himself Indian. This seems to be what annoyed a reviewer on a Lahore daily paper, who found the essays 'ponderous', 'cursory' and 'superficial', and 'done from an angle of vision with which majority of Indians will not see eye to eye'.[17]

Looking to the contributors to the second volume, predominantly academics who were themselves Indian, this Lahore-based critic was confident that they would provide 'a truer picture of India and her ills, which had been mostly manufactured for us by an unsympathetic oligarchy for the betterment of their own people at the expense of India and Indians'. These writers indeed displayed greater expertise, and broadly shared the nationalist perspective of the reviewer. While the tone of the volumes was progressive, this was by the standards of the October Club very mild fare. Some of the contributors were on the left, but there was no hint of communism or revolution in *India Analysed*. That's unlikely to have been at the publisher's behest, as Gollancz published several Marxist and communist writers, but the choice of the editors. Their aim with these volumes was more to inform than to agitate; to create an awareness of India's current difficulties, particularly economic and fiscal, which in turn would help shape discussion about the country's future.

The tone of *India Analysed* became more partisan over time, as any hopes vested in the Round Table conferences faded. Brij Narain, writing about currency in the third volume, asserted that the history of the rupee's exchange rate provided 'a good illustration of the conflict between British and Indian interests which has been the chief feature of our economic life in recent years. ... We [ie

India] believe that we are the best judges of what is good for us.'[18] Another professor of economics, K.T. Shah, railed against the iniquity of imposing a financial burden on India to meet the costs of British wars and military endeavours. 'Mr Gandhi proclaimed, at the Round Table Conference, that India would pay with the last drop of her blood whatever was found justly to be due from her. But she cannot be asked, in fairness, to shoulder burdens which are not hers in reality, which were imposed upon her originally as a piece of injustice and inequity, and which afford no proportionate benefit to the people of India.'[19] This was a more assertive style of Indian nationalism assembling its intellectual armoury.

A multi-author project, especially with such eminent academics across two continents, would have been daunting and enormously time consuming: the process of commissioning, chasing, editing and arranging the chapters would have been anything but straightforward and Gollancz would have expected disciplined observance of the publication timetable. Freda and Bedi received no advance from the publishers, but as they were editors rather than the authors that was perhaps not surprising. For them, this was not about making money but about serving a cause. Even more, it was the joy and camaraderie of a shared project. This was, in the most literal of meanings, a labour of love. They must have used every sinew of their contacts, and of the address books of their academic friends, to attract such a rollcall of contributors, and it would also have been a huge distraction from their academic studies.

The proofs of the first volume of *India Analysed*, devoted to the country's international standing, reached the editors at the end of May 1933, as Freda and Bedi were preparing for their finals exams—and for their wedding. Nevertheless, the book was ready to go to press just ten days later, and it was published in July—at about the time that the couple were heading off on honeymoon.[20] The subsequent two volumes followed promptly. In the second volume, devoted to economic facts, Freda used her married name. The preface was written from Berlin on 5th October 1933—the same day as Freda's letter to her mother-in-law. The couple put the finishing touches to the third volume, about 'economic issues', in April 1934—by which time Freda was eight months pregnant. It appeared at about the time the Bedis and their newborn son were on their way to India. It is a tribute to their determination and resilience that they saw through these three volumes amid the turbulence of exams, moving countries, getting married and having a baby.

The series didn't attract much attention in Britain, which may have been disappointing to the editors but given the dry, academic tone of *India Analysed* was perhaps not surprising. The stridently nationalist temper, particularly of the third and final volume, did not however go unnoticed. It attracted a long and hostile review in the *Times of India*, which argued that the essays were out of date, incomplete, biased and unduly pessimistic.[21] *India Analysed* had adopted an unspoken but very evident nationalist perspective, carefully argued though at times with a polemical edge. This was clearly not to the liking of those happy to place confidence in the benevolence of Imperial rule.

Seeing through all three volumes of *India Analysed* would have been a drain on the time of both Freda and Bedi, but it also must have given them status within the Indian student community in Berlin. Not many students in pursuit of a doctorate had such an impressive list of publications to their name. Berlin was, in the late twenties and early thirties, one of the commanding European capitals, bursting with intellectual energy. Some Indian students preferred it to London, not least because they wanted to escape the embrace of an Empire to which they were opposed. There was also an Indian emigre community in the German capital, politically engaged in ending Imperialism and sometimes working alongside Germany's powerful Communist Party. The rise of Hitler's national socialists changed all this—but not overnight.

Bedi's research scholarship at the old-established Friedrich

Wilhelm Universitat (now the Humboldt University) brought him a modest stipend of 110 Reichsmark a month, supplemented by financial support from his older brother. His research topic was about the development of classes and castes in India under the supervision of one of Europe's most renowned economists and sociologists of the time, Werner Sombart.[22] The university was popular among Indians studying in Europe. Zakir Husain, later independent India's first Muslim president, was awarded a doctorate there in the 1920s. Ram Manohar Lohia, who went on to become a commanding figure in Indian socialism, was a doctoral student at the university until early 1933.[23] There was in the early 1930s an active network of left-wing and nationalist Indians in Berlin—and of informers passing word of who was doing and saying what back to the British authorities. The British embassy in Berlin kept a close eye on the activities of Indian students and the Indian police were keen that nationalist students should not be forced out of the city, as that would disrupt the flow of intelligence. The League Against Imperialism, established in 1927 on the initiative of communists and with the active support of Nehru and the Indian National Congress, was based in Berlin until it was raided at the end of 1931. This was an important initiative aimed at creating links between nationalist movements in countries such as India, China and South Africa, western socialists who were campaigning for 'colonial freedom' and the international communist movement, and while it eventually dissolved amid political and factional recrimination, it was the sort of initiative which put the British authorities on edge.

By the time Freda and Bedi headed to Berlin there were clear indications of the worsening political atmosphere. There was a book burning at the university in May 1933, a portent of political and academic intolerance. Even more alarming, a few weeks earlier A.C.N. Nambiar was arrested, and also roughed-by by members of the Hitler Youth. He was a journalist and long-term resident of Germany who had been the administrator of the Indian Information

Bureau, the rallying point for the Indian left in Berlin. The British ambassador felt obliged to protest about the ill-treatment of this British national, albeit one who was working against British rule in India.[24]

The prospect of a child and the changing political climate in Berlin discouraged Bedi from any sort of political activism which might attract the attention of the authorities. But his social circle certainly included Indian nationalists living in or passing through Berlin. Both he and Freda got to know Subhas Chandra Bose, the key figure on the radical wing of the Indian National Congress, and when in India they both published an article by him and publicly defended him from accusations of fascism.[25]

For Indian leftists, impatient with what they saw as the quietism of Gandhi and his allies within the Congress and demanding a more militant form of nationalism and anti-Imperialism, the rise of a race-based populist nationalism caught the eye. When in Lahore, B.P.L. Bedi wrote about the Hitler Youth in a style more descriptive than denunciatory, explaining why Hitler put such importance in organising young Germans and how he had managed to attract four million youngsters into his youth wing.[26] At the time of Bedi's stay in Berlin, his supervisor Werner Sombart—who had once spoken of himself as a convinced Marxist—published *Deutscher Sozialismus* ('German Socialism', though the English translation was published as *A New Social Philosophy*). This clearly looked to the Nazi party to achieve a new style of socialism which placed 'the welfare of the whole above the welfare of the individual'. Sombart asserted that '"a new spirit" is beginning to rule mankind'. There could be 'no universally valid social order but only one that is suited to a particular nation'—and German socialism required that 'the individual as a citizen will have no rights but only duties.'[27]

Freda seems to have imbibed something of this indulgence of totalitarianism. In a review of books about European fascism, she expressed understanding—sympathy almost—for the rise of National

Socialism. 'Germany is making a determined fight for equality and national self-respect,' she declared. 'Her desire for equal arms is only an expression of it—she has no desire to make war.' And citing her 'year of observation in Nazi Germany', she argued that one of the authors had misunderstood his topic:

> He has judged Germany by the standards of democratic countries. He has seen very clearly the German love of organization, of uniform and of bands. But he has not rightly understood that the passion for discipline in Germany is a question of internal order, something ingrained in the cleanly, thorough German character—and not an expression of an agressive [sic] spirit that is a danger to European peace.[28]

It was, alas, Freda who had failed to understand the character of German fascism.

In the same review, she wrote approvingly of Oswald Mosley and British fascism. 'It is useless to deny that Fascism will have a hold in England,' she declared. 'Leaving aside the personality of Mosley— there may be differences of opinion on that—the fact remains that a vital nationalistic policy, put forward by a group of men determined on the idea of service, has never yet failed to stir a nation to action and to progress.' She repeated this chilling endorsement of fascism in the conclusion of the review:

> Fascism in its national aspect can be sure of an ultimate success, but English Fascism must beware against inheriting an imperialist tradition, with all its evils and abuses. Mosley and his men may see before them a Greater Britain, but there are others equally sincere who see before them a Greater India. And the dynamic national consciousness of India will attain its ultimate victory just as surely and thoroughly as Italy has done, and Russia and Germany. English Fascism will only succeed in so far as it limits itself to the borders of Great Britain.

Freda spoke later of the 'fascist horror', but at this stage she appeared to acquiesce in the rise of fascist movements. It was an extraordinary and unsettling argument she advanced: for its endorsement of a militaristic style of nationalism; for its insistence that this did not bring a heightened risk of war; and for the supposition that British fascism could be decoupled from Empire to the extent of tolerating the national ambitions of the colonies. While fascism was not yet tainted by the visceral anti-semitism that produced the Holocaust, by the time Freda's book review was published some of her fellow members of the October Club had been involved in pitched battles with Mosleyites at Olympia and elsewhere. Fascism had been unmasked, and the brutality that underlay it was already apparent. Freda's comments emphasise that her burning political commitment was to Indian nationalism and that her broader political outlook at this time could best be described as confused. This was a short book review not a well-developed political treatise, but it suggests an alarmingly naive and uncritical approach to the rise of the most monstrous of twentieth-century totalitarianisms.

Her most pressing task, however, was preparing for the baby—and doing so in a new home, in a foreign country, with no family beyond her husband at hand. She made two good German friends who helped in making baby clothes and gave sound advice. One of them, Nora Morrell, recommended a nursing home—Hans Dahlem, a well-regarded Catholic institution with its own way of doing things. 'It was an extremely good nursing home,' Freda later recalled, 'but they had this theory that one shouldn't give too much anaesthetic to young mothers. But they didn't on the other hand teach one how to have painless childbirth and give one the sort of exercises which are regularly taught these days.'[29]

The baby was born on May 13th 1934: a boy, delivered after a fairly uneventful four hours in labour. 'He was a healthy child, weighed about eight pounds, and had the most astoundingly beautiful eyelashes and a little cap of dark hair and rosy cheeks.' Freda's mother came over to Berlin for the birth—the earliest photo of the baby is at three days old, in his grandmother's arms. Mother and baby came home nine days after the birth; his cradle was Indian, swathed in cotton and blue bows. This little boy was born in the German capital to an English mother, but he was from the moment of his birth Indian. That was reflected in his name, Ranga Trilochan Bedi. Trilochan was the name of Bedi's older brother. The name Ranga, his mother recalled, was after a liberal politician who had been the editor of an Indian daily paper rooted in moderate nationalism. When news of their engagement had become public the previous year, at a time when many Indian public figures were in London in the aftermath of the Round Table conferences, it had prompted discussion about inter-racial marriages among students:

> At that time we were told by friends that Rangaswami Iyengar, who was the editor of *The Hindu*, Madras, had staunchly supported us and had said—'Why shouldn't our boys marry the best English girls, why must they always marry girls who are not in the university? I think they should get married. Why not!' And hearing of that, when we went up to London next time we called on him and thanked him and we became friends.[30]

Rangaswami Iyengar had died by the time the baby was born, and the naming of the child was in part 'because it was the name of this great statesman who had helped us so much.'

Ranga's birth merited mention in the *Tribune*, the more nationalist minded of Lahore's English language daily papers. Its anonymous correspondent in the German capital described the Bedis as 'two very conspicuous figures in the Indian community of Berlin', destined soon to make the journey to Lahore, and gave a flattering, almost swooning, pen portrait of the couple:

> Mr Bedi is a strong, impressive personality of fine manly presence. His scholarly attainments are no mere abstractions, no mental

achievements that go straight to sleep after their birth in the brain of an unoriginal mind. They are blooming realities of sterling worth that struggle again and again into fruitage in the microcosm of his mind under the percussion of the macrocosm around him. In addition to his manifold activities in the University and the seminaries attached to it, Mr Bedi is doing excellent constructive work in the Executive of the Indian Students' Association. Mrs Bedi has been very busy learning the Hindi language at the University since her arrival in Berlin. She reads Premchand's short stories fluently and corresponds in Hindi with her mother-in-law and sister-in-law in India.[31]

Mother and baby 'are progressing well', the letter added more prosaically. It was an embarrassingly verbose commendation of the Bedis, but clearly well informed.

Freda and Bedi lovingly assembled two baby books for their first-born, replete with anecdotes, photographs and letters and telegrams of congratulation from India and England. More than eight decades later, Ranga Bedi has them still. Among the letters was one from Lucie Zimmern in Oxford, who had done so much to encourage the couple to have faith in their love. 'My dear children,' she wrote, 'How happy I am for you + how much we are looking forward to meeting this little baby who carries with him such a rich + extensive heirloom. May he witness a better use made by men of their minds + spirits + may you both be inspired to guide him.' The letter was signed 'grand maman', grandmother—the Zimmerns took an almost proprietorial interest in the romance they had helped to nurture.

The Bedi family lived a quiet life in one of the more verdant Berlin suburbs. On their first wedding anniversary, they took the baby, then five weeks old, on his first outing—to the zoo. Another outing, with Freda's mother and stepfather, was to Sanssouci, Frederick the Great's splendid summer palace at Potsdam just outside Berlin. It must have seemed at times that the wider political situation, and above all the racial and political intolerance of Hitler's administration and the free rein given to his supporters, was receding into the distance. But inevitably, the darkening clouds intruded into their lives.

President Hindenburg, the only real constraint on Hitler's assumption of absolute power, died on August 2nd 1934. The cabinet had decreed that on his death the office of president would be merged with that of chancellor, which was already held by Hitler. He was duly declared to be Germany's fuhrer. The Bedis had been contemplating heading to India that autumn, but Bedi had kept his options open by enrolling at the university for a further year. This additional step towards a Nazi dictatorship unsettled him:

> I remember B.P.L. put down the paper and said: tomorrow we get on the train and go to Geneva, it's not safe any more. He was not taking part in any active politics but he was friendly with the Indian students of Berlin … And he knew that Hitler's ways were such that he could swoop down on the Indian students—and precisely that did happen. He had a prophetic vision of it really.
>
> So the next morning—literally I was packing all day. You can imagine the state I was in—packing and getting everything ready in one day, and B.P.L. going and getting the visa to Switzerland. But he put me on the train all right, and the next morning I was on the train and Nora on the platform to wave, say goodbye.[32]

In one of the baby books, there's a photograph taken on the station platform in Berlin. Freda and Ranga are in the carriage, just visible at the window, while Bedi is standing with Nora and some Indian friends, one of whom made the journey to Geneva with them. They had been forced to take refuge from fascism. It was not a happy way of saying goodbye to their first real home as a married couple and the city where their baby was born. But in Switzerland they were safe.

Through friends, the couple had the use of a flat in Geneva, which gave them some thinking time after the hurried departure from Germany. Bedi had to abandon plans for a doctorate, and leaving Berlin also meant forsaking his scholarship stipend. They had always intended to make their home in India and they decided to sail east as soon as they could. After just a few weeks in Geneva, the young family travelled to the port of Trieste and embarked on the SS Conte Verde. This sizeable ocean-going liner operated by the Lloyd Triestino line called at Bombay on its way to Shanghai, and had space for more than seven hundred passengers. Ranga was just four months of age and a little young for a tough two-week sea journey. 'The nightmare was to get milk for myself to drink, because I was feeding the baby. And I remember the millions of cockroaches that used to come out at night in the ship's kitchens—I used to go in and attempt to get milk.'

The photos they took on board showed Freda in a sari looking after Ranga, and there were some group photographs—it seems that two Chinese men who the Bedis knew from Oxford were also on board. 'On the ship my chief work was to prevent the discipline of [Ranga's] little life, his regular sleep, from being disturbed by a stream of affectionate passengers who could not resist him—in particular by a charming party of Indian girl students returning from a tour of Europe, and some young nuns going East for the first time.' The voyage also offered an opportunity for Freda to reflect on and adjust to the country and the extended family which awaited her and to talk through hopes and anxieties with those sharing the journey and the experience of an inter-racial relationship:

On the boat there were three more international marriages—an American woman with a Bengali husband and an eight-year old son; a German girl from Munich going out to join her doctor husband, 'I have left my little girl in Munich,' she said, 'with my mother. I could not bear to bring her out to strange and difficult

new surroundings. I shall send for her when I have made a home.'
I have often wondered since whether they met each other again.
The third marriage was a young Berlin girl, a librarian, married
to a Chinese and going to Shanghai.[33]

Freda's intellectual immersion in India, her commitment to the
country's freedom movement and her adoption of the Indian style
of dress helped to ease the shock of experiencing India—'so when I
arrived in Bombay I felt, at least outwardly, at home. The port was
just as I had imagined it, the jostling crowd of coolies and the faces
of friends at the side of the ship. It was hot and sticky.'

On disembarking, the customs officials at Bombay had an
unpleasant surprise in store. 'We had been listed as "politicals"
because of our activities in London, mild though they were. And
we were subjected to body searches ... and even Ranga's little
napkin was taken off and searched because they thought I might
be carrying messages in it.'[34] Her husband recalled that for seven
hours, they searched the boxes of books they had brought, their
personal possessions and the baby's nappies. 'Even in Hitlerite
Germany,' he commented angrily, 'the search was never so thorough
as here.'[35] One of the pre-occupations of the India Office was to
prevent communist and militant nationalist publications from being
smuggled into India and to disrupt links between leftists in India
and allies abroad. To Freda, it must have seemed as if from the
moment she set foot on Indian soil, she was viewed by the Raj as
suspect. It must also have reaffirmed her identification with India
and its politics, and her rejection of Empire and the indignities it
imposed on those it ruled.

4

Your People Shall Be My People

From the gangplank disembarking at Bombay, Freda would have been struck by the heat, the humidity, the bustle and noise all around her. The sea passage provided a gradual acclimatisation for her first venture beyond Europe. And the end of the journey offered respite from the narrow confines of the cabin, which had made the task of caring for a four-month-old baby on board ship all the more exhausting. She was now faced with the reality of the country she had chosen as her own. After years of imagining India, reading and writing about it, campaigning for it, romancing it too, here she was on Indian soil at last. This was her future. She was to live twice as long in India as she had in England, and nothing that she said, wrote or did suggests a trace of regret about the choice she made—beyond the distance from her Derby family.

'India is my womanhood and my wife-hood,' she declared, 'and the place where my home and my future is … I too am "dust that England bore, shaped, and made aware". Yet I am living in an Indian way, with Indian clothes, with an Indian husband and child on Indian soil, and I cannot feel even the least barrier or difference in essentials between myself and the new country I have adopted. For there are things deeper than labels and colour and prejudice, and love is one of them.'[1]

Although Freda rarely wrote directly about race, she recognised—after her year in Berlin, how could she fail to?—that racial division was an increasingly stark fault line. She also sensed that the pendulum of global power and moral authority was moving away from Europe and North America. While the problems of the current generation were economic, she commented in a book review, those of the future will be about race. 'With the Great War, the White Races lost their unquestioned superiority, and the future lies with the unexploited qualities and potentialities of Africa and the East.'[2] By heading to India, she was not simply embarking on a new life but endorsing the claim of subject peoples and nations to shape not just their own but the world's future.

She was also becoming part of a new family—an Indian extended family with a matriarch at its head. When Freda set down her account of her first meeting with her mother-in-law, she used an affecting title: 'your people shall be my people'. It was a simple and sincere statement of her attitude. She was wedded to India and would do what was expected of an Indian bride—to fit in with her husband's family. It was also, as Freda would have known, a quote from the Book of Ruth, in the Old Testament of the Bible, with a very precise analogy to her own experience of crossing borders of nation, race and religion. Ruth was a Moabite, and in addressing her Israelite mother-in-law, she declared:

> Where you go I will go, and where you stay I will stay. Your people
> will be my people and your God my God. Where you die I will
> die, and there I will be buried. May the Lord deal with me, be it
> ever so severely, if even death separates you and me.[3]

Freda lived up to that promise. She did not convert to her mother-in-law's religion, but she did embrace another of India's great faiths. She shared a household with her mother-in-law. And she died in her mother-in-law's country and was cremated according to its customs.

Freda's landing point, Bombay, was India—but it wasn't Bedi's India. It was another 900 miles to Lahore, the provincial capital of

Punjab, where he had been at college before heading to Oxford. In Bombay (now Mumbai), they were welcomed and hosted by K.T. Shah, an economist and nationalist who had been a contributor to *India Analysed*. But this was a brief sojourn before pushing on to Punjab. Bhabooji, Bedi's mother, had after the death of her husband moved back to Kapurthala, a small Sikh-ruled princely state sixty miles east of Lahore. Her family had served as courtiers there. Indeed, they had more-or-less run the place; Bedi's grandfather had served as the chief justice and his great-grandfather had been the prime minister. They were wealthy, stylish and socially (and politically) conservative. It was a sprawling extended family. Freda had written to her mother-in-law from Berlin, and addressed her as 'mother' in the Indian fashion—but this first face-to-face encounter was the litmus test of whether they would be comfortable in each other's company.

The train journey from Bombay took two days and would have been an endurance test for both Ranga and his parents. It was late September, past the scorching heat of summer but still hot enough to sap anyone's energy.

It was about eleven o'clock at night when we arrived. I felt rather sick after the journey, and very dirty. A white cotton *sari* is not the ideal travelling dress, and nursing Ranga had not improved it. All I wanted was a good sleep.

We alighted from the car that brought us from the station into a narrow and busy *bazar*. After climbing a flight of very dark and narrow stairs, we emerged into a big pillared room, full of light, whitewashed and decorated with elaborate scrolls and sculptures. At the head of the stairs an affectionate aunt almost smothered us in jasmine garlands, a heap of piercing fragrance round our necks.

My husband's mother, short but very dignified, came to meet us wearing the tunic, veil, and baggy trousers that the Punjab woman wears. He touched her feet, with the traditional greeting of respect, and I copied him, feeling a little awkward, but all my shyness disappeared when she smiled at us both with tears in her eyes, and embraced us and the child as if she could not hold us close enough.

The room was full of people, Freda recalled—and full of sound, with singing and a drum beating.

We were taken to the centre of the room and sat down on a carpet in front of my mother-in-law. She placed a long scarlet muslin scarf over my shoulders, spreading the end out on the floor in front of me, and various relatives and intimate friends of the family put on them sugar baskets and rupees—the usual offerings to a new bride. Blessings were given, and finally the sugar and rupees were tied up in bundles in the red cloth. We were quite unprepared for such a ceremonial welcome, and neither of us had given a thought to it.

... I could not speak to my husband's mother or to any of the women (the men, young and old, could all speak English) but there was unmistakable happiness in their eyes, and, strange though the whole surroundings were, I was moved by this coming 'home'. I was sure that even the most orthodox bride could not have been more sweetly and sympathetically received.[4]

If Freda was worried about whether her husband's family would accept her, the warmth of the welcome banished that concern. If the Kapurthala household was concerned that an English bride wouldn't make the huge accommodation required, then Freda's wearing of a cotton sari, touching her mother-in-law's feet and her charm and humility won them over.

Over the next few days, Freda was shown the town and was introduced to 'all kinds of relations ... the most venerable being a grand old man, the grandfather, a pious figure of great dignity

sitting cross-legged in spotless white cotton clothes.' She got to
know the two young girls in the joint family who confided 'how
terrified they had been meeting this foreign sister-in-law and what
they had expected me to look like and there I came wearing this
very shabby white sari and all their fears disappeared and we were
soon laughing and talking together.' According to family folklore,
Freda was compared favourably to Bedi's brother's wife, Tara, who
while Punjabi was regarded as very bold and modern. The story is
still told of how Tara went to a Swiss finishing school and on her
first visit to Kapurthala arrived attired in a western-style trouser suit.
Freda's cotton sari was seen as much more in keeping with what
was expected of a daughter-in-law.

'Never once was I made to feel a stranger or an "untouchable",'
Freda wrote. 'We all ate together, and I was taken spontaneously as
a new and very interesting daughter of the family. From the first day,
with many smiles and embraces, my mother-in-law, whom I had
begun to look upon as my Indian mother, began teaching me with
infinite patience to speak Punjabi.'[5] Bhabooji also gave her a sari,
brilliant scarlet and blue and embroidered with sequins, while other
women in the family presented her with salwar kameez and dupattas,
the essential elements of traditional Punjabi dress for women.

As Freda got to know her mother-in-law, she came to appreciate
that Bhabooji had been through an even more cathartic experience
on marriage. She too had made real the pledge that 'your people shall
be my people'. Brought up in an elite courtly family in Kapurthala,
Bhabooji moved as a child into a very different type of home.

She was ten years old when she was married and went to a strange
household for her first visit. The daughter of an aristocratic
Hindu family from an Indian State, she had been the darling of
the house. ... Her venerable grandfather, a great statesman and
diplomatist, had preached Hindu-Sikh unity and intermarriage,
and the simplification of expensive ceremonies. To prove his

principles, he had given his only grand-daughter to the son of a very old Sikh family, living in the birthplace of the first Guru.

It was a great change for the little girl. She who had been the pet of a cultured family, living in a rich small State where all the luxuries of food and clothing were taken for granted, was sent to a rough Punjab village circle, where lands and birth were the touchstones of village society.[6]

For the first six years of the marriage, before it was consummated, the girl journeyed backwards and forwards between her old and new homes. Bhabooji's mother gave her advice, which Freda herself took to heart: "'My daughter, now you are going to another mother. She bore your husband, and you are her daughter. Serve her devotedly for all the days of her life, and the blessings of God be upon you.'"

By the time Freda met Bhabooji, she had been a widow for a decade or more, and was very much the traditional Punjabi mother—running the household, the kitchen and the cooks and servants, but preferring to eat alone on her string bed after the rest of the family had dined. 'In spite of the seeming stillness of her pose, the bright black eyes, missing nothing, show that inside this mountain is a volcano of activity. Not a person moves in the cool mudded courtyard and not a thing goes on in the house that her eyes do not see. Not a grain of rice, not a handful of flour or a bit of vegetable is used in the kitchen without her knowing it, and every spoonful of the precious *ghee* is extracted from a locked box in her presence.'[7] Although Freda doesn't mention it, she was traditional in another of her practices. Throughout her life, she would not eat food cooked by a Muslim. She would welcome all her family's Muslim friends, would hug and greet them, but once they left would ensure that any utensils they had eaten from were ritually cleaned. Such attitudes were not uncommon among the old school Punjabi Hindu and Sikh elites but they jarred uncomfortably with the progressive mindset and lifestyle of her son and daughter-in-law.

After an initial stay in Kapurthala, Bedi and Freda went on to Solan, a small town five thousand feet up in the hills north of the Punjab plains where Bedi's brother, T.D. Bedi, was then living. He and his wife Tara—both well-educated and Europe-returned—also offered a warm welcome, 'a very modern welcome' as Freda remembered it, in the 'typical home of the English-educated intellectual. ... The only thing Indian about it really was the food—and of course the saris my sister-in-law wore.' T.D. Bedi was in the elite Indian Civil Service and seems by nature to have been rather aloof, with a passion for Urdu literature and fine food. B.P.L. Bedi was close to his brother, but Freda doesn't seem to have warmed to him or to Tara. There was one more crucial family journey to make—to Dera Baba Nanak, the village where Bedi grew up, to introduce his wife to the Sikh side of her Indian family. That too seems to have gone well and helped Freda settle herself in to her new homeland.

The hurried journey from Europe meant the family had arrived in Punjab without any clear plans for the future. No home had been arranged, no job set up. So for their initial months in India, they stayed in Kapurthala and Solan:

we lived in a joint family circle: my mother-in-law, my husband's brother and his wife and ourselves. I learnt a good deal ... of Indian ideas and ways of living; it was a valuable and interesting lesson to me, and I enjoyed it, although I will not minimise the difficulties and the strangeness, which would have been the same anywhere for someone used to independent living. We all learned to know and understand one another as we should never have done if we had lived in separate houses, and, from hearing the language spoken continually around me, I picked it up very quickly.[8]

Bedi, however, needed a job—and the sort of academic posts which would attract him were not going to be found in the smaller towns of Punjab. There was an added difficulty. The family broadly fitted in with both British and princely rule. They had done well out of the old order; they were not nationalist minded, and not particularly eager to see the British pushed out of India. The colleges similarly were looking for teachers who would not rock the boat. There were of course plenty of professors in India, the Bedis' friends and academic collaborators among them, who had managed to combine a political voice with a college career. But Bedi saw himself as a leftist and a nationalist, and didn't want to take a post which could constrain his political activity. With his brother's help, Bedi got offers of jobs but none that suited him. 'He was offered the post of professor of economics in the Khalsa College, Amritsar,' Freda recounted, 'but again this was a college which depended on government support, and if he had taken that job it would have meant giving up all his nationalistic ideas and all his idealism about Indian independence. So he said: "I can't do it".'[9]

Bedi had to do something, however. While the family was well-off, their wealth was in land and property more than money in the bank. And it hardly felt appropriate for the couple to live off their neo-feudal family status. To make the issue more urgent, Freda was expecting another child. They decided to move to Lahore, which offered the best opportunities for work in teaching and journalism. At first they moved in with Bedi's brother, who had been transferred there—not the most comfortable of arrangements given Bedi and Freda's leftism, as Bedi himself recalled:

> my entering into politics was a big shock not only to my family but it used to be a big shock to the British governor as well. Every time my brother ... went to see him, he said, 'Look, what is your brother doing? How is he making the name of the family mud?' He used to turn around and say, 'Your Excellency, the matter is very simple. We sent him to the most conservative university, Oxford, and there he became a communist: I have to ask you, what have you done to my brother, rather than you asking me what is your brother doing? And how a daughter from your country

and this boy is painting the country red here, making me feel uncomfortable, making the family uncomfortable; so what am I to do about it?' That used to be the joke of the situation.[10]

It was, though, an awkward cleavage in the family. 'It's almost like a Bollywood film where one joins the British and the other fights the British,' in the words of the film star, Kabir Bedi. Freda and Bedi soon arranged to rent their own house in Model Town, then a new and prestigious development on the outskirts of Lahore. Bhabooji came with them. So too did another member of the extended family, Berindernath Dewan—Binder as he was universally known—a young boy who Bedi's mother had informally adopted. Binder was a couple of years older than Ranga. His mother had died when he was a few weeks old; his father had been posted away from Kapurthala. The arrangement was supposed to be temporary—but Binder looked on Bhabooji, and in time Bedi and Freda too, as if a parent.

In September 1935, a Lahore daily paper published a photograph of a heavily pregnant Freda along with Bedi, welcoming to Lahore one of their Berlin friends, Nora Morrell.[11] '"I have loved India all my life and have looked forward to this pilgrimage," their German visitor declared. "I am so happy to find myself here in the midst of those people whose ancient spiritual heritage has always attracted me so much."' By this time, Bedi had secured some writing work and set up himself up as director of the Institute of Public Affairs, a forum for lectures and not quite as imposing as the name might suggest. He recalled 'expounding the Marxist theory of the state, and I started speaking Punjabi. Shouts followed from the students, "English, English, English!" I said, "My friends, I do not see any white face here. I have to live with a white face every day. There I have to speak English perforce, but here I thought I will have my Punjabi out with my friends."'[12] It was a good anecdote but these lectures brought in next-to-no income and he had found nothing in the way of regular paid employment. 'Everybody was too frightened to appoint a nationalist in any job which depended on the government for money,' his wife lamented.

She was the one who eventually found regular employment. 'There was a women's college just opened in Lahore called the Fateh Chand College for Women which prided itself on being the first nationalist college for women. ... They offered me the post of lecturer in English. I felt that I wasn't very well qualified in literature but when I saw the syllabus, I realised that more-or-less what we study in the last years in school—Shakespeare and the poets and so on—were the texts which the girls used and that I should be able fairly easily to teach.' By the spring of 1936, she was head of department. 'I give three lectures a day there on English texts, which is good fun,' she told her old friend Olive Chandler, Ranga's godmother, in a gossipy letter. 'I am very attached to the girls. Of course the standard isn't Oxford ... and I would rather teach politics or economics, but this was the only vacancy and it is interesting anyway.'[13]

'I expect you are dying to know what I think of India,' Freda wrote—and then answered that question with political caution but personal enthusiasm, an assessment of India and her engagement with the country after eighteen months on its soil:

> India is in a very bad way, and constitutions for all the fuss made over them are not going to help her at all. It will need something much more radical. Spiritually one lives on a precipice here. Both P.L. and I are determined that in our lives the fight for Indian independence is to be the one and only aim. There is no good or satisfaction in massing money or possessions even if one wanted to, when people with any independent political opinions are liable at any minute to be either imprisoned or to have their goods confiscated. So we live in a happy-g[o]-lucky fashion, and thoroughly enjoy ourselves because we love the work. The only bribes Government has got for the unwary are fat jobs and those we are supremely uninterested in, so there is no danger for us.

Strangely enough, I am happier here for all the hardness of the life from the point of view of Western amenities than I ever was before. I get a satisfaction in all this writing, speaking, ... and feel very happy with the Indian people. The more I see of India, the more I realise that I was not built to live in the West ... the kind of happiness I feel in an Indian bazar [sic] I never felt in an English street. I am picking up Urdu and Punjabi by degrees, and hope to have a good teacher in the future. I shall be thrilled when I can get fluent in them.

Freda had also seen an aspect of India which enchanted and intrigued her even more than the city bazaar:

I have had a glimpse into Indian village life, in the village where P.L.'s father's home is. A lovely place on the wide Punjab plains, surrounded by the grain fields and with the Himalayas stretching covered with snow in an unbroken line only fifty miles away. To see them in the melting heat of a summer day, suspended as it were in the haze of hot air is unforgettable. But when you get in the home of the peasants—unbelievable poverty. They live on three pice—1d. at a liberal estimate—per day everything inclusive. Just ground down by starvation and the money lender.[14]

The main purpose of Freda's letter was to give news of the baby, another boy, born at the end of November 1935. He was named Tilak Zaheer Bedi—Tilak after a pioneering, and radical, Indian nationalist, and Zaheer after Sajjad Zaheer, their communist contemporary at Oxford. With those names, Freda told Olive, 'he should be a pretty good revolutionary'. He was thinner and less jolly than Ranga, but had his brother's large eyes and outsize lashes. 'He is a pale cafe-au-lait in colour (most attractive)—a sort of golden mean between my skin and P.L.'s.' The astrologers had declared that Tilak would be a lucky and successful child. 'I can see a smile on your face,' Freda wrote to Olive, 'but these Indian astrologers have a disconcerting habit (at least for rationalists) of telling the truth.'

On this occasion, the astrologers got it tragically wrong. Tilak didn't live to see his first birthday. He died of dysentery in a summer diarrhoea epidemic—'it was a big shock,' Freda told Olive, 'but then I am philosophical about these things. I see too much of life in all its forms not to believe that such troubles are "all in the day's work", and at that I must leave it.'[15] Among the family photos are two elegant, professionally taken portraits of Freda, heavily pregnant, wearing a sari and her head partly covered. These appear to have been taken in Model Town, and suggest a spacious house and a comfortable lifestyle. The photos seem to have been sent to the family in England—one bears on the reverse a note: 'me—a week before Tilak came.' But Tilak himself is strikingly absent from the baby books and family albums. Many photos must have been taken, but it seems none have survived. Freda and Bedi appear to have responded to the shock and hurt of their loss by excising their second son from the family record.

Ranga believes that his mother 'never forgave herself for being unable to take care of [Tilak]'. This bereavement less than two years after arriving in India shook both parents. While she shrugged it off at the time as just one of those sadnesses that can't be avoided, the impact was lasting. It was 'really one of the turning points in our life,' Freda confided many years later, 'and we had decided that in the life that we dedicated ourselves to, it wasn't fair to have children unless we could give them our wholehearted attention, and until the day dawned when I needn't go out to work to keep the family.'[16] She stuck to that resolve. It was another decade before she had her next child.

Tilak's death prompted Freda's mother to make the long journey out to Lahore to offer solace and practical support—the only journey any of her Derby family made to visit her in India. Nellie would have known instinctively how deeply her daughter was affected by the loss of her baby, and how lonely and vulnerable she must have felt in what was still a new and at times unfamiliar environment. It was also a chance for her to get to know Ranga, by now a happy and outgoing toddler, and to meet Freda's Indian family. 'One incident in these years stands out in my memory,' Freda wrote. 'It was the day when [my mother] was leaving again for England. While saying goodbye to my mother-in-law, she cried and said: "Tell her to look after you." The reply was: "Tell her she is my own daughter, as dear to me as my son," and they both cried together.'[17]

While Freda began teaching—to which she added both writing and occasional lecturing—Bedi took the lead in his own publishing venture, taking its cue from the *India Analysed* books. Freda and Bedi persisted in the intention of producing the planned fourth and final volume of this series. But the couple's repeated upheavals—the hurried departure from Berlin followed by a sea passage to India, settling in to a new home with a young baby and then the added complication of a second pregnancy—frustrated that goal. More than that, they found a more compelling format for articles about Indian current affairs than a London-published five shillings specialist volume—one which had the added value of providing Bedi, who had reached his mid-twenties without ever having earned a living, with a purpose and at least the prospect of an income.

At the start of 1935, the couple established a journal, *Contemporary India*, which in time took the sub-title 'a national quarterly', though 'nationalist' might have been the more accurate term. The idea had taken root before they left Berlin. It was suggested by Werner Sombart, who lamented that India had no quarterly magazine of intellectual calibre. 'That very day I came back home, discussed the situation with Freda and decided that we must have a quarterly magazine immediately on our return,' Bedi said.[18] The new journal was political, polemical at times, but much in the style of *India Analysed*, consisted in large part of substantial and rigorously researched articles about India. Bedi took the role of editor; Freda was managing editor. Between them they wrote most of the book reviews, and Bedi's brother and cousin were among the contributors. But this was much more than a kitchen table publishing venture. *Contemporary India* was the most innovative and impressive, the most intellectually ambitious, of the publishing ventures that the Bedis pursued over the decades. The journal 'brought us some fame in university circles and among the journalists in India,' Freda recalled. It was also the moment when they made common political cause most effectively. Several of the most important political articles in the journal were in joint names. They were in every sense a team.

Bedi assembled an impressive list of contributing editors—nine Indian professors and senior academics, several of whom had contributed to *Indian Analysed*. The journal was substantial—approaching two hundred pages each issue. There were no photographs or graphics, but a touch of colour on the cover helped it stand out. The journal's agenda included scholarly, statistics-laden articles on the Indian economy, but it was much broader than *India Analysed*, extending to caste, gender, sport, literature, religion and politics. Freda's influence was evident not simply in the serialisation of her landmark translation of Voltaire's writings on India, but also in the securing of a series of articles by Devendra Satyarthi who was collecting and collating traditional song and folklore. From time to time, poetry was published, including several verses by Balraj Sahni, who went on to become a prominent figure in Indian cinema. As the journal's title suggests, India was its focus, but not its only concern. Several articles explored developments in Soviet Russia, and one issue republished in full the Soviet Union's new constitution along with Stalin's speech explaining and applauding it. Other contributions discussed the rise of African national consciousness and the plight of Palestine.

Contemporary India on occasion published keynote nationalist texts, such as Nehru's addresses to annual sessions of the Indian National Congress, but most of its content was specially written.

Subhas Chandra Bose, the commanding figure on the radical wing of the Congress ('undoubtedly India's coming man' in the journal's judgement) wrote for the journal about 'India Abroad':

> The impression that has been created in many circles all over the world as a result of prolonged hostile propaganda is that we are an uncivilized people—that our women are enslaved and that we are not a nation, as our Society is seething with dissensions. Can we shut ourselves up in a room and remain indifferent to what the world thinks of us? We cannot ... it is indispensably necessary that a systematic propaganda, backed by the Indian people, should be undertaken. There are Indians abroad who are determined to do this work with the limited resources at their disposal. The only question is whether the Indian National Congress will take charge of this all-important work and do it in a more effective and efficient manner.[19]

It was quite a coup to persuade Bose to write for the quarterly. Freda and Bedi had met Bose in Berlin and discussed his single-minded determination to drive the British Empire out of India. They jointly wrote a prominent article for *Contemporary India* seeking to refute suggestions that Bose was a fascist.[20] That was a 'whispering campaign' and 'mischief-making'; they weren't to know that a few years later Bose would raise an army of Indians, largely expatriates in South-east Asia, which would fight alongside Imperial Japan against the British.

As the journal became better established, the Bedis found a more assured political voice. They echoed Bose in criticising the Congress leadership for timidity, and urging a more militant, activist and explicitly socialist approach. 'The Congress has so far gathered momentum on the wings of middle class enthusiasm,' Bedi argued. 'So far it has been its strongest point. In future this very thing will turn out to be its biggest limitation. The time has definitely come when the Congress programme should be re-cast and based on a much broader basis so that it makes a much more powerful appeal to the millions of peasants who have so far remained indifferent towards the Congress aims.'[21] The editors explicitly endorsed the Congress Socialist Party, a new group within the Congress umbrella in which both socialists and communists mustered. 'If the peasants and workers are to get an adequate voice in the national movement of their country which is inevitable,' they argued in a joint article, 'the Congress Socialist Party must be the penetration point by which the fusion can occur of mass needs and the Congress demands.'[22] The journal also published the All-India Kisan Manifesto, an aspect of peasant activism and organisation which became an increasing pre-occupation for Bedi.

For all this record of innovation and achievement, *Contemporary India* never achieved financial stability. Freda told a friend at the close of the 1936 that the journal was 'self-supporting, and growing every day'[23]—but that was putting a positive gloss on a fairly precarious situation. Its ninth issue in the spring of 1937—the one which gave such attention to Stalin's constitution—gave a hint of the constraints under which the quarterly was labouring. The Postmaster-General's office had confiscated two books sent from London for review, both communist inclined—*The Letters of Lenin* and Stephen Spender's bestselling *Forward from Liberalism*. More alarmingly, Bedi warned readers that the journal was facing 'difficulties' because of subscriptions being dishonoured and would-be subscribers seeking discounts. The writing was on the wall. The journal simply wasn't achieving the revenues to sustain publication. This may well have been the last issue of *Contemporary India*.[24] Other publishing ventures followed, but the highbrow nationalist and progressive platform which the Bedis' had developed first with the *India Analysed* volumes for Gollancz and then with their Lahore-based quarterly was lost for good. With it closed the most successful and rewarding aspect of the intellectual partnership between husband and wife.

One aspect of the *Contemporary India* enterprise that never came to fruition, but offers an insight to the Bedis' lives and aspirations, is revealed in a full page notice which appeared in the journal—a three-month 'Round Europe' tour through the summer of 1936, to be 'personally conducted by Mr. and Mrs. B.P.L. Bedi'. The intention was to take in eight countries and more than thirty cities, all for a little under 2,000 rupees. Perhaps the Bedis were looking for a way of funding a visit back to Europe. This ploy would have got Bedi to Berlin for the Olympics in August 1936. Freda would have had an opportunity to visit her mother and renew her English friendships. But the plans for a round Europe tour came to nothing—it was always a pipedream, and Tilak's death made it impossible to contemplate.

The *Contemporary India* venture was only one aspect of the Bedis' publishing activities in Lahore. In 1937, Freda's translations of Voltaire were published in an elegant 90-page book as *Voltaire's Fragments on India*.[25] This was a work of real scholarship and endeavour. 'It was in 1934 that my husband, studying for his thesis brought home from the Oriental Section of the State Library in Berlin, a small, yellowed, calf-bound volume called *Fragments sur l'Inde*,' Freda explained in a foreword. This was among the less well-known of Voltaire's later works, an account of France and England's tussle for supremacy in India in the eighteenth century which was first published in 1773 and had never before been translated into English. For Freda, there was the excitement of rendering into English a brief work about India by one of France's most important writers and political philosophers. And she found within it a political agenda—'remarks on the economic basis of Imperialism have an almost modern flavour,' she said—which chimed with her current concerns. 'Had I lived in Paris or in London rather than in the heart of the Land of the Five Rivers [Punjab], I might perhaps have made a book of more academic value, and had a greater personal satisfaction in so doing. But a hard political and journalistic life does not allow me such luxuries. Instead, I have presented the book in the way I

hope it will be read—as an intensely personal and acute summary of
Indian affairs in the eighteenth century from the pen of a brilliant
Frenchman and a brilliant satirist.'

If the Voltaire book was the most scholarly of the Bedis'
publications, another fruit of their scouring in Europe's libraries was
probably their best-seller. They assembled into a 64-page booklet
all the letters about India which Karl Marx had contributed to the
New York Daily Tribune.[26] 'Why they were not collected so far by
scholars of Marx, we do not know,' the Bedis commented in a joint
introduction. 'All we know is that it was the most taxing job we
undertook in our Oxford days. It was hard to sit patiently looking
through column after column and issue after issue of the New York
Daily Tribune in the Newspaper Section of the British Museum in
London. ... The reader, however, can now share the joy which we
felt, after these letters failed to arouse the curiosity of the Customs
Police who searched our belongings.' Bedi provided a note on 'Karl
Marx: the man' whom he described as the 'greatest thinker of all
time'; in a genuflection perhaps towards his own wife, Bedi also paid
tribute to 'Jenny Marx who stood by the side of Karl Marx'. This
smart but inexpensive paperback gave the Bedis standing within the
left in India and beyond. The present writer's copy once belonged
to Rajani Palme Dutt, the leading theoretician within the British
Communist Party, who was of Indian descent and served as both
guru and godfather to the Indian party prior to independence (and
indeed for a while afterwards). Although there are now other editions
of Marx's letters, Freda and Bedi's selection is still available. It was
the couple's most abiding contribution to Indian socialism.

5

The Huts Beyond Model Town

When Jawaharlal Nehru, in the months leading up to India's independence, sent a note to Freda Bedi, the address was wonderfully concise: The Huts, Model Town, Lahore.[1] That's where the Bedi family lived for the greater part of their years in Lahore—in traditionally built huts without any electricity in fields adjoining Model Town. It was the defining aspect of their life in Lahore, a move born partly out of economy, and also a desire—Freda's as much as Bedi's—to be unencumbered, and to live in something of the village fashion within the bounds of Punjab's principal city.

The collapse of *Contemporary India* indicated how hand-to-mouth the Bedis' existence was in their early years in India. They couldn't easily meet the rent on their house in Model Town so they moved out and, with the permission of the owner, built a simple hut on a plot which hadn't been developed. This was not the model on which Model Town was planned, and the Bedis were told that their hut didn't comply with the rules for the development. So they moved again, just beyond Model Town, and built another hut, indeed a suite of huts. Bedi also made clear to his relatives that he would not be part of the old customs and traditions. 'The family had realised that this boy was not going to follow the old feudal pattern,' he recalled. 'So we were almost left out from being dragged into family functions.' He also forsook a stake in his family's wealth, telling his civil servant brother that 'we, husband and wife, have taken a decision that we shall live strictly on what we earn ourselves'—though of course Freda was the more reliable bread-winner. 'I was the happiest person,' he recalled, 'because Freda took to it so enthusiastically. ... No question of resistance; there was jubilation and fullest support; she looked forward to it and we just put up three huts ... and we started living there.'[2]

'The Huts' was the Bedis' address for ten years or so until Partition and the upheaval that accompanied it forced them from Lahore. This was not the sort of place of which Freda's mother would have approved—'I think my living in huts would have upset her if she had seen it'—but it was the home where the family was most content. Life in the huts was both happy and beautiful, as Freda remembered it, with a canopy of trees and, beyond, the mustard fields which were a hallmark of the Punjab countryside. 'Under those trees we designed and got built reed huts with plastered mud floors ... and we didn't have to pay rent because we built it in what was known as the green belt. We cultivated vegetables and had a rose garden and sat out under the trees on the string cots of the Punjab. We had the living complex where a dining room and bedroom combined in one big hut; we had a guest hut; and we had a hut for my mother-in-law and Binder.'[3] Over time, there was a retinue of domestic staff—a gardener, a cook and a secretary: 'In India,' Freda explained to a friend in England, 'there are always too many servants, because they are so cheap + inefficient!'[4]

Without electricity, reading, writing and marking papers in the huts was restricted to daylight hours. Reading 'almost stopped in the house at dusk, which could be pretty early in the winter, later in the summer,' Freda said. 'And I used to read in the early morning hours as we got up with the birds, and that again was say 5 a.m. on summer mornings.' There was no room, however, for the Bedis' large collection of books and periodicals which they had assembled with such care and in the spring of 1938, their 'nice personal Library of about a thousand books' was given to the Servants of the People Society, a nationalist-minded social welfare organisation.[5]

The huts were a statement that the couple had rejected the sort of comfortable, establishment life that Bedi had been born in to. They were a curiosity, a talking point, an emblem of a Bohemian lifestyle. The journalist Som Anand, in his childhood a close friend of Berinder, left a vivid account of the place in his memoir of pre-Partition Lahore:

> It was a picturesque sight. Half a dozen thatched huts built on a large tract of land with trees all around gave the place a somewhat romantic look. This austere style of life in a neighbourhood of palatial bungalows seemed a little exotic. It naturally aroused the curiosity of all the upper middle class people who passed that way.
>
> To me, Berinder's house was a new world completely. What struck me most was the stark simplicity of the place. The huts had no electricity and everyone used kerosene lamps … There were no fans, no electric heaters and none of the fashionable furniture which is found in every middle class house. Mud floors and sackcloth curtains completed the unadorned beauty of the house.

While the Bedis had rejected the luxuries of upper middle class Lahore, their lifestyle—as Som Anand commented acerbically—was very different from that of the urban poor. He found the huts' inhabitants every bit as striking as their habitation:

> Mr Bedi was tall and hefty and dressed in his 'shalwar' and 'kurta', with a 'chaddar' thrown around his shoulders, he looked like a Biblical figure. Another thing which impressed me about him was his chaste Punjabi. It was surprising that he could speak so fluently in rural idiom after such a long stay in Europe.
>
> Mrs Freda Bedi also looked graceful in her 'shalwar-kameez'

and 'dupatta'. The ease with which she wore her clothes made her look almost like a Punjabi; her blue eyes and English accent were the only signs which revealed that she was British. ... I saw little of her as she remained busy writing or conversing with visitors in her room. Occasionally a handsome figure would emerge from behind the sack-cloth curtains and a sonorous English voice reverberated in that vast open space: 'Ranga, come learn lesson.' And Ranga, who generally played 'guli-danda' with the sweeper's son, went running to his mother's hut.[6]

Anand was also struck by the curious accommodation between the two women of the household, the mother-in-law obliged to live in a thatched hut 'without any of the comforts she was accustomed to' and a daughter-in-law who showed great respect to the older woman:

Sometimes I went to my friend on my way to school in the morning. I now had the opportunity to hear Freda Bedi discussing the day's cooking programme with her mother-in-law in her English-accented Punjabi. It was very amusing to listen to that conversation as every word she uttered in Punjabi seemed to become a part of the English language. ...

It was nothing new or unusual for me to see a British wife in a Punjabi home, but nowhere had I seen a white woman trying to be a typical Indian, or rather Hindu daughter-in-law. It surprised me to see Mrs Bedi coming to bhaboji's hut in the morning to touch her feet. In household matters she respected the old mother's inhibitions. Strict observance of the rules of Hindu conservatism must have been taxing for a young English wife, but Freda Bedi had learnt the art of adaptability. Her mother-in-law was an equally large hearted person; despite all her conservatism she had accepted a Christian into the family without a murmur.[7]

One area in which the family suffered no privations, Som Anand noticed, was in its cooking. 'Eating had become a passion with the Bedis. ... In no other non-Muslim family have I seen such a sophisticated taste for non-vegetarian food ... and from pickle to the most ordinary dish, everything seemed to have been made with some kind of meat.' If the Bedis shared a weakness, it was an appetite for rich food, and the huts were no impediment to that. Bedi kept poultry and milk came from Clarabelle the buffalo. Indeed, there was a menagerie of animals: goats, ponies, rabbits, guinea pigs and two shepherd dogs called Pug and Snug to keep wild animals at bay.

'There was looking back on it a certain rishi-like quality in life in the huts which those who came to visit us, and there were many who stayed a night in the simple guest hut, never failed to notice,' Freda said. Rishis are Hindu sages and ascetics, and there was certainly (food apart) an element of renunciation about the decision to live in such a simple and unconventional manner—much more a pragmatic and political than a religious act but with a spiritual undertow. Rishis are also writers—traditionally of Vedic hymns. Freda didn't write religious verse at this stage in her life, but she did compose rhymes—nursery rhymes. She found that traditional English nursery rhymes meant nothing to Ranga, a boy growing up a world away from the reference points in those ditties. So she wrote her own 'Rhymes for Ranga'—simple children's verses about Bhabooji, the animals all around, flying kites, celebrating festivals and all the adventures and experiences of her young son. 'These rhymes grew up with you, Ranga,' his mother wrote, 'and they grew out of you, because it was sometimes the little words you said, and the nonsense songs you sang, that quickened something in me and gave them birth.'

Clarabelle the buffalo, acquired by the Bedis when she was a one-year-old calf or 'cutty', featured in one of the rhymes:

Miss Chambeli Clarebelle Cutty
Has eyes of blue

She lives in a personal private hutty
Does Miss Chambeli Clarebelle Cutty

One rhyme was prompted by Ranga asking how granny's parcels
from England managed to reach them in Model Town; another
by the sight of an outsize boot marking a cobbler's shop in central
Lahore, which the young child thought must belong to a 'big' man
such as Gandhi. A handful of the rhymes were directly political.
'So India is marching, Straight to her Freedom Day,' one declared,
'And nobody shall stop her, And nothing shall bar the way.' In
another, a peasant who cultivates the mustard fields explains what
has happened to his money:

It goes to the landlord
It goes to the shop
It goes to pay taxes
Drop by drop
It goes to the barber
It goes to the priest
And all that is left
Is a beggar's feast.

One of the verses mentions the name Ranga had bestowed on
his mother and by which she was known within the family ever
after: Ooggee. This was it seems a child's corruption of 'oh, ji', the
interjection Bedi used so often in the home that his son came to
believe it was his mother's name.

Rhymes for Ranga was Freda's very personal bond with her first
born but it was also intended for publication; Freda told Olive
Chandler in the spring of 1940 that it would be out by the autumn.
The book only appeared much later, towards the close of the 1950s,
and in Urdu. That edition won an Indian government award for
children's literature.[8] A handsomely illustrated English edition finally
appeared in 2010—by which time Ranga was in his seventies.[9]

Lahore sweltered in the summer, and the huts offered little respite from the blistering heat. The Bedis took refuge in the hills of the Kangra Valley, 130 miles east of Lahore. At Andretta, an Irish woman, Norah Richards—an actress and theatre enthusiast, and thirty-five years older than Freda—had established a modest homestead which became the hub of a cultural and artistic community. Norah's own home was as simple, perhaps more so, as the Bedis' in Model Town, with mud walls and a thatched roof. In the mid-1930s, she was given a small estate, and here poets, potters, artists and writers set up home. Freda remembered Norah as 'a great old lady and a great friend'—a friendship which persisted until Norah's death in 1971. 'Norah had wanted to prove, Tolstoyan fashion, that one could live in the countryside wearing country homespuns and one needn't go to the town for intellectual life. ... She gave us a piece of land there on the hillside, and we built our first mud cottage there ... and though she had some misgivings about our political ways, we assured her we didn't bring them to Andretta and that we came there to rest. ... She was interested, as I was, in the simplicities and beauties of rural living, in cooking and in not using anything except local products, earthenware plates and homespun cloth.'[10]

In the summer of 1939, Freda and Ranga were in the Kangra Valley, with Bedi joining them at weekends when his political work allowed. 'I hate being away from him for the hot months, and we both feel lonely at times,' she confided to Olive Chandler, 'but there is really no alternative, as I find the hot weather quite takes the life out of me.' And the Kangra Valley had charms that Freda was keen to share with her correspondent:

This year we have built our own mountain cottage on a bit of land given us by a friend ... We are on a minor hill-slope overlooking the valley, our house site being partly hollowed out of the soil, and the snow range of the Himalayas stretches like a great wall on the other side of the fields. I am writing this letter in my favourite position—sitting on a cushion before a low table in the doorway—facing the mountains.

The cottage is a great triumph, built of local stone + sand + mud bricks + bamboos, cement-washed + roofed to keep out the rains. ... There is a big spacious living room ... with a dining niche, a kitchen + a bathroom + with two verandas for outside sleeping. Later we shall add two sleeping cabins—possibly after the rains when our finances have had time to recover.[11]

When Freda published a selection of her writings as *Behind the Mud Walls*, several of the articles were about the Kangra Valley: the gentle rhythms of village life; the dignity of the hill women; celebrating Christmas in the valley (Freda's insistence on marking Christmas as traditionally as possible was a legacy of her English upbringing which persisted in Punjab, as was her baking of cakes and making of fruit trifles); and the adventures on third-class rail journeys on her way to and from the hills. Freda was much more captivated by the Kangra Valley than by the bustle of Lahore. She saw in the village the essence of India—its spirituality, its creativity, its social values—and it must have carried an echo too of her own childhood on the rural fringes of Derby.

Freda was not unusual in being an outsider who was trying to come to terms with a new culture, cuisine and rhythm of life—not to mention the heat and dust which came as such a shock to newcomers. She was surprised how many mixed marriages there were in Lahore. Privileged young Indian men had often returned home with a European wife as well as a European degree. 'I remember once counting the foreign wives in Punjab at the time when I was there and there must have been about 300, and that's not a small number,' Freda recalled—and not all made the transition easily or comfortably. 'They came from all over Europe, from Sweden to France to Germany to England and from the States. The English wives seemed to settle more readily and the Germans and the Scandinavians a close second, but the French wives tended to get tired and to long for their own cultural setting within a few years.'[12]

Within the progressive artistic and political circles in Lahore in which Freda and Bedi moved, there were a handful of foreign wives. The renowned poet Hafeez Jullundhri was a close friend. He had two households; his concurrent wives lived, none too comfortably, in houses almost opposite each other in Model Town. His younger second wife Anela, an English woman of Lithuanian descent, found an ally and confidante in Freda, and her daughter Zia has affectionate memories of Freda. 'She used to come, this beautiful lady in a sari and I used to see her—usually it was a white sari, and cotton, and she always looked very fresh, and even in the heat looked cool ... I was very fond of her. Auntie Ooggee, Auntie Ooggee, I used to go rushing to her and hugging her on her legs.'[13] Another close friend, the artist Roop Krishna, married a British artist, Mary Oldfield. The Bedis would also have known the sisters Alys and Christabel George from near London, who married two of the most influential leftist writers and intellectuals in Lahore, the poet Faiz Ahmad Faiz and the writer and educationist M.D. Taseer.

Inter-racial marriages were not common, but nor were they so unusual as to attract particular comment. It was much more exceptional for foreign spouses to embrace nationalist and leftist politics, and to take to the platform, join processions and write articles in support of India's independence. The foreign wives and companions of South Asian revolutionaries who embraced their partners' politics have been described as 'a group almost lost to history' because so little is known, and written, about them.[14] Freda was clear long before she settled in India that she would be active in pursuing India's cause and so became part of a significant but slender tradition of white women who gained prominence within South Asian nationalist movements.

Of that tradition, Annie Besant was pre-eminent. She was the wife of an English vicar who walked out on her marriage, became a noted radical and freethinker, and eventually settled in Madras (now Chennai). She was a pioneering Theosophist and a powerful advocate of Indian nationalism and served as president of the Indian National Congress. There are striking parallels in the lives of Freda Bedi and Annie Besant, who both in turn showed commitment to radical politics, Indian nationalism and Eastern spirituality. Besant died a few months before Freda reached India, but Bedi had made a point of meeting her before he came to Oxford, and Norah Richards knew her and was influenced by Theosophism. A closer contemporary of Freda was Madeleine Slade, the daughter of a British rear admiral. She spent many years supporting and working with Mahatma Gandhi and took the name Mirabehn. Freda met Slade several times and regarded her as a friend. 'Her name was high in Indian nationalist circles. She was a woman of great dedication and lived a life of some self-sacrifice.' Freda's life also bears an echo of that of Nellie Sengupta, a Cambridge woman who in the years before the First World War married a Bengali student who lodged with the family, Jatindra Mohan Sengupta. He was a prominent member of the Indian National Congress and mayor of Calcutta and died in 1933 while in jail on political charges. Nellie subsequently served as Congress president and was active in politics in Calcutta and, after Partition, in East Pakistan (later Bangladesh). She died in 1973.

In time, Freda became a role model for English women who followed in her footsteps. Nancie Jones met and eventually married a Punjabi socialist studying in England. Immediately after the Second World War, she came out to India to be with him and took not just his surname but changed her first name, becoming known as Rajni Kumar. By the time she reached Lahore, Freda was well established in the city and held up 'as a model of how to adopt myself to Indian life and culture, and how to involve myself in the struggle':

> I visited Freda in her delightfully simple and ethnic home along with some of the women activists of the Communist Party. ...

I have vivid recollections of the simplicity of their life, the rural touch of the place, the string hammock where the baby was sleeping ... and the jute beds and the books stacked everywhere. I remember too, the deep involvement and concern that all of us shared regarding the course of the freedom struggle which was fast nearing its end. Freda made a deep impact upon me, and I resolved that like her, I would try to adapt myself fully to Indian ways and culture, and become a real Indian woman. I was already wearing thick khadi Punjabi clothes as she was.[15]

Seventy years later, Rajni Kumar still recalls Freda Bedi's advice. 'She told me that the best way to become a part of the Indian struggle is to be a part of it yourself. If you Indianise yourself enough—and people think you are with them, you are part of them—you've overcome all the prejudices.'[16]

6

A Martyr Awaiting Execution

Freda Bedi did not take easily to Indian politics, nor was she at first comfortable on the platform speaking a language which many in the audience would struggle to understand. It was, at times, an ordeal. But as with so much else in her life, it was a challenge from which she didn't shy away—she broke through barriers and crossed personal borders. Freda had been involved in politics at Oxford, but not prominently. She had no track record as a public speaker and the extent of her politically engaged writing was modest. In Berlin and initially in Lahore, the challenges of starting and raising a family, running a household and earning a living squeezed out any sustained political activity. But she was political by nature and a determined opponent of Empire, and when the opportunity arose to campaign for India's national cause, and for Indians caught up in the iniquities of imperialism, she didn't let it pass by. Initially, this was largely in support of Bedi and the causes he adopted. But she also came to pursue her own political interests and agenda—notably championing civil liberties. Both husband and wife developed into accomplished orators—Bedi relying on his ready wit and rustic turn of phrase, while Freda was more thoughtful and reserved but no less effective. Unlike her husband, she had no great political ambition; where he was a communist, she never lost her admiration for Gandhi; he had presence on the platform, she was more measured in her language—though both on occasions gave vent to what contemporary leftists would have described as class anger.

Freda's induction into progressive politics in India was moulded by her husband's political loyalties and activity and by the cross-currents of the nationalist and communist movements. B.P.L. Bedi returned to his home province of Punjab in 1934 with political allegiances quite different to those with which he had left Lahore. A loose identification with nationalism had hardened into a determined anti-imperial mindset. He was a Marxist and a communist; his style of politics was not bound by Gandhian civil disobedience. Two events at around the time of his return shaped his political involvement. The Communist Party in Punjab was declared an unlawful organisation a few weeks before he left Europe—the province being the first in India to invoke these measures.[1] For the next eight years, the party operated underground. At the same time, the international communist movement moved out of a period of intense sectarianism, when social democratic parties in Germany and elsewhere were denounced as social fascist, to advocacy of the united front. This meant working alongside non-communist parties for specific purposes, such as opposing fascism, and on occasions working within these parties.

In India, this opened the way for collaboration between the Congress and their fierce critics to the left, the communists—and in Punjab both needed the other. Lahore was the city of Bhagat Singh, India's most celebrated revolutionary nationalist.[2] He killed a British police officer in Lahore and after months on the run was involved in throwing two fairly harmless explosive devices into the Central Legislative Assembly in Delhi. After a trial which had the effect of galvanising nationalist opinion, Bhagat Singh was hanged in the grounds of Lahore jail in March 1931—just as Bedi was preparing to head to England. Singh was 23 and came to be widely regarded as a martyr for the national cause. 'One's elemental urge went entirely Bhagat Singh's way,' Bedi reflected in later years, 'and one's inner conditioning ... coming from a religious family, went more towards, perhaps, Gandhiji's path.'[3] That inner conditioning was largely superseded during his years in Oxford and Berlin by militant leftism. Two political forces in Punjab fed into India's incipient communist movement—the Ghadar (or rebel) party, a largely Sikh organisation which gained prominence in the years immediately after the First World War; and the Kirti Kisan (workers and peasants) party, which remained an influential radical and socialist force in rural Punjab. But the left was not particularly strong in the province, and the Congress was distinctly weak. The dominant political force through much of the 1930s was the Unionist Party, representing the landed elite and antipathetic to nationalism. When the Unionists were eventually eclipsed, the beneficiary was Muhammad Ali Jinnah's Muslim League, whose demand for a separate nation for India's Muslims was realised with the creation of Pakistan in 1947.

For the Bedis, finding a political home in Lahore was not straightforward—nor was it their immediate priority. 'For the first year and a half, we worked in a very indirect way because it was essential to build up at least a minimum income on which to live,' Freda explained to Olive Chandler in December 1936, 'but for the last nine months we have been doing much more openly socialist work ... among the students and the peasants. Holding study circles, addressing meetings, and P.L. has been holding peasant schools in the villages to instill [sic] a spirit of rebellion into them all (adult schools). We have had inspiring conferences lately ... there is a storm of rebellion in the Sikh peasantry of the Punjab, at present just brewing, but ready for the bursting.'[4]

For both, the introduction to political activity in Lahore was in the lecture hall. When early in 1936, a radical organisation in Lahore organised a series of lectures on 'The Great Contemporaries', Bedi addressed the inaugural session on 'Hitler in the Rebuilding of Germany'. Freda spoke at a later meeting about the Irish nationalist and republican Eamon de Valera, at that time head of government of the Irish Free State—the comparisons with Indian nationalism were unstated but clear.[5]

It was a big step for Freda to move from talking to relatively small groups much in the fashion of a college lecture to addressing mass meetings on contested political issues. Bedi was a natural orator, with a powerful voice, an ease with words and command of Punjabi as well as English. For Freda this was a skill she needed to develop. She recalled that her first big meeting was a student gathering at one of Lahore's principal nationalist venues, the Bradlaugh Hall:[6]

> B.P.L. said oh, you know, they want you to talk—it's nothing, you just talk as you talk in a debating society at Oxford. And when I got there I was petrified to find that there were 24,000 people waiting, and this crowd of 24,000 had a very definite opinion about what it should listen to and what it shouldn't. And if it didn't like the speaker it would start beating the ground with sticks and the soles of the feet and making a noise so the speaker would have to go down.
>
> Anyway, I decided that the reason they didn't like a number of speakers was that they couldn't hear them and the best thing would be to speak pretty loudly ... So I stood on the platform like a martyr awaiting execution and I suddenly began speaking—I think it was about the proctorial system in Oxford or something like that, which they'd asked me to speak on—in a very loud voice, and I can still feel the shock that went through the whole 24,000 heads when this slight western-looking person suddenly bellowed into the microphone, must have been out of sheer fright. And that established me as a speaker. I found I could go on speaking and not be drummed out of existence by the sticks and the feet.[7]

In November 1936, Freda addressed a similar event—a large audience 'consisting mostly of young men' at the Lajpat Rai hall in Lahore at the inaugural meeting of the Punjab Youth Association. Again she traded off her student years at Oxford: she 'was tired of hearing from people that the Punjab youth was fond of fashions because she had begun to feel that the heart of the Punjab youth was very sound':

> She told the students that they could form an organisation, just as they had done at Oxford, and influence the politics of their country. She wanted them to organise a united anti-imperialist front in the Punjab. They were a force and they could do wonders.[8]

Freda was in some demand to address these large meetings. She had a certain novelty value—a white woman in her mid-twenties—but she also had a natural authority and the ability to command an audience.

By this time, Bedi—and probably Freda too—had joined first the Punjab Socialist Party and then the more substantial Congress Socialist Party. The CSP was an uneasy alliance of socialists who wanted to win the Congress to a more activist-based style of politics and of communists whose allegiance was to the underground party and to Moscow more than to the Congress and its leadership. While this wasn't always a sharp or distinct divide, Bedi was in the latter camp. The Bedis' quarterly journal *Contemporary India* was not a party publication but its allegiance to the CSP was crystal clear, as was its advocacy of political work among the kisan, India's peasantry. Bedi had grown up in a village, he was comfortable with the colloquial, village style of the Punjabi language and he understood the rural radicalism of the Kirti Kisan party. It was a style of politics to which he could relate.

Bedi relished organising and lecturing in the Punjabi countryside. He convened kisan schools, designed both to increase political awareness among rural workers and to identify and train a cadre of activists. The first school was held in Lahore, and the initiative then spread out to other areas. The courses stretched over fifteen days, with a mix of formal sessions and of looser political conversation. Food was provided either by Sikh gurdwaras or by local collections. The syllabus consisted of the study of three revolutions, those in America, France and Russia—Bedi said he wrote a very simple Punjabi primer about the Russian revolution. Basic Marxist theory was supplemented by a look at economic history, showing how Britain had exploited India. This was leavened by issues much more directly linked to peasant life: about the law, rights and what police could and couldn't do.[9] Freda got involved in this outreach work:

[I] went out a great deal into the villages to help the peasants in their demands for remission of land revenue and various demands of that kind and for civil liberties in the villages. I later became the secretary of the first civil liberties union in the Punjab and had to travel a great deal to protect villagers against very heartless police officers ... It became part of my life to spend weekends also going out and to protect people against police beating by bringing this to the notice of the towns. And the Punjab peasant became familiar to me and a friend. So when I say in those days I addressed meetings of not just thousands of villagers but hundreds of thousands, I am not telling an untruth. And it became part of the way of life.[10]

This civil liberties advocacy was Freda Bedi's first independent political activity in Punjab—the first marking out of her own political space as distinct from that of her husband, who as a leading figure in establishing an India-wide leftist peasant movement became joint secretary of the Kisan Sabha (peasants' assembly).

The Indian Civil Liberties Union was established by the Congress's Jawaharlal Nehru in 1936—two years after the National Council for Civil Liberties was established in Britain, harnessing radical, communist and pacifist concerns about illiberalism and an intolerance towards political dissent. Freda was diligent in seeking out breaches of civil liberties and became the most prominent activist in Punjab of a movement which she insisted was non-party and non-denominational 'welcoming all shades of opinion in its rank'. By the spring of 1937, Freda was on the national council of the Civil Liberties Union and in June she was the principal organiser and speaker at a widely reported civil liberties conference in Amritsar. The purpose of the Union, she explained, was 'to throw the spotlight of publicity on any encroachments of the legal rights of the people, and to consolidate public opinion so that we are in a position to demand redress from the authorities concerned. Its function is therefore, mainly as a propagandistic body.' So the aim was to work within the system more than to challenge it. She talked of the civil liberties movements already in place in Europe and America 'and we can count on their help and co-operation in this fight which has in reality no national boundaries, but is concerned with man and his relation to the state. We of the Colonial countries'—she declared in an emphatic expression of her identification with India over England—'may be more in need of such organizations, but it is only a matter of degree because wherever there are rich and poor, wherever in fact Capitalism raises its head, the need is urgent.'[11]

Once established as a speaker, the demands on Freda's time became relentless. She and Bedi both spoke at a Congress Socialist Party meeting in Lahore on the anniversary of Karl Marx's death; she described him as 'a brave fighter who fought all his life for his convictions'. A month later, both spoke at union meeting of sweepers in Lahore, where Freda's remarks were particularly militant, insisting that 'there were two worlds and not one':

> One was of the rich who enjoyed life and the other of the poor who had not enough to eat. The rich were mosquitos who lived as parasites on the blood of the poor. But if the poor people stopped work for a day all the rich people of Lahore would come and fall upon their feet. The real power, therefore, which made the world move were the people who worked with their own hands. It was for them however to mobilise their strength.[12]

She also urged the sweepers 'to bring their women folk with them to such conferences as they were as hungry as they—men—were and their difficulties were the same as those of men.' A month after that she was outside the Khalsa College in Amritsar—where Bedi had turned down a professorship—as students protested against the political victimisation of some of the teaching staff. 'Mrs Bedi said it was their right to protest if any of their beloved professors was maligned ... Had such a thing happened in Oxford or in any country other than India the whole population would have come forward and taken up the cause of the students. In the end Mrs Bedi advised the students to remain firm until their demands were fully met.'[13] Another month on, and she was presiding at a meeting of striking bank and insurance workers. She was developing a reputation as a radical activist. While Bedi will have had a higher profile in the rural areas of Punjab, in Lahore—where Freda's limited Punjabi was less constraining—she was probably as well-known as her husband. Not that all this came entirely naturally to her. 'It was not an easy position for an English girl married to a Punjabi to, as it were, float on that ocean of great national feeling,' she recalled years later. 'But I felt as an English person I should be dedicated to something that really was a matter of pure democracy, real democracy. And I believed in the ideals of Mahatma Gandhi.'[14]

The temper of politics was becoming more turbulent. The stalemate over India's demand for independence increasingly turned the country's intelligentsia against their colonial masters. The tussle for control of the Congress was being won by more radical figures, notably Subhas Chandra Bose, who was elected the Congress president—in spite of Gandhi's misgivings—in 1938 and again the following year. Freda attended some of the most crucial and contested Congress gatherings—an Urdu language newspaper published a photograph of her at one such event with Bose also in the picture. The public order situation was at times precarious, with newspapers reporting police using lathis, their over-size truncheons,

against demonstrators, and of fights and stone-throwing between
rival groups at left-wing rallies. Towards the close of 1938, Bedi
was named president of the Punjab Trade Union Congress, and
after the hoisting of the red flag, he both praised the Congress and
quoted from Lenin as he urged the need for a 'broad and powerful
Anti-Unionist Front'.[15]

Bedi was not always guarded in his oratory—his language was at
times flamboyant, some critics might say incendiary. A new aspect
intruded into the Bedis' life and political activity. 'B.P.L. suffered
his first term of imprisonment, could be about 1937, because of
some particularly provoking speech he had made at some kisan or
peasant conference,' Freda·recalled:

> And I began to see his prediction come true—living naturally
> always in a state of worry as to how things would go in the jail.
> By and large, the jails, at least the ones we came into contact
> with, were not unduly oppressive, and often there were some
> enlightened Indian officers in charge who were nationalists at
> heart and did not give any hard time to the prisoners. ... B.P.L.
> was cheery and somewhat stoical about these things as were many
> of his friends, and he had many good friends, and usually there
> were one or two like that in jail with him. So I carried on with
> my usual routine. I've no doubt my mother-in-law, because of her
> age and generation, suffered more than I did about this.[16]

Ranga has childhood memories of his father being detained by the
police—sometimes for a few hours, sometimes a few days, occasionally
longer. Freda and her colleagues in the Civil Liberties Union made
the plight of political detainees a focus of their activity.

To eke out a living, both Freda and Bedi wrote school and college
textbooks. Freda recalled that she wrote one about the art of precis
writing. Bedi took on some more ambitious commissions, the most
successful being his biography of the Sikh civil engineer, architect
and philanthropist, Sir Ganga Ram. This remains the work for which

he is best known in Punjab.[17] There was another new publishing project, a new political paper, which engaged much of Bedi's energies and Freda's too—and which added to their reputation in Lahore. *Contemporary India* had been highbrow; his new title *Monday Morning* was determinedly popular. As the name suggests, it was a weekly. They had spotted a gap in the market. The Lahore daily papers did not at that time work on Sundays and so did not publish a Monday edition. So a weekly hitting the newsstands first thing on Monday didn't have much in the way of direct competition.

No copies of *Monday Morning* have been located so it's difficult to judge its style and political agenda but for a while, at least, it sold well. 'Some English friends at the time called it laughingly a rag—I suppose it was a bit of a rag,' Freda said, 'but it was a very outspoken, interesting weekly paper which came out on Monday morning and successfully deprived us of every bit of rest that we might have had on Saturday and Sunday as a result. ... I learned a tremendous amount ... about how to bring out papers and press schedules and proof reading and a number of other things and we got a lot of fun out of it. And this helped the family finances somewhat because advertisements began to come in.'[18]

Monday Morning became a serious irritant to the authorities. 'This magazine had a very profound effect, because it was very militant,' Bedi recalled, 'totally anti-fascist in character, because anti-fascism was the wave of the times, and naturally it had to be anti-British, and it became one of the big exposure magazines. Any exposure which nobody would publish, we would publish.' Bedi claimed, with perhaps a measure of exaggeration, that the weekly achieved a circulation of 40,000 after six months, and so alarmed Lahore's main nationalist daily, the *Tribune,* that the paper tried to coerce newsagents into not selling their weekly rival. Bedi's main collaborator on the paper was Jag Parvesh Chandra, later a prominent Congress politician in Delhi. He recalled gathering with others at the Bedis' huts to work out how to start the paper, and the excitement of its early impact:

'the paper became a mouthpiece of the nationalist movement and was a success from the start.'[19] Another of the *Monday Morning* team was the actor Balraj Sahni, then in his mid-twenties and something of a political innocent. Bedi insisted that he warned Sahni against getting involved in the messy world of political journalism. 'I said, "My Dear Balraj, look here. This is politics. If it were a literary magazine, I would say gladly come. Running a political weekly without any funds is a dog's job and we are dogs, we are out to be whipped by our own choice. You are an artist."'[20] Balraj duly bailed out after three months. His younger brother, the novelist Bhisham Sahni, gave a somewhat jaundiced account of the hand-to-mouth launch of the paper:

> the editors had neither the resources nor the know-how of a weekly journal. Their enthusiasm and youthful energy were their only assets. It was planned that the paper would cover, besides news, cultural events and contain stories and poems, as also articles projecting socialist thought and ideology.
>
> We waited eagerly for the first issue of the paper, but when at last it came, my heart sank. It was a two-sheet paper, full of printing mistakes. ... The second issue, a week later, was even worse, so far as printing mistakes were concerned and we feared that such a paper was not destined to last long. ... Meanwhile we received a letter from a relative living in Lahore, saying that he had met Balraj inside a printing press, where he sat on the floor, unshaven, in high fever, correcting proofs and that Balraj looked tired and exhausted.[21]

The family was greatly relieved when they learned that Balraj had walked out on *Monday Morning*. 'The experience had left him sad, but a good deal wiser.'

As the international situation became more tense, and the prospect of war loomed, the left in Punjab organised against military recruitment. This deeply alarmed the Imperial authorities who were in any event finding the enlistment of new soldiers more difficult, in part because of the growth of nationalist sentiment. Recruits from Punjab constituted fully half of the soldiers in the British Indian army.[22] They had proved their worth in France and Flanders in the First World War and were again to be conspicuous on battlefields far from India in the Second World War. In September 1938, Bedi's involvement in anti-recruitment activity prompted his most serious clash with the authorities—as Freda explained in a letter to her old friend Olive Chandler:

> Bedi got arrested on a political charge … Some hirelings of the Punjab Government broke up an Anti-Recruitment meeting at which Bedi was presiding (also breaking his head from behind, quite a nasty cut!). Later they had the audacity to arrest him, along with twenty-seven others, for rioting!! Just a ruse to prevent Anti-Recruitment propaganda, at a time when it was quite legal … To cut a long story short, Bedi + the others were finally allowed bail + the case has been dribbling on (without coming to any conclusions) for the last nine months. It is what is known as a 'harassment case', trying to put everyone to the maximum amount of trouble. When it will end, + with what result we don't know—they have only a very rocky concocted case again[st] them all, but the Government has got away with worse.[23]

The saga ended eighteen months later, when Bedi was convicted by a magistrate in Lahore of 'delivering an alleged anti-war speech in a public meeting outside the Railway Station' and was sentenced to two years rigorous imprisonment—though by then he was already behind bars.[24]

By the time Freda wrote that letter to her old Oxford friend in the summer of 1939, *Monday Morning* had folded: 'after terrific hard work, sometimes from eight in the morning to eight in the evening, with scarcely a day's break, it has had to stop. Journalism in India is a tragic struggle against advertisers + newsagents who sit on bills +

never pay up + it's practically impossible to carry on without strong financial backing which, as all over the world, a "left" newspaper can rarely get!'[25] It had survived for about eighteen months.

7

Behind the Mud Walls

Freda Bedi's wartime incarceration in Lahore Female Jail is the act of valour which forged her reputation as a nationalist icon. Thousands of Indian nationalists and leftists were detained for opposing India's participation in the Second World War. Vanishingly few of these were English and white skinned and so identified in the public mind with the coloniser rather than the colonised. Freda was, of course, both undeniably English and unequivocally on India's side. She was jailed as a deliberate act of protest and renunciation—offering herself up for arrest under an initiative launched and overseen by Mahatma Gandhi, who personally approved all those who were to be his satyagrahis, or disciples of truth. She was the first, and perhaps the only, European woman to be part of this phase of Gandhi's non-violent protest against the Imperial power. For her, as for so many others, jail strengthened political resolve and extended the network of nationalist sympathisers. It also provided a window on the lives and tribulations of those so often beyond the view of middle-class India—the women who shared the prison grounds with her not out of political commitment but because of the desperate acts they had been pushed to by a profoundly unequal and patriarchal society. That, as much as the informal political meetings and study classes, was a part of Freda's education in jail.

War was declared in September 1939. The tensions within the Congress Socialist Party between communists and others were by

now acute. But all agreed, initially at least, on the need to oppose
the war—the Congress because Britain's Viceroy in New Delhi had
declared that India was at war with Germany without the agreement
(or indeed seeking the agreement) of India's political leaders, and
the communists because Moscow, in the wake of the Nazi-Soviet
pact, had declared that this was an imperialist war. By the end of
October 1939 more than 150 Punjabi politicians were in jail, and
by the end of the following year that number had swelled to many
hundreds. Punjab led the rest of India in the number of communists
and socialists detained—generally on the grounds of their anti-war
and anti-recruitment activities.[1]

B.P.L. Bedi was, by his own account, publishing anti-war
literature and using his contacts in the rail unions to help get the
leaflets circulated around the country. He was not among the early
wave of arrests, but he knew that he was likely to be detained before
long. That knock on the door came in early December 1940. 'I had
just come from Lahore and the British Superintendent of police
had arrived,' Bedi recalled. 'Soon after my servant told me that
there seemed to be some peculiar movement of people round the
bushes so I immediately sensed that the moment of my arrest had
come. Within ten minutes of his announcing this, he arrived and
in a very British way said, "I am afraid I have to arrest you."'[2] In an
even more British manner, Bedi asked the police officer to sit down
and have a cup of tea while he packed a blanket, some clothes and
a few books. Bedi was at this time on the national executive of the
Congress Socialist Party and his arrest under the Defence of India
Act was front page news in the *Tribune*. It reported that as he was
being driven away in the police car, 'Mrs Bedi raised loud shouts of
"Inquilab Zindabad"'—a communist slogan which best translates as
'Long Live the Revolution'.[3]

Bedi was held briefly in the jail in the town of Montgomery (now
Sahiwal), still in Punjab but some distance from Lahore, and then
was sent more than 400 miles away to Deoli, a remote spot on the

edge of the Thar desert in what is now Rajasthan. A Victorian-
era military base there had been turned into a detention camp—a
concentration camp, the communists complained—for political
detainees from across India. It had a long history of being used to
lock-up 'undesirables', and continued to fulfil that role in later years.
From 1942, the camp housed prisoners of war—and in 1962, it was
used to intern Indians of Chinese origin during a brief India-China
border conflict. As soon as he reached Deoli, Bedi began to protest
against his detention—refusing to carry his bags into the camp as a
statement, in his own words, that the 'revolutionaries' had arrived.
'At Deoli were nearly four-hundred persons, who were all Leftists
... From the moment we arrived we started planning to create more
trouble and a hunger strike was on the agenda.'[4]

Freda can hardly have been surprised by her husband's arrest, but
she was certainly angered by it. 'On December 4th, 1940, the lights
in the huts went out,' she recalled:

> Bedi was taken away for indefinite detention for being a Socialist,
> for hating Fascism, for hating the Imperialist exploitation of
> India. There was no oil in the lamps when the police came, and
> we groped around in the dark getting a few clothes together. Pug
> drooped his tail dejectedly when he said goodbye.[5]

A couple of days later, she announced that she too intended to
flout the wartime emergency regulations and was happy to take the
consequences. The *Tribune* reported that she had sought Gandhi's
permission to give herself up for arrest. 'Should Mahatma Gandhi's
permission be secured, Mrs Bedi will be the first English lady to
offer satyagraha in the civil disobedience campaign.'[6] Freda regarded
Gandhi's campaign as 'halting and incomplete'—but it was at least
action on a nationwide scale. 'There should have been a great, a
magnificent up-surge of the nation. Gandhiji decreed otherwise,
and chose his men with the greatest care. Only the few were to go

to jail to protest for the many. It was to be a demonstration to the world of India's national right.'[7]

At the end of January, Freda heard that Gandhi had agreed to her request—she believed she was the fifty-seventh volunteer to be chosen as a satyagrahi in this stage of the civil disobedience campaign. This was Freda's boldest political act—she was putting herself forward for arrest and imprisonment to protest against her native country's treatment of her adopted country. 'She said that she was born in England but had adopted India as her mother country,' the *Tribune* reported, 'and would wish to be known as an Indian woman.'[8] It was also an impetuous move. She had a six-year-old son whose father had just been detained indefinitely, and rather than be around to offer support and reassurance, she decided that the political imperative was what mattered most. She admitted being torn about what to do. 'It was a terrible blow to lose B.P.L. and his cheery daily support in life's problems. And his mother, my son, the adopted boy Binder and myself were left alone in the huts. I didn't want to make things worse on the domestic side but on the other hand I felt that I should back up the nationalist movement in whatever humble way I could, even if it meant suffering some months in prison. I felt I could trust my mother-in-law to look after the boy and my brother-in-law to see that the family did not lack support at that time.'[9] So the family arranged to move from the huts to Bedi's home village where they would be able to live comfortably with many members of the extended family there to help. In the carefully choreographed way of these protests, Freda wrote to the district magistrate in the town of Gurdaspur to tell him exactly when and where she intended to stage her act of civil disobedience. 'Mrs Freda Bedi left for Dera Baba Nanak,' the *Tribune* announced on its front page, 'where she will offer satyagraha on 21st [February] at 11 a.m.'[10]

'So I packed up my little household, put that furniture with this friend, that with another, here my crockery and there my few loved possessions,' Freda wrote. 'I left Lahore station, in a welter of photographs and flower garlands. The women in the women's compartment were inquisitive ... "It is degrading that Indians should be treated like this," I said. "Somebody had to do something: we can't just all sit down and keep quiet about it." "But what does your husband say about it?"one matron asked. "He is in jail himself," I replied. "Ah ..." her eyes were turned in pity towards me, "now I understand." It was the wife following her husband. That was as it should be.'[11] Freda was following in her husband's footsteps not out of blind loyalty; rather in a marriage which was based on intellectual and political camaraderie, she saw it as the natural course of action. Bedi of course did not offer himself for arrest; he was detained as an anti-war activist. It's not at all clear whether they had discussed what the family should do in his absence, but Freda never suggested that he had endorsed her intention to become a satyagrahi.

In writing about the eve of her arrest, Freda lapsed into a reflective mode which points to the complexity of her political commitment and the awareness that she was about to make an act that would come to define her. In the Bedi household in Dera Baba Nanak, she slept alongside Bhabooji, Ranga and Binder in a room lit by a spluttering oil lamp—but she felt lonely and vulnerable:

Little bodies and one big round body were lumped under the fluffy cotton-stuffed quilts. There was somebody still banging pots and pans in the kitchen. I could hear Pug and Snug barking somewhere in the garden. Suddenly, I felt alone, agonisingly alone. I could have wept for my sheer aloneness. I wanted to talk to Bedi, to have his cheery voice near me. What I wanted to say I could not say in my limited Punjabi. I doubt if I could have said it in English, or even mentally told myself what I felt. I suppose in all crises of our life we get that feeling of isolation as though we are treading a path into the future and are treading it, for all the love that surrounds us, quite alone. When we first leave home, when we marry. When we have a choice to make at some cross-roads of our life and endeavour. ... And on the borders of that aloneness, of that feeling of smallness in the face of the immensity of the unknown, there comes another feeling, which is interwoven with it and part of it and yet not part of it, of being given the strength to carry on, of not being alone any more. Of being a part of something greater than the mere individual human body.[12]

This was written within a couple of years of Freda's imprisonment and a decade before she became interested in Buddhism, but there is a pronounced spiritual aspect to her account. Freda became comfortable with the feeling of isolation she describes—it was another border she chose to cross—and instinct, or faith, guided her at what she calls the crossroads of her life, which gave her a sense of comfort that she was on the right track.

'We wrote a letter to the district magistrate,' Freda recalled, 'saying that we would break the law by asking the people not to support the military effort until India became democratic and that India must get her elected government first. But since we sent the letter, we effectively prevented ourselves from speaking because on the day we were supposed to speak we were naturally arrested before this happened.' Exactly what happened in the village that February morning is difficult to establish beyond doubt through the layers of valorous nationalist narrative and family folklore.[13] Freda's own account is both the most straightforward and most credible. Her intention was to shout anti-war slogans in Punjabi in the village streets. She heard that the local inspector had summoned an English officer from Amritsar, thinking it best to have an Englishman to hand when an Englishwoman was placed under arrest. 'At eight-thirty they arrived. In the centre was the local Inspector with a beard. He came forward politely, "regretting that it is my duty but I must arrest you." The turbanned police-officer on his left had a half-smile. To the right was the European Inspector from Amritsar

in an unwieldy topee [hat]. He was surprisingly small and had a
walrus moustache. He looked like Old Bill: I wanted to laugh, and
the corners of my mouth twitched. "Yes, I am quite ready. Take
me along with you.'"

The little procession started towards the Police Station winding
its way back through narrow brick-paved gulleys of the village.
The shopkeepers came to the door of their shops, with their hands
folded in greeting. The women crowded on the flat roofs to see
us go, and sighed in the doorways. A few young men and boys
began to attach themselves to the little group and shouted wildly
'Freedom for India. Long live Gandhiji. Long live Jawaharlal
Nehru. Long live Comrade Bedi. Release the detenues.' We
reached the elegant grey Amritsar car parked under the *peepul* tree
near the only *pucca* road. Garlands were thrown over the radiator
of the car, through the windows. They were removed immediately:
'garlands not allowed'.[14]

At the village police station, Freda was questioned by the police
officer she had nicknamed Old Bill, who she later discovered had
'Irish blood and a kind heart'—though the interrogation was limited
to questions along the lines of 'What colour would you call your hair?'
Under the wartime regulations, trials under the Defence of India
Act could be held straightaway and without any legal formality or
indeed representation. Freda was taken from the police station to
the dak bungalow, the guest house where visiting officials stayed,
and that's where her trial took place that same morning:

It was finished in fifteen minutes. The man on the other side of
the table was quite young still, and looked as though he had been
to Oxford. His face was red.

'I find this as unpleasant as you do,' he murmured.

'Don't worry. I don't find it unpleasant at all.'

'Do you want the privileges granted to an Englishwoman?'

'Treat me as an Indian woman and I shall be quite content'
… The room was deserted but there was a noise, and two Congressmen walked in. They had been allowed at the last minute to attend the 'public trial'. They carried a round shining brass tray filled with flowers and sweetmeats.

'Wait until you have heard my judgment, perhaps you will not want to give them then.'

Six months Rigorous Imprisonment.

'She cannot have the garlands. Give her one or two of the sweets.'[15]

Freda had expected the jail sentence, but not the specification of rigorous imprisonment. 'Hard labour was the point,' she said many years later, 'and none of the Indians arrested got hard labour in the Punjab except myself. None of the women at least. Whether it was the ignorance of the young civil servant, Englishman, who gave the sentence, very regretfully and with many apologies. … Or whether it was that they wanted to make an example of me because I was the first, maybe, western woman to offer satyagraha at that time.' Once the sentence was pronounced, Freda was put back in the car which was mobbed by well-wishers, many of them members of the Bedi clan, as it set off to Lahore jail.

News of Freda Bedi's arrest and sentence once again made the front page of the *Tribune*, complete with a posed portrait photograph. The following day's paper offered a fuller account of her arrest and sentence—which emphasised the level of local interest in and support for her action, reporting that she was 'profusely garlanded by the public' after sentence was passed in a trial in which she had refused to participate. The Reuters news agency eventually picked up the story—and a few weeks after the event, the jailing of 'the first Englishwoman to join Mr Gandhi's passive resistance movement' made front page news back in Freda's home city with the headline: 'Derby Wife of Indian Sentenced'.[16] Freda of course regarded herself as Indian but her act of protest gained attention and achieved impact precisely because she was not Indian. It's a paradox which didn't greatly perturb her. She seems to have managed to negotiate these conflicts of identity without a lot of soul-searching. However much she might seek to forsake the special status accorded in colonial India to those with white skins, it was an indelible aspect of her life there. Inspector Price, the moustachioed Irishman, had been sent from Amritsar to Dera Baba Nanak to be present at Freda's arrest because it felt inappropriate for a white woman to be detained simply by Indian policemen. It was another example of the awkwardness of the British authorities in India in the face of a British woman who had sided with India. They had dealt with British men who had allied with and supported Indian leftist and nationalist movements—indeed there were three British communists among the defendants in the long-running Meerut conspiracy case which was widely discussed in both India and Britain in the early 1930s and for which Oxford's October Club had collected money—but a white woman directly challenging Imperial rule was a much rarer phenomenon.

Freda wrote luminously about her time behind the mud walls of Lahore's female jail (after her release, she and a fellow prisoner persuaded the authorities to rename it, with greater verbal precision, as Lahore women's jail). Within days of her release, she began a short series 'From a Jail Diary' in the *Tribune*, concerned particularly with the 'criminal' prisoners—she was a 'political'—she met there. This developed into a much more ambitious account of her time behind bars—a day-by-day jail diary which is the spine of her book *Behind the Mud Walls*, and is the most resonant and affecting of her writings. She weaves into her account of imprisonment the personal, the political, the observational, with reflections of the temper of Indian nationalism and more so about the inequity, the gender injustice, which consigned so many of the non-political inmates to long terms of confinement. It is one of the most remarkable and readable accounts of Indian nationalist endeavour at this time. The jail diary is a well-established literary form and as the struggle against colonialism led to the detention of intellectuals who would otherwise be unlikely to land in jail, there are many nationalist narratives of imprisonment. Few are quite as compelling, as simple and unadorned, as the account Freda Bedi published as 'Convict No. 3613'.[17]

'The mud road to the "Female Jail" was long and dusty,' Freda wrote. 'The gates looked like the Lion House at the Zoo.'

The gates opened. We went in. They shut. It was cool like a cellar in the entrance room. Beyond was a second door: a sheet of solid iron like a safe. To the right the Deputy Superintendent's room. I was motioned towards the door. It was bare and depressing. A cold stare came from the aging woman in a drab frock on the other side of the table.

'What is her crime?'

'Political ... Six Months Rigorous Imprisonment,' said 'Old Bill'. After a few minutes, he turned and left.

The world beyond the barred gate seemed a long way away.

'Give over all your jewellery and money,' said the Deputy Superintendent.

'I haven't got any jewellery.'

She pointed to my left hand.

'That is my wedding ring.'

'It is also counted as jewellery,' she replied.

I looked at my wedding ring. It had never left my hand since that day in Oxford when Bedi put it on. Reluctantly, I used my last weapon.

'I am an A Class prisoner. Are you within your rights in taking it away?'

... There was a shuffling sound, a sort of subdued commotion, on the other side of the inner iron door. I could see an eye glittering through the peep-hole. Shouts of 'Gandhiji ki Jai' [Long live Gandhi] and lots of 'Zindabads'. It seems the 'politicals' had found out that I had arrived.[18]

The small group of political prisoners in the women's jail banded together: on Freda's first evening 'behind the mud walls', they spun together, 'our common badge and discipline as satyagrahis'. On one occasion they staged a twenty-hour spinning relay—Freda declared herself 'not very thrilled at the idea, but doing something has got its moral exhilarations ... I took my turn at 4.30 a.m.' There was also collective reading of Hindu scriptures and talks, meetings and education sessions. The camaraderie among these women activists was intense and nourishing. They were responsible for their own cooking, and the jail regime was sufficiently relaxed to allow them to meet fairly freely, staging informal political gatherings and on one occasion having a picnic and dance in the prison grounds.

Freda practised yoga in the mornings. 'I am doing them with no "spiritual" intent, only to keep healthy in the roasting months ahead of me. Find they are simple, rhythmical, and invigorating.' She read alone from Hindu religious writings and from novels by Aldous Huxley and John Steinbeck—'feel the lack of political books,' she noted, 'we forget how dependent we are on them.' She described herself on entering the jail as a professor of English and college connections sometimes resurfaced in surprising ways. 'The new Deputy Superintendent came to-day,' Freda wrote in her diary. 'It seems she was one of my old B.A. pupils. She is touched that I am here. I feel amused.'

Alongside the fairly unexacting routine, for the political prisoners at least, was the hardship of the raging summer heat which turned the very basic sanitary facilities into a 'horrible' ordeal. 'I was trying to decide the other day what annoyed me most, physically, here, and I decided it was the dilemma of sitting in the latrine with (1) either my face in a dirty sacking curtain; or (2) throwing up the curtain and being frightened of somebody arriving quietly and catching me. The latrines are uncovered to sun and rain and we are exposed to the elements. ... One can get used to anything, and one has to shut one's eyes and ears and brain to it, but if I give way to what I really felt, I could be sick every time I go near the place.'[19]

Freda made two strong political friendships—with the peasant leader Bibi Raghbir Kaur, described by Freda as 'my political mother-in-law', and with the renowned Aruna Asaf Ali, who was about Freda's age and had form as a political prisoner (after her release from Lahore jail she famously went underground as a pro-independence activist). Aruna was from Delhi, and housed in a different block, but they arranged to meet regularly. 'Aruna came for tea,' Freda wrote in her account of jail life a month into her imprisonment. 'She is a comfort, and I am happy with her. With her I can exchange thoughts—she's the only one who can give me that satisfaction. Although I manage in Hindustani, I know so few words that it is a continual frustration to try and express myself. Besides which, quite apart from speaking to her, or any question of language, I am fond of her.' As a team they worked well, all were leftists as well as admirers of Gandhi, and they managed to hold a May Day meeting inside the prison:

A few words from me on its significance. Attari Devi sang 'Inquilab Zindabad'; Raghbir Kaur spoke in Punjabi on the peasant and the worker; Aruna a little on Lenin and the significance of the Russian revolution. A funny rambling affair, but we did manage to celebrate it. Had a gnawing feeling inside me because of newspaper reports on Deoli, couldn't eat properly, felt like vomiting. The temperature has gone to 116. Mentally, it doesn't worry me.[20]

Concern about the plight of her husband was a constant preoccupation—she was anxious about reports of a hunger strike at the much more spartan and remote Deoli camp and worried when she didn't hear from him for weeks on end. 'In his confinement, he must be thinking of me, and indeed I have felt him almost physically with me these last stirring days,' she wrote on the second day of her detention. The occasional telegram from Bedi gave her a big boost. One came on Ranga's seventh birthday—'Congrats for Bunny Heart'. 'Such a silly telegram and so nice to get it.' Freda missed her son too and was delighted when permission was given for him to spend a few days with her, sharing her bed. Ranga too—who still has notes he sent as a child to his parents in their separate jails, one in Punjabi and the other in English—was thrilled to spend time with his mother. But he wasn't allowed to accompany her during the day as she worked, and some children of the non-political detainees jeered and mocked him, so it was a short stay.

Freda shared a cell with 'two very lovely women of the old type', as she described them—both were brahmins and vegetarians as well as political campaigners. She gave them English lessons, and in return was helped in her Hindi. 'Both Lakshmi and Savitri remain for me an example of beautiful Indian womanhood: self-sacrificing, simple, cheerful. Naturally pure. And it was a great privilege to spend three months sharing a room with them. I shall never forget it. They both excelled in simple Indian cookery, making maize cakes and vegetables, and insisted on doing this little service for me. And I found time in the early mornings to meditate, at dawn under the trees in the jail compound, before my labour started—which took the form of gardening.'

She was fortunate that her hard labour consisted of running the prison gardens—a much more congenial option than the laundry or picking ropes or other punishment labour. 'It's still delirious with young leaves and the scent of orange blossom, the cooing of doves, the screech of parrots, an early owl hooting,' she wrote in mid-March. In a replication inside jail of the class hierarchy outside, she was put in charge of a group of 'criminal' prisoners in tending to the flowers and vegetables in the small prison grounds. Freda liked the work, which brought to mind the huts in Model Town, and she relished the opportunity to get to know the other inmates and something of the circumstances that led to their jailing. Repeatedly in her jail

diary, she relates life stories which were stacked against the women.
'Find our fellow prisoners in the "criminal" barracks most interesting.
Seems a good many of the better-looking are young wives in jail for
killing old husbands. Consensus of opinion seems to be that jail is
preferable to an old husband.'

Among these prisoners, one in particular stood out—by her
appearance, and the curious and exceptional story that surrounded
her:

Met one beautiful woman—yes, really beautiful, of a beauty that
pulled strings inside you. Lallo is a Pathani, from the wild frontier,
cream of skin and undarkened by the sun of the plains.

She wore the brilliant yellow basanti [spring-like] clothes of
those who have been in jail a very long time, and her veil was
thrown twice over her head, as if to suggest purdah, and some
sweet modesty. Her long-lashed eyes had the mystery of beauty
in them, and every movement of her slim erect body had a grace
that cried to the prison walls. 'She has been thirteen years in
prison, since her early teens, when she killed an old husband' I
was told.

There were even more unusual stories about the Pathani. The
young lover who had put the poison into her mind and her hands
had not been convicted: to shield him, she had named another,
and that man, innocent as he was, had suffered with her fourteen
years of exile and disgrace. But in the court-room he had fallen in
love with the girl who had wronged him, and taken his life in her
hands. He had applied for interviews with her every year, and told
her that he was suffering for her, and she must reward him at the
end of his long penance by becoming his wife. And his devotion
was not in vain, because she too fell in love with him.

In another six months, he will leave the prison and its routine.
Six months after that, she too will leave the mud walls, and put
her life in his hands, as once he put his in hers.[21]

There is an innocence about the story and the manner in which it is told that reflects an aspect of Freda's personality: accepting, trusting, caring. It's difficult to imagine that the young prisoner's tale is quite as Shakespearean as is related here, but Freda clearly wants this story to be true, and wants the woman to find redemption.

On other occasions she was simply angry at the blatant gender injustice. 'Saw an Arab girl in the garden,' she wrote. 'Sixteen, married to a 78 year-old husband who had sent her and other "wives" on the streets to beg and for prostitution. He bit off the top of her ear when she ran away with another man, who has since joined the army. Now he has framed this abduction case against her. I really wonder if European jails would be big enough if every woman who ran away with a man was prosecuted and jailed for a few years. ... A stranger in a foreign land. Nothing to go back to; nothing to look forward to. We told her to demand divorce through her lawyers. Anything better anyhow than that old satyr.' This spell in jail, and the insight it gave her into the lives and difficulties of the most marginalised women in Indian society, pushed her towards a feminist emphasis on the need to tackle the built-in power bias towards men and to encourage women to challenge male authority and take control of their own destiny. 'The dread of having daughters is so real, the financial burden of marrying them so great. The social system is Sinner No. 1.' As so often for nationalist and left-wing detainees, jail proved to be part of her political education: 'reactionary' Indian Civil Service rule, she wrote, 'is worse than the most reactionary popular government.'[22] She also, perhaps for the first time, got to know well women from underprivileged backgrounds, and was moved by their plight and on occasion sought to advocate on their behalf. Her time in jail set her on course to the social work she took up in Kashmir and, more determinedly, in Delhi.

In mid-May 1941, word began to circulate in the jail that some of the women were to be released, because of a ruling that an intention to challenge the wartime regulations was not a sufficient basis for

conviction. If activists had not publicly challenged India's involvement
in the war, then they had not broken the law. The rumours turned
out to be true. In her entry for 24 May 1941, Freda wrote:

> My last day in jail. Got up and went into the garden very early;
> did my exercises. Packed, with some difficulty, my little household.
> All went and had a breakfast of pooris and vegetables and halwa
> with the Delhi people in Aruna's tiny courtyard opposite the cell.
> We sat on mats on a white sheet with the thalis [plates] in front
> of us. The Superintendent arrived half way and sat talking to us.
> There was an atmosphere of regret: we were parting, after so long
> together, in an intimacy that only jail life gives. Who knows which
> of us will meet again, have the same talks.[23]

After a little over three months in detention, Freda emerged from
behind the mud walls. A large number of male political detainees
were being released in Lahore on the same day, and for the same
reason: in all, fifty-three satyagrahis emerged from Lahore jails,
thirteen of them women.[24] The local Congress party wanted Freda
and other women set free to go to the men's borstal and journey
with them to a big rally at the Bradlaugh Hall. She didn't feel like
a big fuss, so she made her excuses, phoned and sent telegrams to
give word of her release, and then went to Fateh Chand College:
'the girls crowded round me like bees: we were so happy to see each
other again.'

A few days later, Freda travelled to Dera Baba Nanak, where
Bhabooji had been presiding over the family. The local Congress
committee, led by one of her husband's relatives, organised a grand
procession which welcomed Freda at the railway station and paraded
her across the village.[25] 'A terrific fuss, including a brass band and
innumerable garlands to welcome me,' Freda recorded.

> They did it out of love, but I felt embarrassed, with so much
> motia [jasmine] round my neck, walking through the almost

unbreathable dust in a procession back to the village. All the
village seemed to be there, making a deafening noise. They carried
Ranga shoulder high and took us first to the Darbar Sahib [Sikh
temple] to offer a rupee and get the sugar in return. We went
on to uncle Ram Das's house and still the crush continued, the
women and children flooding the rooms and refusing to go,
although I folded my hands in entreaty, longing to be left alone.
They called it darshan but after an hour or two it [felt] like being
in a zoo.[26]

During the procession, Freda addressed the crowd: she urged them
to wear homespun cloth, join the Congress and appealed to Hindus
and Muslims to join together to achieve India's freedom. Immediately
on her release, Freda rang Mian Iftikharuddin, a friend, fellow leftist
and president of the Punjab Provincial Congress Committee. She
was seeking political instructions. She told him that she was 'ready
to do whatever the Congress wanted me to do. He said I should first
go and interview Bedi, and see him on my return.' So Freda planned
a journey to visit her husband at the Deoli camp, and decided to
take seven-year-old Ranga with her.

Ranga's recollection is that Freda had to fight for permission to
make a family visit to Deoli, and that they made the trip 'in the
blistering heat of June' by third-class train, buses and then a lengthy
walk.

The camp was run and administered by the army, not the police,
and they had no information regarding our visit or the permissions
granted. There was perceptible discomfort among the British
junior officers in the guardroom, caused by Ooggee being British.
They were certainly overawed by her being in a khadi [homespun]
salwar kameez and the fact that she was the wife of a dangerous
political criminal. They were polite, made us comfortable under
a fan, and got some tea and nice biscuits. A short while later, we
were escorted to the office of the commandant, a strapping British

colonial. The commandant's discomfiture was greater than that of his juniors, he could not permit the visit without confirmation from the local headquarters.

Freda's skin colour worked to her advantage. She and Ranga were put up in a room set aside for senior officers on inspection visits; she declined an invitation to dine in the officers' mess. The visit to Bedi the following day didn't happen—Ranga's memory is that his father and other political detainees were on hunger strike, and an attempt to force feed Bedi ended with him grabbing the medical officer and dislocating his shoulder. "'Didn't you know he holds the all-India hammer throw record and was a wrestler in his college days?'" Ranga recalls his mother telling the camp commandant when she was informed why the visit wouldn't be possible.

The following day, a compromise was reached—Bedi agreed to call off his hunger strike, and Freda and Ranga were given exceptional permission to visit the detainee, still weak but adamant that he would not use a wheelchair, in his room.

> Two junior British officers were assigned to escort us to ensure that we did not communicate with any other prisoners or political detenues. Papa's barrack was quite a distance … He was in the last corner room, right next to the security fence and a watchtower, the sole occupant of a ten-by-ten foot room with a mattress on the floor, no furniture of any description, no curtain on the solitary window, no attached bathroom. Papa received us with hugs and kisses. Two rickety collapsible steel chairs were brought for us to sit on. One could see why the M.O. had refused permission for him to walk to the visitors' room. He was positively unstable on his feet.

They had ninety minutes with Bedi. All their books and gifts were seized for inspection. The camp provided a truck to drop Freda and Ranga at the main road, where they could catch a bus. She thanked the commandant, and left a small packet of raisins—a welcome gift in wartime—for the injured medical officer.

Freda went back to teaching at Fateh Chand College. She was allowed to live in at the college and—an even bigger concession—to bring Ranga to live with her. He was bored by the absence of playmates, but fussed over and spoiled by the other staff and the students. He remembers with particular affection Teji Suri, another lecturer and close friend of Freda's who lived close to the college. 'Aunty Teji was a commanding personality, young, vibrant, beautiful and always immaculately turned out. The girls idolized her. Even at that age, I thought she was God's gift to man.' Teji Suri had visited the Bedi family in the village when both parents were detained, and had looked after Ranga in Lahore on his visit to his mother. When Freda was working late at college or going out, Ranga would go home with Teji Suri, and often served as a young chaperone when suitors came to call. He always imagined that the dashing, smartly dressed army captain would win out over the soft-spoken poet in a crushed kurta pyjama and well-worn open sandals. He was wrong. In 1941, Teji Suri married Harivansh Rai Bachchan and left Lahore. In October of the following year, their son Amitabh was born; he became the biggest Bollywood star of his era.

The notoriety that Freda had attained, both by her own activism and time in jail and her marriage to a prominent communist, made her a target for police surveillance. Ranga's recollection is that plain-clothes police officers came regularly to the college and questioned staff about what his mother was up to.

Administration staff members were called to the police station to check whether Ooggee was preaching sedition. Friends and relatives were not permitted to visit us in college, and our room was subjected to surprise searches to monitor her writings. At the college gate, a book was maintained in which Ooggee would have to log where she was going and for what and who she would be meeting. On one occasion, a hostel sweeper was manhandled in the local police station. She marched off, with me in tow, to take the police inspector to task. She also forcibly made an entry in the complaint book. That evening, a British police officer visited college and threatened to arrest her for defiance.

This pattern of intimidation did not prevent her recommencing writing for the papers. Within days of her release, she resumed writing for the *Tribune*, for which she once more became a regular contributor. She commented, in a more nuanced manner than a card-carrying communist would, about the Soviet Union. 'Let us not think of Russia as a paradise,' she wrote as part of a 'Spotlight on Russia' feature in the *Tribune*. 'It had the debris of the past to clear away. It worked with ordinary human beings, and human beings make mistakes. Russia has made mistakes. Some she has admitted to and some she has not. To name a few of the most publicised, she collectivised agriculture too rapidly and too tactlessly, she invaded Finland, she antagonised world opinion with her "man hunting" purges.'[27]

There was no such ambivalence a few weeks later when she expressed her sorrow at the death of the Nobel laureate Rabindranath Tagore, who had helped to arouse her interest in India and its culture and beliefs. 'I first saw him at Oxford lecturing on the highest philosophy before some of the greatest savants and philosophers of the West. He sat on a low platform with the rare light of the late evening falling on his face and making an aureole round his white head. I was very moved by his understanding, his dignity, the way in which he seemed to distil the essence of India into the small hall and with it the essence of all that is highest and universal in man.' And she made a political point of out Tagore's passing. 'It was a pity ... that a country which could produce such a great man and a genius could still be denied the right of freedom.'[28]

Her main political concern, however, was Deoli, and the fate of her husband and hundreds of other leftists who remained locked up there. She became a member of a Central Aid Committee, set up amid reports of another hunger strike. At a regional gathering of the All-Indian Women's Conference she 'drew a sorrowful picture of the difficulties encountered during the journey to such a distant place … under dust and burning sun and held that the expenses incurred in going to Deoli and coming back to the Punjab were such which were beyond the means of the wives of the prisoners. If anything, the Government should at least open a separate camp in the Punjab so that the miseries of the poor wives of the hunger-strikers were not augmented.'[29]

A few weeks after Freda emerged from Lahore jail, the war took a turn which had direct repercussions for both her and her husband. Hitler launched Operation Barbarossa in June 1941 and attacked the Soviet Union, his erstwhile ally. Communist parties which had already carried out one contortion when the Molotov-Ribbentrop pact became public knowledge and changed overnight from describing the conflict as a war against fascism to an imperialist war were again wrong-footed. The British party quickly fell in line with Moscow and came to hail a people's war which needed to be prosecuted zealously, not least to protect Soviet communism from the Nazi aggressor. The Indian party was slower to respond to the changing contours of the conflict—in part because of a reluctance to make common cause with the Imperial power, and in part because the detention of so many leading left-wingers hampered debate and decision making. By the close of 1941, Indian communists were coming to accept the need to support the allied war effort against Germany and Japan. In April 1942, the communists confirmed their change of strategy, and so decided to support the war and all it entailed. Three months later, the Communist Party of India was legalised.[30] This support for the prosecution of the war was not a popular move in India. 'It alienated us completely from the national movement …' Bedi recalled, 'but at the same time the conviction was so deep that anti-fascism struggle had to be carried on.'[31] It also sharpened the distinction between communists and other progressive strands of nationalism. In August 1942, Congress launched the Quit India agitation which placed achieving independence ahead of fighting Germany and Japan, and which also entailed the detention of most Congress leaders for the remainder of the war; in that same month, the more radical nationalists led by Subhas Bose established the Indian National Army to fight alongside the Japanese in an attempt to evict Britain from India. The communists stood aloof from both endeavours.

Towards the close of 1941, a Friends of the Soviet Union association was established in Calcutta. Freda Bedi promptly took to the platform to endorse the campaign; her earlier misgivings about aspects of Soviet policy were set aside. 'The spirit that animates Russia in her magnificent resistance to Nazi barbarism will never die,' she told a students' conference at Lahore's Bradlaugh Hall at the end of November. She read a telegram from Bedi sent from Deoli, and passed by the censors there so in a sense approved by the British authorities: '"Convey students glowing greetings towards peace and progress through vigorously functioning Punjab Friends of Soviet."'[32] Within weeks, the new association had established a regional organisation in Punjab and Freda became the provincial organiser. It was the most prominent position she took in Indian politics, and her profile was eminently suitable for a communist front organisation of this period. She was not publicly associated with the party and she had a standing and reputation which helped the pro-Soviet, anti-Nazi, message percolate beyond the immediate ranks of the still underground CPI and its supporters. She had another considerable advantage—she was an exceptional organiser as well as an accomplished orator. The British communist intellectual Victor Kiernan was in Lahore at this time and regarded Freda highly, considering that she was 'emerging as one of the most effective of a new generation of Party leaders'.[33]

Victor Kiernan's comment prompts the question of whether Freda Bedi ever held a party card. If she did, that was more out of deference to her husband than devotion to the party. To judge from Bedi's own comments, it seems she was a member of the CPI, though briefly:

No meeting was held in Lahore those days where Bedi did not speak or Freda Bedi did not speak. She joined the communist party just out of loyalty to me, because I had joined the communist party. The party did not utilize her even to this extent. I do not think Freda Bedi addressed more than two/three meetings in the big city of Lahore after her association with the party which lasted for a limited time because they did not want her name to be more and more popular among the people. That was their small heartedness.[34]

'Our platform is non-party,' Freda insisted, not entirely convincingly, when seeking support for the initial conference of the Punjab section of the Friends of the Soviet Union, 'and the object of the organisation is to draw together all those who sympathise with the Soviets in their epic struggle against the Nazi hordes, whether on cultural, political or humanitarian ground.'[35] On another occasion she spoke of the Second World War as an 'international civil war' and asserted that 'it is to Russia that the poor and neglected of the world look'.[36] She spoke widely, warning that India would have 'greater troubles' if Japan triumphed while also raising money for medical supplies for the Soviet Union and—as a civil liberties activist—continuing to campaign for the release of political detainees.

The detention camp in Deoli served, as Imperial jails and detention camps so often did, as a recruiting ground for communism. The factionalising on the left evident before the war was played out behind the barbed wire too. But the communists were the best organised and intellectually the most confident, and the bulk of the detainees rallied to their standard. The communists had already made a determined attempt to take control of the Congress Socialist Party at its conference in Lahore in April 1938. Bedi's own account was that, in Punjab at least, there was no real need for the party to capture the provincial CSP, because most of its members had been won over to communism. He also details, however, how the CPI acted as a caucus within the wider party—establishing its own line on issues of policy and organisation and distributing secret circulars not to be shared with those with non-communists in the CSP.[37]

It was at Deoli that Bedi's allegiance to the CPI deepened. He entered the camp as a party sympathiser; he left it as a party apparatchik. By his own account, he was an important figure in the excited debates about communist strategy which helped wile away the long hours in the barracks. And he aligned himself with the hardliners in the party, such as B.T. Ranadive, and urged loyalty to Stalin and active support for the defence of the Soviet Union.

With communists now one of the few organised political groups in India to support the allied war effort, there was little purpose in keeping so many of their leading cadres locked up. A handful of Punjabi communist leaders were released in April 1942—even before the ban on the CPI was lifted. Bedi appears to have been part of the group. There were extenuating personal circumstance. Ranga was ill with a prolonged bout of typhoid which led to unsightly abscesses, and Freda strenuously sought her husband's release on compassionate parole.

By early May 1942, B.P.L. was back in Lahore. He was guest of honour at a function arranged by 'prominent citizens' where he thanked the people of Lahore and all those 'who had helped detenus [sic] by keeping up the agitation for release and rendered other help.'[38] Far from being chastened by his sixteen months in detention, he was back on the podium and even more militant than before. He presided over an 'anti-Japanese Day' meeting in Lahore and stormed that 'guerilla bands should be formed in the Punjab, especially among the rural area for the protection of their hearths and homes. Mr Bedi declared that he would enrol ten lakhs of guerillas in the Punjab.'[39] This was more rhetorical than practical, and perhaps not the wisest of declarations from a former political prisoner released just days earlier. Although the Japanese threat to British India was real, and an invasion was attempted from Burma, Japanese troops never got within a thousand miles of Lahore. But it was a declaration of militancy, or political fervour in repulsing the Axis powers and so defending Soviet communism.

On a personal level, Freda and Bedi had overcome a long period of enforced separation. They now had to re-establish their household in Lahore and offer their son and Binder a sense of security and stability after a couple of turbulent years. Bedi had come out of detention still more committed to political activity and to communism. Freda now had an opportunity to gather breath and reassess her priorities, and to spend more time on an activity she found still more rewarding than organising and addressing meetings—her writing.

8

From a Woman's Window

When early in 1947 Freda Bedi applied in Lahore for a British passport, she described herself as a journalist. She had spent years teaching English at a girls' college, and was to resume that line of work in Kashmir, but in the mid-1940s, writing and reporting was her main occupation. The family circumstances changed for the better. Bedi's writing and publishing, ranging from textbooks to ghost writing, started delivering an income and that, Freda said, 'enabled me to take a rest from the rather hard routine of lecturing in the college and travelling backwards and forwards so many miles a day. So the years '42 to '46 were years when I was more at home and writing.'[1] She relished the chance to have a calmer, more settled domestic life. Indeed she commented of the political activity in Lahore which now became a less prominent part of her life: 'I didn't particularly enjoy doing all this. I would have preferred, frankly, to sit at home and have a more peaceful family life. But it was the way life was, and there was no choice.' Whether this was a downplaying of the political expressed later in life when the spiritual aspect was foremost, or reflected a disdain for the rough-and-tumble of a political existence which was born more of duty than conviction, it's difficult to say—probably a bit of both. She also faced another political difficulty—as the Communist Party, and so her husband, fell out of step with the rest of the nationalist movement, husband and wife were also increasingly at odds about how best to achieve an independent India committed to social justice.

As a writer, Freda achieved a prominence to match her political reputation—and it was the work she most relished. In her student days, when her friends were talking excitedly of their personal ambitions, Freda's goal was to write. She published two books, largely collections of her writing for newspapers and magazines. As a columnist, she addressed women's issues with a directness which was startling. Throughout 1943, she had a weekly column in the *Tribune* entitled 'From a Woman's Window' which tackled issues—such as childbirth and breast-feeding—which rarely surfaced in the mainstream media at that time. But her focus on gender, and the unfair and unequal burden on India's women, was evident much earlier. Throughout her adult life, she sought to extend the bounds for women in public life. It would be difficult to describe Freda as a feminist. In her marriage, she willingly embraced a subservience to her husband and his personal and political ambitions. When she argued for women's interests, it was not on the basis of a principled demand for equality but of a measure more equity and respect. As a Tibetan Buddhist, she eventually found a comfortable niche with a distinctly patriarchal spiritual tradition which—as with most major religions—limited and confined women's role. Yet her championing of women, and her campaigning for the redress of women's grievances, was a consistent aspect of her life, and first became evident as an activist and writer in pre-independence Lahore.

In the spring of 1936, eighteen months after arriving in India and just a few weeks before Tilak's death, Freda was prominent in a public debate on the desirability of birth control clinics. The event was organised by the medical college students' union, and addressed a pressing issue in an era of large families and high infant and maternal mortality. 'Mrs Freda Bedi said that birth control did not mean no babies, it meant better babies; it did not mean no motherhood, but sensible motherhood. Birth control clinics should really be called "sensible motherhood clinics". Motherhood should be a glorious fulfilment of all that is best in woman and a source of vitality and joy and woman should not be condemned through relentless and machine-like production of children. The way to ensure this was to have efficient birth control clinics established in the Punjab where the service should be absolutely free.'[2] There was lively opposition to her argument, with speakers expressing concern about birth control being sinful, leading to sterility and frustrating India's need for a large army, but the chair of the meeting declared that the general sentiment was in support of the clinics.

A couple of months later, Freda wrote for the *Tribune*'s magazine section as part of a debate about the segregation of the sexes. 'All healthy minded people must agree,' she declared, 'that it is best if girls and boys can mix freely socially, while keeping a good attitude towards one another. ... To my mind, co-education from childhood upwards is the only solution.' But swayed by her experience as a college teacher, she was also concerned that women students were ignoring skills such as cooking and sewing.

The trouble with the present system is that a young man is usually faced with the alternative of a young modern educated wife, who has no idea of running a home intelligently or of bringing up children well, or on the other hand of a pretty girl, very uneducated, who can cook, sew and manage and bring up children but will live a life very apart from him, and be quite unable either to act as a hostess to his friends or to educate his children in the way he would like. I believe that in modern India, a wife, if she is to be useful must be educated, but I am shocked at the way girls in college here neglect learning household affairs. After all, the majority of girls are going to be married and it is only kindness to their husbands to be and their children that they should know something of the more practical things of life.[3]

In comments that must have upset some of her students, Freda went on to say that the 'trouble is that, because higher education is something of a rarity here still, girls become swelled-headed and think that they are sure to marry rich husbands and that it is below their dignity to work in the house.' This combination of progressive and traditional outlooks was a hallmark of Freda's take on life, and evident in it is how she saw her own role in the household, as her husband's companion and collaborator, but also as the homemaker.

As for the role of women outside the household—and particularly whether in such a conservative society, where purdah was still common, educated girls should pursue careers—Freda encouraged young women to seek out occupations which did not excite 'undue opposition from the family and society'. When asked which avenues were open to women, she replied: 'All avenues, ultimately. They have to be fought for, or even just recognised. At present teaching, medicine and nursing hold the field. Journalism is also beginning to attract writers. ... Journalism for women, the development of a *women's angle* in a daily newspaper is a work of which any woman might be proud. It is a national service.'[4]

That drew a sharp riposte from a student at Fateh Chand in an article provocatively headlined 'The Amazon, grave danger to womanliness':

It is significant that in its most loathsome and unacceptable form the suggestion for feminine careers has come from Mrs Freda Bedi, a Western-bred lady. Though, happily, she has united herself to an Indian, and she may be thinking she has 'naturalised' herself to Indian sentiments of life and living, yet the Western influences that moulded her in her childhood and adolescent years have indelibly determined the make-up of her mind and by the very laws of her being she cannot but look upon things with a vision that must needs have a taint of Westernism in it. Mrs Freda Bedi, let us not forget, has a good deal of selfless socio-political public service in Indian interests to her credit, and we revere her on that account. But we should be wary of accepting her views that may tend to disturb our accepted notions of social propriety that are peculiar to our native genius.[5]

That must have stung. A student at her own college insisting that Freda was not Indian, could never be Indian, and dismissing her arguments not simply on their merits but because they were tainted by her roots in an alien and uncomprehending West.

The opportunities particularly for educated young women, and the need to balance the desire for a career with domestic and household skills, was becoming an increasing focus of Freda's writing. In the summer of 1938, she published a 150-page book entitled the *Modern Girl's Guide to Home-Making*—an advert declared that this 'profusely illustrated and practical book should be given to every bride in her dowry and to every growing girl for her birthday'. She also became chief advisory editor to a new Lahore-based monthly journal, *Modern Girl*.[6] No copies of either have been located, so their contents have to be gauged on the basis of reviews. The market for English books and journals was necessarily restricted to Lahore's educated elite. This was not an attempt to address village India, or even the emerging lower middle class, but more the graduates of Fateh Chand and their families.

The reviewer in the *Tribune* was unconvinced by Freda's *Guide*. The book addressed the problems of home-making and how they could be surmounted; included recipes, 'exclusively English'; and dealt with home decorating, furnishing and colour schemes in a manner which suggested that 'only a large house and a lot of furniture of different kinds can make a home'. That wasn't the only aspect of the book that jarred. 'She has given an illustration of a typical English kitchen which is rare in India, as also the bath-room and the lavatory. It is submitted that such things are not suited to this country where the poor constitute an overwhelming majority. Besides it is not possible, except for the very rich, to have a sitting-room, dining-room or a bed-room of the type illustrated.' When Freda herself lived so simply in the Model Town huts, it's surprising that she chose to commend a vastly more expensive lifestyle—this was perhaps the brief that the publisher had insisted upon. The book also offered advice about diet and menus, though the food recommended was expensive and made no provision for vegetarians; there was a 'slimming without tears' section; and a guide for domestic staff about 'how to wait at tables'.[7]

The monthly magazine appears to have had a similar style and agenda—though it was received more warmly by the *Tribune*, which said it filled 'a long-felt want in Lahore society circles and should be eagerly read by educated women all over India. As Mrs Freda Bedi has put it, the "Modern Girl" aims at pointing the way to the true modern girl, the Indian wife and young mother, who has the future of the nation in her pretty hands.' The articles in the first issue covered fashion, the 'place of art in Indian homes', and a topic 'dear to every young girl … "How to become a Modern Venus"'.[8] The journal didn't prosper. A year after its launch, Freda wrote on 'Modern Girl' headed paper to tell Olive Chandler that the magazine had closed.

> I had no financial interest, being in an advisory capacity only, but it had a lot of me in it, + really fulfilled a long felt need—practical home-keeping, child-upbringing, modern news + views, for that rather pathetic creature the 'educated' Indian girl, who is brought up on books + examinations + is often unable to create a new + satisfactory home life for herself in the midst of old prejudices + antiquated methods. It was widely appreciated + quite unique but alas! However, I don't despair. They are seeds, + somewhere, somehow, they will bear some kind of fruit.[9]

Freda had identified a need, and a way of addressing it, but the readership simply wasn't there in sufficient numbers. It was another twenty years before *Femina* found a way of making a women's magazine work in the Indian market.

She was on safer ground with the broader agenda that she addressed in the *Tribune*, and a range of other publications, including film magazines and short broadcasts on All India Radio. Book reviews were initially her staple contributions, along with the very occasional short story. Factual writing, though, was her forte, and particularly the personal reportage that constitutes the finest of her published work. In the summer of 1941 she wrote a series of articles 'From My Village Window' for the *Tribune* which were quite the opposite of the 'Modern Girl' approach. These were not about how the Anglophone elite should mould their lifestyle, but vivid, compassionate pieces about the lives of the rural poor, and of women in particular—often based on first-hand experience which would be unfamiliar to many of her readers, such as travelling in what she described as the 'poor man's club' of third-class train carriages:

> The little one and myself had to sleep in the women's compartment, as the mixed compartments were overcrowded with men returning from a big fair on the banks of the Ganges at Hardwar. As usual we had a very jolly time.
>
> When I first got in and spread our beds on the seat, there was nobody there. Soon two '*burquas*' came in, 'walking tents.' From the young-looking shoes and the fashionable bordered *salwar* peeping out at the bottom, I guessed they were young women. Soon afterwards came a happy party of hill women, also returning from Hardwar. They were two young wives, very smiling and peaceful, with a son and a daughter each.
>
> Their menfolk invaded even the sacred precincts of the women's compartment to give the last rupees to the children, the last glass of water, the last treasured words before an unfeeling ticket collector with an eye on the rules shuffled them out.
>
> Back in the village they would have so many tales to tell of Lahore, and the children would wear their shining rubber slippers until the last shred had come off their feet.

When the train started, there was yet another surprise. From inside the '*burquas*' emerged two very lively young persons who made the whole compartment ring with their laughter. The children responded, and soon the whole train was like a fairground.[10]

In her writing as in her life, Freda displayed compassion and humanity. There is at times a sentimentality, a reluctance to address the rougher, ruder, uglier side of life, but as a columnist she helped the urban Indian elite to see another vantage point on the village and on villagers, with whom she had such an evident affinity.

The personal turbulence surrounding Freda's and her husband's detention forced a pause to her writing. With B.P.L.'s release from Deoli in April 1942, the Bedis were together as a family for the first time in eighteen months. The priority was to re-establish a domestic routine. Freda had moved out of the Model Town huts shortly after Bedi was arrested. They now decided to move back there, and retrieve something of the arcadian style of life which they both treasured. And that meant—Ranga Bedi recalls—building new huts. 'After two years "in the wilderness", we moved into our real home the other day,' Freda wrote in the *Tribune*. 'We lit the kitchen fire in the huts again on Basant, the first day of Spring. It was a beautiful day, lyrical. All around us the young corn was making the countryside green, and we took a handful of the surson [mustard] and placed it in the hut where its living colour lit up the neutral reed walls. It was, quite simply, home.' And the lyrical turn of phrase also extended to her 'reckless marriage'—as she imagined the world might see it—'because the only thing I or my husband cared about was that we loved one another.'[11]

It was not an easy time. In recordings made towards the end of her life, Freda recalled that the period when the family 'went back to our huts in the green belt of Model Town and tried to pick up the threads of life again' was also 'the gloomiest time of all really—the time when the national movement went into the 1942 stage and when the movement within the Indian states became acute.'[12] The gloom was above all political. The Congress launched the 'Quit India' movement that summer and most of its leadership was put behind bars. Communists kept their distance—their priority was to defend the Soviet Union from Germany's invasion and so to support the allied war effort. It was a dramatic political about-turn. The political force which regarded itself as the most militant was now making common purpose with India's rulers and criticising those who were detained for putting the national issue ahead of prosecuting the war. Freda remained active in the Friends of the Soviet Union—though much less vigorously so after her husband's release from Deoli—but this acute tension between communists and Congress must have caused some domestic friction. Bedi was now publicly and firmly allied to the communist cause; Freda's foremost concern was freeing India of British rule and she must have had an instinctive sympathy with the Quit India campaign. It was just the sort of mass mobilisation that she had wanted to see in the early stages of the war. The family's recollection is that she was uncomfortable with the CPI's repudiation of Congress and of Gandhi, and distanced herself from it. 'He was the more radical Marxist,' Ranga says, 'whereas she was supporting him by being a member of the party.'

Once Bedi was back in Lahore, he resumed his publishing work and had some success in securing writing commissions. There were other ventures; the Bedis' advertised a writing service in the *Tribune*: 'HAVE YOU WRITTEN A BOOK? Is it on your table or at the bottom of an old trunk? Are you press shy? If so, we can help you. We can prune, polish and publish it for you.'[13] Away from the routine of teaching English to college students, Freda had the time and space to take on more ambitious writing assignments. The first of her weekly columns under the title 'From a Woman's Window' appeared in the *Tribune* in January 1943. As with so much of her most effective writing, the tone was often personal and reflective.

'For me, the Old Year was a strange patchwork. I sat a good part of it away by the side of a sick-bed. But it brought the blessing of a completed family again. That is saying a good deal, when half of it is submerged in the dangerous whirlpool of the West, and the other wove into the tempestuous East.'[14]

'From a Woman's Window' continued for much of that year. It was unusual for a woman journalist to have a weekly column devoted to women's issues. Freda used it well. Her style was gentle and persuasive. Her range of topics included a fierce denunciation of dowry, Punjabi women's dress and her own adoption of Indian garments and the striving for greater space for women in public and professional life. Some of the sentiments expressed were almost apologetic about women and their shortcomings. In an article entitled 'Our Sillier Qualities', she accepted that 'the majority [of women] can be depended upon to behave in an illogical way, and mix argument with emotion'—but then went on to pose a wider question of why women were that way, and what potential could be realised if bars to their development were removed.

Freda's column repeatedly addressed personal issues about women's lives and choices (or the absence of choices) in a manner that was arrestingly direct. Women's education was a particular concern. 'My own mother, who was very wise in such matters ... used to say "The time comes for every bird to fly away from its nest". If all mothers could understand things as she did, a good many of the tragedies of daily life could be avoided,' she declared in advocating access to higher education. 'I know a good deal about the kind of education that is given in the average college, not only in the Punjab but all over India, and I have my very serious doubts about the worth of the very mechanical book-knowledge imparted to the girls who throng there. But if I had a daughter, I would never hesitate for a moment to send her to college because, as I see it, girls who go there do get the very atmosphere of freedom about them. And freedom I mean in a good sense. It is as though some stillness leaves their bones.'[15] In writing that, Freda must surely have had her in mind her own years at St Hugh's and the manner in which that exposed to her a different world, and to the people and causes that brought her to India.

The column touched on still more personal issues, delving deep into her own experiences of motherhood and its joys and discomforts. It was almost nine years since she had given birth in Berlin to Ranga and the memory remained potent.

> I remember my own feelings when I saw the face of my baby for the first time, when I was giving it milk and my body was racked with pain. It was a symbol to me not only of the beauty of life, but its cruelty, its mystery, its fierce struggle. Here was this little being scarcely conscious that it was yet alive or separate, feeding itself avidly, careless of the pain that was shooting through my body. Eager to live. To breathe. To move. To kick. To survive. And as a mother, there was no resentment in the pain I suffered. It was full of pity and longing and an almost unbearable tenderness for the little atom that was so much part of me, and yet starting on its own stony path, alone, as every human being is alone.[16]

She returned to this issue of the pain of childbirth in an article with the unsettling title 'Going to Bed with a Coffin'. 'I remember lying in child birth with waves of pain seizing my body, and as the crest of the wave went down, and the other was gathering strength, turning the world over in my mind. … It darted through my mind that all the girl child grows to, and blossoms for is just this, this lying in torment.'[17] She believed that in these 'moments of great love or great agony' a sensitivity develops which means that 'many things in life which were hidden to us we see in a blinding flash of understanding.' There was a searching aspect to some of her columns in the *Tribune* which points to her turn to a spiritual path a decade later.

'The Edge of a Naked Sword' was the title of a column devoted to marriage—and Freda wrote in a manner which must have carried some echo of her own experience.

> Marriage is such an intimate affair that, ultimately speaking, it is impossible for two normally constituted human beings to get on together unless they have a very strong physical attraction for one another to begin with, and some other bond of the spirit that will hold them together whatever ill or catastrophe may befall them. Common interests are a good deal. But they are not always essential, as a wife can and does often grow into her husband's life and ways of thought.[18]

Freda had certainly adapted to Bedi's 'life and ways of thought'—without all that much sign of a commensurate adaptation by her husband. She once commented that 'nearly seven years of rubbing about in what is known as "the outer world" has worn off some of my sharper corners. But the process was not a painless one.'[19] And the 'passive demeanour' of the wife could turn into a powerful force once galvanised into action, 'whether it demands simple things like grain for a hungry family or whether it demands great and difficult things like the expulsion of an enemy from a native soil.'[20]

She also reflected on the difficult political situation of a country unwillingly at war. She wrote powerfully of the emotions aroused by one of Gandhi's fasts in support of political demands, reflecting that the response demonstrated the distinction between what might loosely be called a political leader and a truly national figure. 'In every town and village of India the menace of losing Gandhiji, with India a threatened island in a world at war, had shaken people, more than they ever dreamed they could be shaken. During the worst days of the fast I happened to be at Sialkot. There, in spite of efforts to stop it, women and children gathered night and morning in their dozens to pray for the precious life. I also went one night, and leaving aside the quibble of whether or not prayer is any help, the very passionate urge of the heart of those who went shook the air around us. Gandhiji's suffering united India in those twenty-one days.'[21] She understood the political importance of moral authority—indeed, her political outlook was more moral and ethical than ideological.

Towards the close of 1943, Freda assembled a selection of her journalism and writings; it was published by her husband's imprint in Lahore, Unity Publishers. *Behind the Mud Walls* consists of more than twenty articles, mainly written for the *Tribune* and other papers—though the greater part of her jail diary, the centrepiece of the volume, appears to have been previously unpublished. The more personal of her pieces—coming to India, getting to know her husband's family, and then the perils of arrest and jail—are a powerful and elegant account of defining chapters of her life. The book was dedicated 'to the two who have mothered me in England and India', her mother and her mother-in-law. The exigencies of wartime publishing limited the reach and impact of *Behind the Mud Walls*, and (to date) it has never been republished. It is without question the most impressive and revealing of Freda's books and pamphlets. 'Freda Bedi, though an Englishwoman, is one of us,' commented the reviewer in the *Tribune*, 'sharing with us our joys and sorrows in our march to freedom. ... Under the veil of her simple and touching descriptions runs the enthusiasm of the socialist and the reformer.'[22] Once again, the dominant element, besides the personal, was the plight of Indian womanhood, and the often inspirational manner they responded to the challenges they faced. The 'national service' that Freda had identified as an option for her students—journalism by women, about women and for women—was one that she herself undertook with determination.

9

Bengal Lamenting

Freda Bedi's increasing profile as a writer opened new opportunities, the most challenging of which was an assignment to report at first hand on the most terrible of India's wartime tragedies. From the summer of 1943 onwards, newspapers carried accounts of famine in Bengal, where crop failures and cyclone damage were exacerbated by official indifference, a preoccupation with the war effort, and a determination to ensure that if the Japanese army—already well established in Burma—managed to invade they would be denied stockpiles of rice and the boats so essential for local transport. A huge number of Bengalis—perhaps as many as four million, Freda believed—died of starvation or succumbed to diseases which if well-fed they would have resisted.[1] The Communist Party was particularly active in drawing attention to the famine and demanding relief. In December 1943, both Bedi and Freda addressed meetings in and around Lahore on behalf of the Bengal Central Relief Committee.[2] By the end of the month, she was on the spot, sent by the *Tribune* to give a sense of the human consequences of the disaster. Freda didn't speak Bengali and she was almost certainly accompanied when travelling from village to village. Her job was 'to make the famine a reality' for newspaper readers in Punjab rather than 'a bundle of figures' by writing reflective and descriptive columns from the areas worst affected.

In a letter to her old Oxford friend Olive Chandler, Freda recounted that she spent a month 'tramping the villages and seeing the worst spots, something so horrible that an Airgram can't hold it.'[3] She had seen plenty of human suffering, but nothing remotely like this. The paper carried Freda's articles as a series under the title 'Bengal Today' and within a matter of months these were compiled as a slim book. *Bengal Lamenting* was published not by the Bedis' own imprint but by the much larger Lion Press in Lahore. Accompanying the articles were deeply unsettling images. The cover was designed by the progressive artist Sobha Singh whom the Bedis would have known from Andretta. It was a stark and arresting drawing, depicting a naked and emaciated woman with the wasted body of her son on her lap. Pinned in to the book were five photographic images of the famine, one of which showed a dog gnawing on human remains.

In her travels across Bengal and Orissa (now Odisha), Freda made a point of venturing off the beaten path. At times, she travelled by bicycle, 'a perilous affair with inactive brakes. It was in addition a man's cycle and I couldn't get off easily. So I quietly fell off whenever the crowd got too great.' This allowed her to see something of life and suffering in the villages, 'always the barometer of Indian life. There, in one of the hundreds and thousands of huddles of mud huts away from the main road, barely reachable by a muddy path, lies India's destiny, her life, her death, her intolerable longings, her inertia, the remnants of her joy of living, and her last and most bleeding despair.' Her account of the individual stories of loss and destitution gave particular force to her writing.

At every door I stopped to hear the same pitiful theme, with its hundred variations. 'Here the men have gone away to work in Assam: the women have nothing. They make a bare occasional living working at marriages and festivals. In between they starve' ... 'Here they have all run away: the men to the town, the women to beggary and destitution and the gruel kitchens.' I shuddered. There was a lot behind that inadequate word, destitution. Humiliation, demoralisation, casual prostitution, disease. And behind it the face of abandoned children.

We came across a hut without its corrugated roof. It had been casually torn off, the room gaped dully to the sky. In reply to my half-formed question they pointed out a dried up husk of a woman cowering in the next hut. 'Her husband died a few days ago,' they said. 'Her children died before that. She sold the roof, her last possession, to buy him a coffin.'[4]

As so often, her particular focus was village women: those who had seen their menfolk head out to 'get food' and had no idea whether they were alive or dead; those forced by despair and the plight of their children to sell themselves. She reported on the manner by which young girls, some of them infants, were sold for sex. 'The need to take people from beggary to self-supporting work is a real one. In the case of women, it is the only road open to them if they are not to become mere cattle in the markets of human flesh.'

Freda was more an essayist and columnist than a reporter and she was not used to disaster journalism. Her writing from Bengal was vivid, compassionate and resolutely non-sensational. Her challenge was to break through with her prose the barrier that she herself identified—that middle-class readers on the other flank of India had become 'famine weary'. She spoke warmly of the Friends' Ambulance Unit, the People's Relief Committees and all the other local efforts—religious, secular and military—to provide food and medical relief to those in gravest need. There is also a pervasive anger running through *Bengal Lamenting* at the greed and hypocrisy she witnessed amid the many generous and selfless initiatives. 'Doctors who profiteer on patients, and traders who profiteer on foodstuffs and medicines, deserve no mercy at the hands of the people. Peaceful as I am by temperament, by the time I had been round a few villages and heard [the] same stories I felt even transportation for life would be too mild a sentence for them.'[5] In Calcutta, Bengal's capital, the poor and emaciated had been pushed out of the city to harvest the next rice crop—and also, she surmised, to be hidden from the view of the urban middle class. 'Calcutta is a lady with a painted face,' Freda wrote. 'She is hiding her ugliness and her sores under a coating of powder and the red on her lips is the red of the people's blood.' And even as one famine was starting to ease, everyone was talking about the next one round the corner.

In the foreword to *Bengal Lamenting*, Freda declared that her book 'is more than a cry of pain, a call to pity, a picture of another tidal wave of tears that has wrenched itself up from the ocean of human misery. It is a demand for a reconsideration on a national scale of that problem that cannot be localised, a plea for unity in the face of chaos, one more thrust of the pen for the right of every Bengali and every Indian to see his destiny guided by patriots in a National Government of the People.'[6] This was reportage with a political purpose. She dismissed conspiracy theories that the British had allowed Bengal to slip into famine to punish the home province of Subhas Chandra Bose, whose supporters were fighting alongside the Japanese. But she argued that the official response to the Japanese invasion of the rice-exporting regions of Burma, and the policy of 'denial' to ensure that advancing Japanese troops would not be able simply to commandeer river transport and grain, 'meant the sealing up of Bengal from the world rice market.'

Actually what happened was that artificial scarcity in Denial and cyclone areas ... combined with dislocated transport, over-burdened with war responsibilities, created local panics that translated themselves into, on the one hand, exaggerated private-hoarding by the middle classes and, in particular by the big rice-growing landlords who are the king of Bengal's rice, and on the other, profiteering and hoarding by local trades people, backed up by the big commercial rice firms. Add to this inflation, and you have chaos complete. Money flowed into the Stock Exchange; rice became a commodity of scarcity value; and the sharks of Big Business made their daily thousands by trading in the people's life-blood—their staple food.

From this she made the obvious argument that if India was governed by those whose first concern was the welfare of India's citizens, the tragedy would not have been on anything like the same scale. 'There is no argument left for the *status quo* when it has failed so miserably, and there is no doubt about it that any patriotic team of Indians could have averted such a terrible loss of life. The Indian demand for a National Government at the Centre has become not only insistent, but a matter of life and death.'[7]

Freda ended the book with a quote, unacknowledged, from one of the great political poems to come out of the Spanish Civil War. Cecil Day-Lewis's 'Nabara', published six years earlier, was an account of a fascist-aligned warship intercepting and destroying a convoy carrying relief supplies to the Republican-controlled Basque country.

> Freedom is more than a word, more than the base coinage
> Of statesmen, the tyrant's dishonoured cheque, or the dreamer's mad
> Inflated currency. She is mortal, we know, and made
> In the image of simple men who have no taste for carnage
> But sooner kill and are killed than see that image betrayed.

She implied some moral equivalence between the brutality of the supporters of Franco in Spain and of the misery British imperialism forced on Bengal.

Freda also began to spend more time in another of India's troubled regions, Kashmir. The family travelled to Kashmir occasionally from the late 1930s, in part as a summer retreat from the scorching Lahore summer but also to support the nascent progressive nationalist movement in this princely state. After Bedi's release

from Deoli, Kashmir loomed increasingly large in their lives—and
their engagement with the Kashmir Valley merits separate attention.
It was while in Kashmir Valley in the summer of 1945 that Freda
discovered she was pregnant. Ranga was by then eleven. The family's
more settled life near Model Town made this a propitious moment
to have another child. 'I got to know I was having a child when I
was up in Haji Brar beyond Pahlgam ... where we often used to
pitch our tents during the summer months,' Freda wrote nineteen
years later in a 'coming of age' letter to the son she bore:

> ...when the signs came on my body and I knew that a child was
> really coming ... I also knew that it would be another son—a
> third, because little Tilak had died that cruel summer of 1936.
> Everyone said you must be wanting a girl and I smiled, because I
> knew the time for the coming of a daughter had not yet arrived.
> We were still in the straw huts and tents, and girls don't like
> that sort of thing.
>
> Later in the summer I came down to Srinagar to Nishat Bagh,
> a little garden cottage full of cherry trees. I could feel you inside
> me, kicking quite hard. It was a beautiful autumn. I had not had
> a baby in my arms for so long, that you were more than welcome.
> Sometimes I would meditate + a stream of bliss would run through
> my body ... I read the lives of the mystics, Gita, Koran, the
> conversations of Sri Rama Krishna. There was something warm
> and peaceful and beautiful.[8]

Back in Lahore a few weeks before the birth, another newcomer
joined the family—a Great Dane pup called Rufus. 'Papa said "That's
the baby's *chowkidar*". He was such a huge good-natured bumbling
creature, and when he tried to be puppy-like and sit on people's
laps he looked like an elephant on a stool.' Kabir Bedi was born in
a Lahore nursing home on the 16th January 1946. His name came
from a book by Rabindranath Tagore—the *Songs of Kabir* was his
translation of the poems of Kabir, a fifteenth-century poet and

mystic, whose writings influenced or reflected Hinduism, Sikhism and Sufism.

In the final stages of Freda's pregnancy, Bedi was once again preoccupied by politics. The end of the Second World War, and the return of a Labour government in Britain, heralded India's independence. The Bedi family were 'all hoping that the New World will have something for India,' Freda wrote to Olive Chandler. 'She has suffered enough.'[9] Few expected, however, that the pace of change would be so rapid and overwhelming. In January 1946, provincial elections were held across India. The communists decided to contest and hoped to poll well in Punjab with Bedi among their candidates. This was unduly optimistic. The party had very limited strength in the province—the British communist Rajani Palme Dutt, in private notes made during his visit to India later that year, suggested that out of a total CPI membership of 53,700, just 1,600 were in Punjab.[10] 'I hope Bedi is successful in the elections,' Freda's brother Jack wrote from on board ship in Australia, 'there is a worldwide swing to labour and about time to[o]'.[11] He wasn't successful. The outcome was humbling for the communists. Across India, they took less than three per cent of the vote and won only eight seats—none of them in Punjab.[12] It was widely seen as a punishment for their support of the war effort and repudiation of mainstream nationalism. In Punjab, the Muslim League emerged as the largest party in the assembly, a result which enormously strengthened Jinnah's hand in his pursuit of a separate Pakistan.

Although communists had lost out at the ballot box, the temper of political activity was intense. The Bedis were part of a lively left-minded social circle in Lahore which included poets, writers and academics. It was an exciting time. Pran Chopra, then a journalist in his mid-twenties, recalled B.P.L. Bedi as 'a florid individual, physically as well as mentally. You never had a dull moment in a half-hour sitting with others where he was present too.' He was not at all sure how well Bedi fitted in with the disciplined structures

of a highly centralised party. 'B.P.L. would not be a cadre person
for any organisation; he was too much his own man'. He knew
Freda better and was impressed by her. 'One knew that she was
a very serious person—serious in pursuit of her interests. ... She
was in fact a force behind B.P.L. ... She was quieter. She was the
disciplining force behind B.P.L. ...'[13] London-born Rajni Kumar met
the Bedis in Lahore in 1946 and recalled Freda as a very intelligent
and determined woman with 'very deep, penetrating eyes and soft
expression'. But she found B.P.L. more fun:

> Bedi, her husband, was delightful. I loved Bedi. He was huge—
> absolutely huge. He was a scream. I remember going to some of
> these big rallies, kisan [peasant] rallies, in Jalandhar and Ambala
> and Ludhiana. And there was a big communist movement in the
> villages and politicising the rural peasantry and I used to go with
> the girls, the Communist group ... Oh, they were so exciting
> for me, when I saw those big peasants going round, you know,
> 'Inquilab Zindabad', and the shouts and the excitement and the
> feeling of revolution, it was really very exciting.[14]

She also heard of another side to Bedi—his reputation with women.
'It was inevitable in a way because he was that kind of person, he
was that kind of personality. ... Freda was much more, you know
what I mean, controlled. She was a controlled person. She did not
give vent much to her emotions outwardly as Bedi [did]. Bedi was
outgoing. So he could also indulge.'

Bedi's reputation as a communist activist was considerable. He
wasn't a national figure but in Punjab he was well known and
widely respected. Som Anand, who as a youngster used to sell the
communist paper *People's Age* in Model Town, considered Bedi to be
'an orator of some standing'.[15] With his prominence as a leftist came
the renewed attention of the authorities. 'The residence of Mr B.P.L.
Bedi, organiser of the provincial Communist Party, was searched
by the police last night,' the *Tribune* reported in January 1947. 'A

contingent of women police was also present. The search lasted nine and a half hours. Nothing incriminatory is reported to have been recovered, but the police removed certain books and papers.'[16] Such a protracted search was clearly a warning to the Bedis—that they were being watched and had better tread carefully.

Early in 1947, shortly after Kabir's first birthday, Freda chose to make a journey back home to Derby. It was fourteen years since she had left England, and a decade since she last saw her mother. Nellie had endured some difficult years during the war—Freda had at one point told a friend that her mother was 'very very ill'—and there was no prospect of her coming out again to Lahore. The end of the war made international travel feasible once more, and Freda wanted to show off her new child. Leaving Bedi, Binder and thirteen-year-old Ranga behind, Freda and her baby set off for London. Travelling that huge distance with a year-old infant was a daunting prospect—but nothing like as difficult as the ship journey out had been with a still younger Ranga. Many years later, Freda set down for Kabir how that journey came about:

It was at that time that stories came of Independence being given to India in 1948, + Papa felt I should go home + see Mother who had not met me since her visit to India in 1936-7. 'There might be trouble during the transfer of power' he said, 'and we should be together. So go now.'

I remember giving you your last little drop of Mother's milk in the hut. You were looking up to me with a very sweet expression in your eyes. And I thought: 'He does not know he is not going to get any more.' You were one year old: I could imagine the horror if I arrived in England feeding a year old baby. Out of the jungle! All English babies are weaned on to bottles at nine months. But I really hadn't the heart to stop the milk before. You liked it too much!

So still in your wicker Moses basket we boarded the Boat

Plane in Karachi, February 1947. We landed in England in the middle of a terrible snowstorm + you celebrated your first fortnight in Derby, near your adoring Grandma + Grandpa, by getting measles, which you had caught from a child with the snuffles on the Lahore-Karachi train.[17]

Before boarding the plane, Freda dropped a line to a friend asking for advice about what to do in London. Jawaharlal Nehru, who by the end of the year was to become the first prime minister of independent India, sent a brief reply to her at The Huts. 'I hope you will enjoy your visit to England after 14 years,' he wrote. 'You should certainly meet Krishna Menon, I cannot suggest what you might do there, but Krishna Menon will, no doubt, be able to do so.'[18]

Having made the arduous journey back to Britain for the first time, Freda planned to stay in England for several months. Kabir was clearly feted by his Derby family, as the surviving photos from the visit demonstrate. Freda had occasional reporting assignments. Derby's evening paper noted that she was covering the British Labour Party's annual conference for an Indian newspaper and included a photograph of her in Punjabi-style salwar kameez. In her absence, the pace of political developments in India picked up furiously. Lord Mountbatten, the last Viceroy, set a much earlier date than expected for independence. Freda must have been anguished to be out of India when its national aspirations were finally realised on 15th August 1947; and anguished also that India was to be partitioned and that her home city of Lahore was to be in Pakistan. Communal tension and killings erupted in Punjab in March 1947, and became much more intense in the weeks after Partition as huge caravans of refugees made their way in both directions across the new international border. It's now believed that in Punjab alone more than two-million people may have been killed amid the mayhem which accompanied Partition. Somewhere approaching fifteen-million Punjabis became refugees.[19] Lahore, the provincial capital, was in flames. It had been

a lively and diverse city with a Muslim majority, but where the large
Hindu and Sikh minorities had made a conspicuous contribution to
culture and commerce. It became almost exclusively Muslim.

For the return leg, Freda and Kabir were on the passenger list
of a P&O liner which had served during the war as a troop ship,
the 'Strathmore', departing Southampton for Bombay on 26th
September 1947. But they didn't make the journey. The turmoil in
Punjab was so severe, with Lahore suffering such acute upheaval,
that returning there with a baby would have been reckless. Freda
stayed in England a few weeks longer—no doubt anxiously reading
the reports of communal violence in Punjab and waiting for word
from her husband. She took advantage of the extra time to meet
old Oxford friends. At the beginning of December, she sent Olive
Chandler a postcard—the picture was of their old college—thanking
her for a memorable visit: 'Had lunch with Barbara [Castle] today
+ fly tomorrow.'[20] She had been away for nine months.

Freda's visit had a charming codicil. A year later, her mother
received a last minute invitation to meet India's new prime minister.
'Summoned to a reception at India House, London, to meet
Jawaharlal Pandit Nehru, Mrs. F.N. Swan ... cooked a meal for
four, prepared the next day's food and then found time to go out
and buy herself a new dress and a new hat for the occasion before
catching a train to London less than seven hours after receiving the
invitation,' reported the *Derby Daily Telegraph*. Mrs Swan told the
paper that her daughter was 'well known to Pandit Nehru' and she
said her proudest moment came when Nehru stopped at her table
and shook her hand.[21]

Bedi's firm intention was to stay in Lahore after Partition. He was
in Simla on independence day, in what was to become the Indian
part of Punjab, but was determined to return to Lahore and resume
his political activity. 'There was grave danger to my life, I realised it,
but I felt my duty was there.'[22] Amid the spiralling violence, Ranga,
Binder and Bhabooji were sent to stay with Bedi's brother, then

a sessions judge in Jalandhar, on the Indian side of the Partition line. Bedi on several occasions helped families to safety. Anela, the European wife of his friend Hafeez Jullundhri, found herself on the wrong side of the new border along with her seven-year-old daughter Zia. Her husband was a Muslim, and indeed a proponent of Pakistan, and they were at acute risk in Indian Punjab. Anela abandoned her salwar kameez for European dress. Both Bedi and his brother came to their aid. Zia recalls a shot through the window of the house in which they took refuge. They were brought to Jalandhar and put on a train, but even then they were still in peril:

> I remember my mother was wearing a dress then which I thought very odd, and we were in a carriage in Jalandhar, we were going somewhere, and a door opened and a Sikh was there with a sword, and he said: 'Voh Musalmaan—' [You Muslim]. And Baba [Bedi] lent his dog to my mother—he was called Rufus, he was a Great Dane—to be our helper and security guard. ... I was under my mother's skirt, underneath, and I could see. And he was looking for Musulmaan [Muslims]. And my mother said: 'Jao, jao, idher koi Musulmaan nahii hain. Dafar ho jao.' [Go away, there are no Muslims here. Get out.] And Rufus barked ... and he went away.[23]

On another occasion, Bedi travelled to Kapurthala to help a Muslim family make a safe return to Lahore, and required all his powers of oratory and persuasion—and of Punjabi idiom—to quell a restive crowd.[24] Som Anand, who related that story of Bedi's bravery, was also the beneficiary of his help. A few weeks after Partition, the family's home in Lahore was targeted by a group of Pathans, and Bedi along with Hafeez Jullundhri ensured that everyone was moved out. 'Hafeez Sahib made a hurried trip to our house to see the situation. He came back with the news that it was still dangerous for us to go back. Someone in the neighbourhood had told him that the Pathans were still keeping a watch on the area. What then was to be done? Mr Bedi suggested that we should go to Delhi by air, leaving everything in Hafeez Sahib's charge. There seemed to be no other way, and father agreed to it. By the afternoon of that day, we were in Delhi telling my brother the story of our narrow escape.'[25]

Partition ruptured some longstanding allegiances. Hafeez Jullundhri not only embraced Pakistan; he became the country's unofficial poet laureate and author of its national anthem. The friendship was strained almost beyond repair. Even a month or two after Independence, with by far the greater number of non-Muslims forced out of Lahore, Bedi was still minded to stay. He said later that it was Pakistan's decision in October 1947 to fight in Kashmir, to repulse not only India but also the progressive strand within Kashmiri nationalism which Bedi championed, that finally persuaded him to leave. A few weeks later, he managed to make the hazardous journey across the new border to Jalandhar. When Freda and Kabir finally managed to get a flight back to India, they also went straight to Jalandhar. The Bedis never lived again in Lahore. B.P.L. made one visit back years later[26] but Freda never returned. She never saw the Model Town huts again. The independence she had so eagerly and enthusiastically sought had brought down the curtain on the family home where she and Bedi were happiest. It must have been a sour-sweet moment. But they quickly had a new mission—personal and political. Within days of assembling together in Jalandhar, the Bedis flew to Kashmir, the former princely state which was being fought over by India and Pakistan. It was to be their home for the next five years.

10

Kashmir in Disguise

By the time the Bedi family moved to Kashmir late in 1947, they had already made a name for themselves there. Freda Bedi had braved attempts by the maharaja's government to expel her from the princely state and had been dressed in Kashmiri bridal clothes in an unlikely attempt to pass incognito when meeting underground political leaders. Her son unwittingly served as a messenger between Kashmiri leaders forced into exile in Lahore and activists seeking an end to princely autocracy. B.P.L. Bedi's most abiding political achievement was as principal architect of the defining document of progressive Kashmiri nationalism—at the time the dominant political force in the Kashmir Valley. Freda and B.P.L. became firm friends and allies of Sheikh Mohammad Abdullah, the commanding figure in Kashmiri politics. When they moved to Srinagar it was to work alongside him to achieve his goal of a secular, democratic and socially progressive Kashmir—and to strengthen India's contested claim to the state.

The Bedis' involvement in Kashmiri politics was partly an accident of geography. From the late 1930s, the Kashmiri capital, Srinagar, became a summer refuge for Punjabi intellectuals. It was more than five thousand feet up in the foothills of the Himalayas, a place of legendary beauty which offered respite from the bleaching summer sun. An attractive alternative to Andretta, Kashmir offered lakes, houseboats and opportunities to camp and trek particularly in the

upper Lidder valley beyond the resort town of Pahalgam. It became
'like a second home for us,' Freda remarked; 'somebody ought to
make a film round Kashmir with the Kashmir Valley as Hero no.
1.'[1] Among the roll call of Punjabis and north Indians who spent
part of the summer in the Kashmir Valley was Faiz Ahmad Faiz,
the pre-eminent progressive Urdu poet, whose nikah or marriage
ceremony with an English communist, Alys George, was conducted
by Sheikh Abdullah in Srinagar in 1941. Alys's sister Christabel had
already married M.D. Taseer, a leftist writer and intellectual at one
time a college principal in Srinagar.[2] The novelist Mulk Raj Anand,
the actor (and veteran of the *Monday Morning* venture in Lahore)
Balraj Sahni and the cultural figure K.A. Abbas were also among
the more renowned of the left-leaning literati who assembled in the
Kashmir Valley.

Kashmiri political leaders similarly spent time in the Punjabi
capital, Lahore. Sheikh Abdullah and many other young Kashmiris
had been students there. Hundreds of Kashmiris settled in the city,
which offered a bigger canvas and more opportunities for educated
Muslims. The poet Hafeez Jullundhri in particular forged friendships
with the coming generation of Kashmiri leaders, and the Bedis too
got to know—and on occasion host—the key figures in Kashmir's
national movement.

At this time, Kashmir was emerging from a long period of
isolation and popular politics was taking root. The maharaja, Hari
Singh, was a Hindu and, in the eyes of most Kashmiris, an outsider,
while his princely state was largely Muslim and the Kashmir Valley
emphatically so. He was also part of a generation of Indian princes
who were much more comfortable hunting, shooting and fishing
than in engaging with social and political reform. The princely
states were not formally part of the British Raj, but in Srinagar—as
in many other princely capitals—a British Resident kept a careful
watching eye and on occasions intervened to seek to ensure political
stability and protect British interests. Princely autocracy and the

accompanying restraints on political activity and public expression were increasingly an anachronism as the temper of Indian politics began to rise. Sheikh Abdullah and a like-minded group of young, educated Kashmiris—most of them from the state's Muslim majority—sought to challenge the oppressive feudalism still prevalent in the villages and to mobilise public opinion.

The Bedis came to see the Kashmir Valley not simply as a picturesque location offering respite from the summer heat but as the site of a political struggle to which they could, and should, contribute. This was probably a mix of personal initiative and prompting by the Communist Party, which viewed Kashmir as a promising place to seek recruits and influence. Sheikh Abdullah had a firm personal friendship and political alliance with the Congress's Jawaharlal Nehru, himself of distant Kashmiri descent. But the communists were keen to help support Abdullah's party, the National Conference, and shape its policy and strategy. When in the summer of 1942 Bedi was released from Deoli and Freda was able to disengage from her lecturing job in Lahore, their involvement in Kashmiri politics stepped up. In August 1942, Bedi was in Srinagar as the Indian National Congress launched the Quit India movement, its biggest civil disobedience movement to date. At this time, the communists were opposed to protests which would hamper the war effort. By his own account—and Bedi was prone to exaggerate his role in the events he recounted—he persuaded the National Conference leadership to keep a distance from the Congress's initiative:

Sheikh Abdullah, [G.M.] Sadiq and Bakshi [Ghulam Mohammad], all three were lunching with me that day. So instead of arriving at 12 o'clock for lunch, they arrived at about 10.30. 'Ah,' they came laughing and joking and said, 'now good-bye Bedi Saheb, instead of lunching we will be behind bars by the time lunch comes, because this is the situation which has come about.' So, we immediately went into consultations and realised that the ruthless administration of the Maharaja was looking for an opportunity to smash the national movement in Kashmir ... We said, 'Leave alone anti-fascism and anti-imperialism, who is there if the National Conference is removed at the moment to stand between the Maharaja's ways and the people and stem the tide of destruction and suffering.' With this argument we completely assessed the situation and came to the conclusion that no 1942 movement could be launched in Kashmir.[3]

Bedi said he was given the job of making the opening speech at a rally that evening to argue the case for standing aloof from the Congress-launched campaign. In the tussle between the Congress and communists for influence within Kashmir's main political movement, the left had won a victory. Bedi's argument that Kashmiri nationalists could achieve more if they were out-and-about rather than behind bars was well made. The Quit India campaign placed the Congress leadership behind bars and out-of-action at a crucial stage in the advance towards independence. 'Whereas in other parts of India the national movement was smashed,' Bedi argued somewhat self-servingly, 'in Kashmir, the national movement emerged with ten times more strength by following this policy.'[4]

The following spring, both Freda and Bedi attended the annual session of the National Conference at Mirpur. Freda chaired a meeting of women activists; Bedi presided over a gathering of student supporters. Freda wrote in her weekly column in the *Tribune* about the difficult journey she made to Mirpur, the final stage of which was a 'shabby' ferry boat across the Jhelum. 'We got across the river being alternately pulled and pushed and rowed and towed in about two hours. For us it was easy enough since we never left the boat. But the other passengers had to get down on the islands and walk across the burning sand, the round hot stones and the spiked grasses.' Unsurprisingly, the main demand of local women at the meeting Freda convened was for a bridge.

It is no joke for old women and mothers with children to face such a primitive journey every time they want to come to the Punjab or the Frontier. They were indignant about it 'and we even have to ride on donkeys' they said with a smile half mischievous and half ashamed. They formed their own committee. So many have tried and failed. Now it is for the women of Mirpur to show that they will not be refused. Alone a woman is helpless and knows it. Together with her sisters bound by common trouble and suffering she can show greater strength than she or the world dreams of, for none can refuse the weak when they band together [5]

From a small incident, she drew a parable which reflected her own commitment to social justice and the agency of women in achieving that.

Freda also wrote lyrically about a journey in Kashmir, by donkey and on foot, retracing the old Mughal route into the valley. Sheikh Abdullah accompanied the group for at least part of the journey, and was welcomed as if a saviour.

The Kashmiri women had found out that their leader had come. They huddled together in a shy group on the roof of one of the huts, as though undecided what to do. Then they started a song of welcome: 'To-day our Rajah has honoured the house with his presence,' they sang. I looked again at their faces lined with poverty, the dirty and ragged clothes on their backs. Had they been as dirty and as poor when the great ones of history ruled the earth? Probably so, for the poor have always been poor. ... The lively, happy faces of the women were sharp before the dark arches: beggars at the door of history, they were singing for the only ray of light they knew. For one who fought for the poor, and would see them ruling in the land of their poverty.[6]

In another 'From a Woman's Window' column, Freda wrote about attending a martyrs' day ceremony with Sheikh Abdullah in

Srinagar, a tribute to those killed by the maharaja's forces in 1931 at the inception of what became a mass movement demanding civil and political rights. Again, her attention focused on the women, about 150 of them, who gathered outside the walls of the cemetery while the men laid flowers on the graves.

> To outward seeming they were like any other crowd of Kashmiri women. Most were in the burqua, with its crown-like head-piece, making it particularly ungainly and ugly. The others were working women, in their loose-fitting tunics, the white thick veil on the back of their heads, heavy earrings, carved circles of silver, hanging in bunches on their distended ears. ...
>
> They were the silent background of the animated meeting. And it occurred to me looking at them that they had been the silent background of all the history of Kashmir and the struggles of its people. ...
>
> It was women such as these who ran out into the streets and became the heroines of those early fiery days. It was such women who rattled stones and frightened the horses of their soldiery. Some village woman, like that plump aging woman over there, took a club on her shoulder and strode at the head of one of the village 'armies' of the people that marched into Srinagar.[7]

She foresaw Kashmiri women coming on to the streets again, 'throwing that power-house of energy which they hoard as a bee hoards its honey into another great movement of the people.' On this, she was right.

Freda Bedi's empathy with Kashmiri women, and her emphasis on their role in political and social change, is striking. Women were also conspicuous in the iconography of Kashmiri nationalism. When the 'New Kashmir' manifesto was published, it featured a drawing of a woman on its front cover, wearing a Kashmiri pheran or smock and with her head covered—not quiescent but politically assertive, wielding the National Conference flag of a hand-plough in white on a red background. It bears more than a faint echo of Delacroix's famous depiction of Marianne, emblem of the French republic, mounting a barricade flag in hand. The Kashmiri woman depicted appears to have been Zooni Gujjari, a local activist from a disadvantaged background who featured in other National Conference publications.

The content of the manifesto was also notably progressive on gender issues, extending to equal wages, paid leave during pregnancy, the right to enter trades and professions, to own and inherit property and to consent to marriage. But this was simply one aspect of a remarkably far-reaching political programme, which has been described as 'the most important political document in modern Kashmir's history'.[8] It was written in response to an initiative by the maharaja to consult about political and constitutional reform. This was the National Conference's submission—a hugely ambitious, forty-four page document which was a draft constitution, an economic programme and party manifesto combined. It proposed a constitutional monarchy with universal suffrage for those aged eighteen and over; equal rights irrespective of race, religion or nationality; freedom of speech, press and assembly; free and compulsory primary education in the mother tongue; state ownership and management of all key industries; and the abolition of feudalism through an agrarian programme of which the key points were 'abolition of landlordism' and 'land to the tiller'. Sheikh Abdullah noted with justification that his party had come up with a much more detailed prescription for the future than the Indian National Congress, or indeed any other movement in the region.

The authorship of the 'New Kashmir' manifesto was, at the time, opaque. Sheikh Abdullah recounted many years later that to 'compile the manifesto we requisitioned the services of a famous progressive friend from Panjab [sic], B.P.L. Bedi. ... Bedi's sharp-minded, elegant wife Freda typed the manuscript.'[9] Bedi worked with a small group of leftists, mainly from outside Kashmir. Although he took credit for the manifesto, which he described as a '100% Communist document', he never claimed authorship.[10] 'There was not much drafting to be done except to write the introduction,' a veteran Kashmiri communist P.N. Jalali recalled, as it was 'almost a carbon copy' of a Soviet document.[11] For the key opening section, the draft constitution, Bedi turned to an item he had published in *Contemporary India* a few years earlier—Stalin's 1936 constitution for the Soviet Union. It was a resourceful rummage through his personal archive. Although this was adapted to meet Kashmir's circumstances, many of the points were simply copied out. The longer economic programme, including charters for workers, peasants and women, was more loosely based on kisan sabha (peasants' movement) documents, which Bedi would also have known well. The only considerable piece of writing to be done was Sheikh Abdullah's foreword. This was even more explicitly communist in tone. 'The inspiring picture of the regeneration of all the different nationalities and peoples of the U.S.S.R., and their welding together into the united mighty Soviet State that is throwing back its barbarous invaders with deathless heroism,' Sheikh Abdullah was made to declare, 'is an unanswerable argument for the building of democracy on the cornerstone of economic equality.'

As far as the communists were concerned, Bedi had carried out a brilliant political manoeuvre. An important regional party with close links to the Congress had adopted a manifesto drafted by communists, staunchly pro-Soviet in content and reflecting the CPI's political line. 'New Kashmir' was for decades the watchword by which Sheikh Abdullah's ambition for a social transformation of Kashmir was known. Sheikh Abdullah himself described it as 'a revolutionary document'.[12] While much of the manifesto remained simply an aspiration, the far-reaching pledges on land reform were acted upon once the National Conference came to power and remain one of the most radical and egalitarian measures introduced in independent India.

P.N. Jalali's recollection is that Bedi had been 'deputed' by the Communist Party in Punjab to 'look after' the communists in Jammu and Kashmir. Kashmiri communists operated not as a separate party but inside Sheikh Abdullah's National Conference, and were particularly influential among students and the trade unions. 'They did not raise their hand [and say] that: here we are, communists. Except that everybody knew they were communists. Even Sheikh sahib knew. ... But we were conscious not to rub Sheikh sahib on the wrong side because he was very sensitive about any parallel political activity.' While B.P.L. Bedi had the greater political influence in Kashmir, Jalali also had keen memories of Freda and her 'very striking' appearance:

> She was a wonderful lady, very modest, and she was very well known throughout the valley in Kashmir. Every summer they would come, early visitors if you call them visitors. And Mrs Bedi used to deliver lectures on the USSR, they used to be very well attended ... weekly lectures. These were very popular lectures ... Strangely enough, they were held in a hall which belonged to the Church Mission Society

On one of these summer visits, the Bedis got caught up in the growing turbulence of Kashmiri politics. They were part of a river procession through Srinagar, a popular form of both demonstration and celebration in the Kashmiri capital, when political rivals standing on a bridge loosed volleys of stones down on the boats. Several of those in the procession suffered nasty injuries, and Ranga remembers his mother lying on top of him to save him from the barrage.

The reputation Bedi gained for taking the lead in compiling the 'New Kashmir' manifesto helped him in his task of securing recruits. Christabel Taseer saw at close quarters Bedi's effectiveness—she recounted that G.M. Sadiq, later a prime minister of the state, 'was motivated to be a Leftist, as were a number of other young Kashmiris, by association with B.P.L. Bedi and his wife, Freda, both dedicated Marxists.' Another Kashmiri leftist with a large popular following, G.M. Karra, told Taseer how he and several others had been 'won over to the Communist cause through the Bedis'. Yet another stated that 'Kashmir's Marxist intellectual scene was dominated by B.P.L. Bedi and his English wife Freda Bedi'.[13] The Bedis were big fish in the small pond of Kashmiri progressives and radicals—and their close friendship with Sheikh Abdullah and his reliance on the left for strategic direction and organisational support gave them huge authority and influence. At the same time, the Bedis were making friends in the political mainstream of the nationalist movement too. A remarkable group photograph survives, taken in Kashmir in 1945 at the annual session of the National Conference, which includes three future prime ministers of India and two future prime ministers of Indian Kashmir: Sheikh Abdullah and his ally Bakshi Ghulam Mohammad are at the back; in front of them are Jawaharlal Nehru—recently released from detention—and his daughter Indira Gandhi; two nationalist leaders in what became Pakistan are prominent, Abdul Samad Khan Achakzai from Baluchistan and Khan Abdul Ghaffar Khan from the Frontier, the latter carrying a young child, very probably Indira's son, Rajiv Gandhi; on one flank is Mridula Sarabhai, an influential supporter of Kashmiri nationalism; on the other is Freda Bedi, smiling broadly and clearly pregnant, with B.P.L. behind her, largely hidden to the camera.

When next the temper of Kashmiri politics boiled over, it was Freda rather than B.P.L. who was on the spot and propelled to prominence. In the spring of 1946, Sheikh Abdullah launched the Quit Kashmir movement. While the Congress's earlier Quit India campaign was directed against the British, Sheikh Abdullah was seeking the eviction of Kashmir's royal family and the establishment of representative government. The maharaja responded with repression. Protests were violently dispersed. Sheikh Abdullah was arrested in May 1946; hundreds of his supporters were also detained. Several of his key colleagues managed to reach Lahore. Some leaders of the National Conference, notably G.M. Karra, operated underground. Bedi was in Lahore and too well-known to make the journey to Srinagar without attracting immediate arrest. Freda, by chance, was in Kashmir on a camping holiday with her new baby, Kabir, then just four months old and still being breast-fed. On Kabir's nineteenth birthday, Freda wrote him a long and intensely personal letter in which she dwelt on the political drama in which he was caught up.

In summer, we went up to Kashmir as usual. Papa left me in Haji Brar, and went down to Lahore again, promising to return. Then the storm burst. Sheikh Abdullah started the 'Quit Kashmir' agitation. He was promptly jailed along with all his followers. I felt I must do something. What, I didn't know. Srinagar was a long way away and all the people I could discuss things with were behind bars. I came down to Srinagar. You were always with me like my skin, tucked up in your little Moses basket. I daren't leave you for a minute so wherever you + I had to go, we went together.

How can I put in words that painful summer? The police wanted me to leave Kashmir as they knew Papa and I were friends of the rebels. So they issued a notice to me to leave. I wrote on the back of the notice that I didn't accept it, as I didn't recognise the people who issued it. From then on they pursued me. C.I.D. watching, following. I was doing nothing, of course; just feeding you. Whoever I stayed with, the poor boatman, were called and harassed [sic] by the Police. It was so difficult: they wanted to protect me, but I was giving them trouble. Finally, to save the boat people, I took a room in a cheap Punjabi hotel in the city, with a Frontierman Manager, some Peshawari Hindu, I've forgotten his name, but he had a heart of gold. 'Just you sit here and feed that baby,' he said, 'and don't worry about anything.'

But the hotel food made me sick, + my milk began to suffer. It was then that that saintly old man, a Kashmiri Pandit, … heard of my plight and sent me every morning and evening a tiffin box full of pure vegetarian food. That kept me going, and you too. …

Once, the 'underground' Kashmiri nationalists wanted to meet me, and I was given a 'burqua' (you were tucked away under it, close to my heart) and slipped out of a house I was visiting by the back door, + so reached a room in the centre of the old city.[14]

In this intimate letter written many years after the events described, Freda downplayed both the bravery and the political significance of her actions. The state authorities' issuing of an 'externment' or deportation order against Freda in June 1946 was widely reported—so too was her refusal to comply.[15] This was a political trial of will, and Freda could not be sure that if the maharaja's police moved in, she would be gently treated. The British communist Rajani Palme Dutt—in Kashmir in late July as a public show of support for Sheikh Abdullah—complained of the 'reign of terror' let loose by the maharaja and his police. He met Bedi in Lahore, noting that he was 'large' and 'robust'. Bedi, in turn, helped to organise meetings for Palme Dutt in Srinagar, including with Freda.[16] 'I saw armed sentries posted on all the bridges and strategic points,' he wrote in *Labour Monthly*. 'An Indian journalist who accompanied me to Srinagar was subjected to a police raid at night by ten C.I.D. men, who made a complete search of his room, as well as of the room of Freda Bedi in the same hotel. The driver of the car which I had used in Srinagar was ... arrested and beaten up to extract from him information as to my movements.'[17]

Freda's secret meeting was to pass on messages between the National Conference leaders—presumably those in Lahore—and those such as G.M. Karra who were operating undercover in Srinagar. In the absence of much of the male leadership of the National Conference, women activists stepped into the breach. At the behest of some of these women, Freda dressed up in clothes which would have disguised her European appearance but hardly made her inconspicuous. '"People wouldn't put me in an old muddy burka," said Freda. "They wanted to dress me in the best they had, and they would go to the bride's chest." In ballooning garments encrusted with embroidery, and with daintily crocheted inserts just big enough for her blue English eyes to peer through, Freda moved about, relaying directives ... Her temporary retreat into purdah had been an experience for her. "It's a strange sensation it gives you," she said. "You're behind a bridge. You have this queer knowledge that you can observe everybody and no one can see you. It's a peculiar mentality that must develop among Muslim women."[18] Sajida Zameer Ahmed recalls escorting Freda, disguised in a burqa, on a horse-drawn buggy around Srinagar to meet underground activists. She also took on another invaluable role for Freda—babysitting Kabir so that his mother could devote herself more fully to the political role she had taken on.[19]

Twelve-year-old Ranga was also embroiled in taking messages to the underground activists—though without his, or it seems his mother's, prior knowledge. This was probably Bedi's idea—he saw a lot of the Kashmiri nationalists in Lahore, and some stayed in the Bedis' guest hut, indeed it seems that the Lahore Kashmir Committee arranged for the building of an additional hut to house activists. 'I saw many of the important and not-so-important Kashmiri leaders as guests of Bedi—Sheikh Abdullah, Bakhsi Ghulam Mohammad, Ghulam Muhammad Sadiq and a host of others,' Som Anand reminisced. 'During the "Quit Kashmir" movement of the National Conference, Sadiq in particular stayed there for a long time.'[20] This was probably how Ranga was press-ganged into the service of the Kashmiri underground. He was told to make a journey by train and bus to Srinagar during term time to visit his mother and baby brother. He had to travel alone—though there was usually someone close-at-hand keeping a discrete eye on the youngster. In his school copy books, hidden among writing exercises and homework, were political messages written longhand in Urdu. Freda was astonished to see Ranga in Srinagar and, as he recalls, 'horrified' when she discovered the purpose. But she passed on the school books, the relevant pages were neatly removed, and the same method used to get messages back to Lahore.

Freda's letter many years later to Kabir rehearsed what happened at the end of that turbulent summer:

> By October, the Police had realised I wasn't to be bullied, so they were not troubling me any more. But Sheikh Sahib sent a message from jail that I should go down to Lahore, + thanked me for all I had done. Just a silent satyagraha, for what it was worth. During that summer, you and I were as close as ever Mother + baby could be. Papa, too, (who was not allowed to re-enter Kashmir) was wanting us. And so we reached Model Town + the huts again.

Freda kept the letter sent by Sheikh Abdullah from Riasi sub-jail in Jammu province, a personal and affectionate letter but expressing his anger at the treatment from 'these devils' his jailers and his political resolve. 'It seems to me that things will hang on in Kashmir for some time more + that my countrymen shall have to prepare themselves for a final onslaught on the citadel ... The cause must win. I am sure that our cause is righteous + we shall win in the end.'[21] Freda had sent the jailed leader a photo of Kabir. 'He will, I am sure, grow as a very handsome boy,' Sheikh Abdullah responded, '+ his forehead depicts him to become a great thinker + a revolutionary.'

When Sheikh Abdullah's supporters captured the citadel, to use his analogy, Freda was thousands of miles away in England. In mid-August 1947, when India and Pakistan gained independence, the maharaja was still dithering about which nation his princely state should join, and wondering whether Kashmir could achieve independence. Both he and Sheikh Abdullah—for very different reasons—were more inclined to Indian rule than to becoming part of Pakistan. In late October, with the connivance of sections of Pakistan's armed forces and new government, a large force of tribesmen from the North West Frontier entered the princely state and quickly overwhelmed the maharaja's army. They were motivated in part by the pursuit of jihad and of loot, and by vengeance for Partition massacres of Muslims in Punjab—and also by a determination to overthrow the state's Hindu ruler and claim Muslim Kashmir for Pakistan. The maharaja promptly fled to the relative safety of his palace in Jammu, to the south of the Kashmir Valley, and once there signed the instrument of accession by which his domain became part of India. The Indian armed forces began an airlift to the rudimentary landing strip outside Srinagar, saving the city from ransack, and within a couple of weeks had repulsed the invading force. But Indian troops failed to evict the tribesmen from the entire princely state which became informally partitioned between India and Pakistan—as it still is.[22]

Sheikh Abdullah, recently released from jail, manoeuvred into the vacuum created by the flight of the maharaja and his courtiers. With communist help, he organised a militia, some of which was trained and equipped by the Indian army. This was both a defence force should invaders again imperil the Kashmiri capital and a demonstration to all that the old regime of princely autocracy had been swept away. Sheikh Abdullah's supporters flooded the streets of Srinagar, and the city pulsed with political energy. 'The National Conference red flag ... decorates every public building in the city,' the *Times of India* reported. 'In the main square in the heart of the city, which has been renamed "Red Square", a giant red flag flutters from a tall mast under which workers and ordinary people foregather at all hours of the day to hear the latest news of the war and exchange political gossip.'[23]

Amid all this turmoil, Sheikh Abdullah received a letter from Freda in England and found the time to write a brief reply from the hotel in Srinagar which had become his temporary headquarters:

> We are facing a grim struggle and the enemy is almost at our door-step. But we are confident that we shall turn the corner.
>
> I think the best you can do for us at present would be to help

us to set up an Information Bureau in New Delhi to work as
the medium of our publicity in the outside world. I do not want
to call you here because coming here at present is unsafe and
unpleasant.

I should love to hear from Bedi. The two of you have done
such a lot for us.[24]

Freda and Bedi took no notice of Sheikh Abdullah's warning to
stay clear of Srinagar. Within a few days of their re-assembly as a
family in India in December 1947, they all moved on to Kashmir.
While the Indian army by then had the upper hand, Kashmir was
a war zone. 'From Delhi we were flown in an army troop carrier,
Dakota DC5,' Ranga recalls. 'No formal seats, fixed benches along
the length of the aircraft and seat belts anchored to the body of the
plane. Our great dane Rufus on the floor shivered out of fright all the
way. When we landed in Srinagar it was a hive of military activity.'
Bedi's role was to work closely with Sheikh Abdullah, both on
policy and propaganda. The family were allotted evacuee property—a
simple but well situated house with the name Dar-ul-Aman ('home
of peace') at Gagribal, close to Srinagar's renowned Dal Lake.

Within days of arriving in Srinagar, the Bedis had a visit from
one of the commanding photo-journalists of the era. Margaret
Bourke-White had provided *Life* with its first front cover in 1936.
She was a war photographer in Europe but turned her back on the
'decay of Europe' and came to India just as it was about to achieve
independence. 'I witnessed that extremely rare event in the history
of nations, the birth of twins,' she wrote.[25] She arrived in India in
March 1946 and spent seven months travelling widely across the
subcontinent, meeting and photographing all the main political
players. She returned in September 1947, as it became clear that
the birth of twin nations, midnight's children, was also a profound
human calamity. Her powerful and unsettling images of Partition—of
migration and massacre—are among her most memorable. She was

determined to record India's passage to independence not only in images but in a book. *Halfway to Freedom*, sub-titled 'a report on the new India' and published in 1949, is a vivid account of India's faltering steps to full nationhood.

When fighting erupted in Kashmir in late October 1947, Margaret Bourke-White was determined to get there. For a photo-journalist, the prime requirement is to be at the heart of the action—there's no other way of capturing the most commanding images. Early in November, Sir George Cunningham, the governor of Pakistan's North West Frontier Province, noted in his diary that two American women journalists from *Life* had been refused permission to go to Abbottabad, the informal headquarters of the invading force, and beyond to Baramulla.[26] That didn't stop her. She managed to reach Abbottabad and to meet and photograph a band of several hundred armed Pathans on their way to Kashmir:

> Unlike higher officials, these tribesmen seemed to know what was going on when I questioned them.
>
> 'Are you going into Kashmir?' I asked.
>
> 'Why not?' they said. 'We are all Muslims. We are going to help our Muslim brothers in Kashmir.'
>
> Sometimes their help to their brother Muslims was accomplished so quickly that the trucks and buses would come back within a day or two bursting with loot, only to return to Kashmir with more tribesmen, to repeat their indiscriminate 'liberating'—and terrorizing of Hindu, Sikh and Muslim villager alike.[27]

A few weeks later, Margaret Bourke-White managed to reach the Kashmir Valley—approaching not from Pakistani territory but from the Indian side. 'Just before Christmas of 1947 I flew over the wild mountain barrier, with guerrilla warfare going on fiercely but invisible among the ravines and chasms below, and landed in the enchanted city of Srinagar. Everyone who has ever visited Kashmir knows it has a special magic. "It is a different world altogether," my friend Bedi, who was my guide in Kashmir, expressed it; "the water and the land combines into one."[28]

The account Bourke-White gave of the turbulence in Kashmir— the political cohesion of its people, the progressive credentials of the National Conference's manifesto and their 'legendary' leader Sheikh Abdullah, 'this good-natured, weather-beaten, eminently practical and rather homely young man'—reflect the political outlook of her guide and host. Indeed, her two chapters on Kashmir capture the high water mark of the progressive New Kashmir movement. She interviewed Sheikh Abdullah and several of his associates, met members of his people's militia, and encountered the key figure in the underground movement during the Quit Kashmir campaign. And of course, she got to know Bedi's wife.

> Freda Bedi is a fair-haired English girl whom Bedi had met and married when both were students at Oxford. She had become deeply interested in the welfare of her adopted country, learned the language, and wore the long full pajama like dress of Kashmiri women. She had her own jail record—acquired for her participation in the freedom movement—which is the proud badge of every patriotic Indian who has worked for independence.

Bourke-White also wanted to see the evidence of the invaders' largely indiscriminate destruction, and having heard about the desecration of a convent at Baramulla and the ransacking of the mission hospital, she persuaded Bedi to take her there:

> It was badly defaced and littered, and a delegation of students from Srinagar was coming next day to clean it up and salvage what remained of the library. ... They would put the Christian mission in as good order as they could in time for Christmas Day.
>
> We made our way into the ravaged chapel, wading through the mass of torn hymnbooks and broken sacred statuary. The altar was deep in rubble. Bedi stooped down over it and picked up one

fragment, turning it over carefully in his big hands. It was the broken head of Jesus, with just one eye remaining.

'How beautiful it is,' said Bedi, 'this single eye of Christ looking out so calmly on the world. We shall preserve it always in Kashmir as a permanent reminder of the unity between Indians of all religions which we are trying to achieve.'[29]

And that's where she left her account of Kashmir—an impassioned, if partial, piece of reportage. She recited uncritically what she heard from Bedi, and this has to be marked down as one of his key successes as a propagandist. There's hardly a whisper of criticism of Sheikh Abdullah and the movement he headed, and hardly a good word about Pakistan or the invaders acting in its name.

B.P.L. Bedi pops up repeatedly in the pages of *Halfway to Freedom* as Bourke-White's friend and guide. In Delhi in mid-January 1948 a couple of weeks after leaving Kashmir, she conveniently caught sight of him when attending Gandhi's prayers during a fast to protest against the communal hatred unleashed by Partition. 'Bedi was a giant of a figure in his billowing wool homespun which swept in coarse, oatmeal-colored folds from his massive shoulders to his Gargantuan feet, bare and crusty in their open sandals.'[30] Another two weeks later, she was again with Bedi in Delhi when she heard of Gandhi's assassination and rushed with her camera to the spot. The following day, Bedi and sixteen-year-old Binder accompanied Bourke-White to Gandhi's cremation, Bedi using his persuasiveness to help get access, and Binder being little short of heroic in guarding the cameras from the crush of the crowd and helping Bourke-White to a vantage point.

Margaret Bourke-White was in her early forties when she arrived in India—vivacious, sociable, successful, determined and with two failed marriages behind her. She embarked on an affair with one of India's best-known journalists, Frank Moraes—handsome, hard living, Oxford-educated with an accent to match. He was a friend

the invaders, as were an English couple (the wife had just given birth in the hospital's labour ward), a patient, a nurse, and the husband of the hospital doctor. Those who survived the initial attack were held in the baby ward of the hospital for ten terrifying days before their evacuation—an ordeal which the novelist H.E. Bates recounted in fictional form.[3] Elsewhere in Baramulla, many buildings had been destroyed and businesses ransacked—there were persistent reports of extensive sexual violence, and a number of young Sikh women were abducted. Ranga, then thirteen, has memories of visiting Baramulla with his mother and cleaning encrusted blood from the floor of the church. He recalls his mother being traumatised by the experience. She had 'already been disturbed by tales of rape, loot, plunder, people being shot, mutilated, missing, all that misery. Scraping dry blood off floors in the chapel, from ante rooms with hacked, broken-down doors, was more than she could handle. Gory stories by locals of the dreadful happening on that day only added to her grief. All this made her morose, retreated within herself, lost sleep and appetite, flagged in energy.' It took about a week, as Ranga recalls, for his mother to regain any semblance of normality.

The women's militia in which Freda enrolled was one of a number of left-inspired initiatives to support Kashmir's progressive government and its ambitions for social change. The men's militia, replete with a political officer, saw active service alongside Indian troops and several of its members were killed. A cultural front encompassed progressive writers and poets from Kashmir and other parts of India and performed hastily written agitprop theatre. 'The atmosphere reminded one of Spain and the International Brigade,' one of the participants recalled a touch romantically, 'where, it was said, writers had come to live their books, and poets had come to die for their poetry!'[4]

The Women's Self-Defence Corps was, as its name suggests, not intended as an offensive force but to help defend Srinagar, and particularly to protect the honour of its women. The numbers enrolling were modest and disproportionately from the Pandit, or Kashmiri Hindu, minority—reflecting the social conservatism of the Muslim community and the preponderance of Pandits in the local intelligentsia and the left. The women were provided with rifles and trained in their use by an Indian army officer; they drilled and paraded in Srinagar's parks and open spaces. An armed women's militia would have been a striking innovation in any part of India—in the conservative and sheltered Kashmir Valley, it reflected a revolution in social attitudes. The Communist Party paper, the *People's Age*, gave proud prominence to the militia. 'I am writing this letter from the Paladium [sic] Cinema which is our headquarters now,' one woman volunteer wrote. 'Down below at the crossing, thousands of Kashmiris are always mounting guard with their rifles. The whole city is mad with joy ... Today four of us girls will be taught the use of rifles. Tomorrow we may be sent to the ... front as field-nurses.' A subsequent issue featured two pages of photographs of the women in training, and declared: 'The women in Kashmir are the first in India to build an army of women trained to use the rifle. By their example they have made Indian history, filled our chests with pride, raised our country's banner higher among the great nations of the world.'⁵

The women's militia never saw active service, though it paraded for and was inspected by Jawaharlal Nehru, now India's prime minister, on his visits to Srinagar. Pathe newsreel footage from 1948 includes a glimpse of Freda on the parade ground with a rifle in her hand.⁶ The volunteers also took on a social role, helping those displaced both by Partition-related upheaval and by the fighting in parts of the former princely state which came to involve the Pakistan army as well as irregular forces. They took up 'women's work' among the refugees, organising milk for the camps, and distributing clothes and blankets, 'all of us,' Freda told friends, 'acting as older sisters to the thousands of children and women suffering not only physical hardships in the desperate cold, but often in mental torture when relations and children had been killed, abducted, or lost on the miserable trek to safety.'[7]

Early in 1949, Freda wrote a long letter from Srinagar to 'Olive darling'—her old friend Olive Chandler—which gave a vivid account of both the excitement and exhaustion which were part of the Kashmir experience:

> I don't know how to recount the last year to you in a letter: it has been a new world, harrowing + yet inspiring. On my return, Bedi + I + Ranga + Kabir naturally (since Lahore was impossible) found our way to Kashmir where our friends of the National Conference had formed the State's first popular Government. It was grim: snow, uncertainty, salt, sugar + rations low. But Kashmir maintained her unity + Hindus, Muslims + Sikhs fought together to keep the raiders out. Last winter I divided my time between the Kashmir Women's Army—military training—+ refugee relief. We had 17,000 refugees in the city and ran 23 milk + relief centres. There wasn't time to breathe + I lost over a stone!! That work finished early summer. I had a month or two's rest. I now am back again running Relief Centres for unemployed in the city.

This last mentioned initiative, she explained in a later letter, gave technical training to the children of boatmen and of domestic workers, accompanied by a monthly cash payment. It was a means of providing wider opportunities to young Kashmiris while also providing a slender income to those impoverished by the impact of war on Kashmir's hitherto booming tourist trade.

The impact of the conflict over Kashmir pervaded Freda's letters—'we are a battle front' she told Olive Chandler—and while a United Nations-brokered ceasefire came into effect at the close of 1948, Kashmir's contested status cast a shadow on the social ambitions of its governing party:

> While a very brutal tribal invasion + hot propaganda from the

Pakistan side has been trying to make the State communal minded, it has valiantly stuck to its democratic ideas, + built up a corner of India where one can truly say an inter-communal life exists. Something to be deeply grateful for after the inevitable frustration + bitterness that followed in the wake of the riots both in India + Pakistan.

All I had by way of books + household goods was either looted in Lahore, or is stored there ... + I can't get it. We had to rebuild from the ground up. But nothing matters—all of us are safe + having been daily with refugees with their heartrending stories of violent death + abduction I feel we have been lucky.[8]

She went on to reflect on the prospect of a popular vote to decide whether Kashmir should be part of India or Pakistan—a commitment that Nehru had made to Kashmiris, though neither he nor subsequent Indian leaders have honoured it. 'Living in Kashmir is like sitting on the edge of a precipice,' she said.

There will be a tough fight when + if a plebiscite takes place. The other side uses low weapons: an appeal to religious fanaticism + hatred which can always find a response. We fight with clean hands. I am content as a democrat that Kashmir should vote + turn whichever way it wishes: but I know a Pakistan victory would mean massacre, abduction, the mass migration of Hindus + Sikhs + I hate to face it. God forbid it should happen. Kashmir with its Socialist Government + its young leaders can lead India, rebuild this miserable Country. I've great faith in it, + love for it, too. It is beautiful, rich in talent + natural resources.

Her next letter to Olive, just four months later, bore personal news—she was expecting another child, which she declared 'firmly' would be a girl. 'It's rather a lot to take on a new baby in the midst of present-day Kashmir but Kabir needs someone his own age—+ there's a lovely garden to relax in + forget sometimes the quarrels +

miseries of the world.'⁹ Her confidence that the boys would have a sister was borne out; Gulhima (universally known as Guli), a name which she told friends meant 'rose of the Himalayas', was born in Srinagar in September 1949. 'So pleased to get the wire with the good news ...' Freda's mother wrote from Derby, 'you are a complete family now. ... I hope she has a kink in her hair. She might because the males have your hair so the female more likely will take after Bedi.' She made sure the birth was noted in the columns of Derby's daily paper.

When opportunity arose, Freda made the most of Kashmir's beauty—she swam from the bathing boats in Dal Lake, and enjoyed the meadows and the spring fruit blossoms. She also made friends among Kashmir's tiny European community, one of whom, the novelist Rumer Godden, became Guli's godmother. There was still a spiritual void, and Ranga recalls that for a year while in Kashmir, his mother practised the Muslim faith, including prayers five times a day. The family still has her English translation of the Koran, a bulky volume bought by her husband who also inscribed it: 'To Oggee—My better self—on Gandhi Jayanti '48.'¹⁰ She then spent a year practising Hinduism. Neither of India's principal religions offered the solace that she sought. It's curious that none of the three great religions of Punjab—Hinduism, Sikhism and Islam—captured her imagination. She read their holy books, respected their teachings and was familiar with their ritual, but it was only when she chanced to visit a mainly Buddhist nation that her interest in Eastern spirituality turned into a clear allegiance to a specific faith.

Bedi's role for the new Kashmiri government was varied, and relied greatly on his easy familiarity with Sheikh Abdullah and his key lieutenants. Christabel Taseer described him as 'Adviser in Chief' to Sheikh Abdullah. The diplomat Josef Korbel, alarmed by the extent of communist influence in Kashmir, put it more strongly, denouncing Bedi as 'the *eminence grise* behind the Abdullah government'.¹¹ After the initial burst of political energy and excitement, he was for several months based largely in Delhi, liaising with India's national government, getting involved in what would now be described as public relations for Kashmir's new rulers, and seeking new markets for Kashmiri handicrafts and agricultural produce to replace those lost with Partition. By the autumn of 1948, he was back with his family in Srinagar, and working almost entirely on publicity. 'Bedi is on Counter-Prop:' Freda told Olive Chandler, 'counteracting the Pakistan attempt to give everything a religious-communal angle + create hatred for the minorities. A beastly enough game.'[12] He had the uncomfortable responsibility of rebutting partisan comments made by one of his oldest friends, who had remained in Lahore and actively championed Pakistan. Bedi recalled that his daily routine 'began by scanning everything that the Pakistan radio was putting over, and then shooting out a reply. I knew from the other side the most pungent things were being said by my dearest friend Hafiz Jullunduri [sic] and on this side when I wrote something, he would in his very nasal way say, "Oh Bediyan: oh baimana hun tun he saanu is taraha dinya galan kahna hain." "O, faithless Bedi, now you are stabbing us."'[13]

Although Bedi, as a non-Kashmiri, was not as prominent as a platform speaker as he had been in Lahore, there were occasions when he continued to make use of his oratorical skills. Shanti Swarup Ambardar, as a young man in Srinagar, knew of the Bedis, 'a curiosity to most Kashmiris as a glamorous couple. Their proximity to Sheikh Abdullah gave them an added air of authority'. But when he skipped college with some friends and went along to a large meeting at Nedou's Hotel, Sheikh Abdullah was the man they wanted to hear. The Kashmiri leader didn't turn up and it fell to the Bedis to calm the crowd. 'Bedi was dressed in a rumpled kurta pajama,' Ambardar recalls. 'He was heavy set, with a pug nose and unruly black hair, and looked more like a Punjabi businessman than an intellectual. He smoked a lot. Freda was tall, thin and fair, had a sharp nose and wore an elegant sari. The physical contrasts between the two could not have been more obvious. ... Sensing the crowd's disappointment at not seeing Abdullah, Bedi leapt onto a table. He launched into a tirade against money-lenders and zamindars [land owners]. The crowd guffawed at his mocking dialogues and animated gestures about expropriating assets without compensation. He had a good command of Urdu proverbs and quoted from Iqbal and Ghalib.'[14]

In his role as propaganda chief, Bedi established a network of paid informers whose role—he said—was to pass on promptly the rumours and gossip circulating in the streets and market places.

At 8.30 [pm], I would call the political committee meeting in which one or two politicians, poets, writers, and artists would participate. I would give the political line on whichever rumour had come, and having given the ideas, the artist would get down to draw his own impression in the art form, the poet would write a little poem and the writer would make a really good thrilling write-up. By 10 o'clock they had to give me that. I would read through it very carefully. ... at 12 o'clock the posters would be sent to the Press ... at 5 o'clock when the town woke up, there would be full-sized posters, answering all the rumours, which had been heard in the town the previous day and mentioning that we all knew what they were talking about.[15]

Although Bedi was proud of this rapid rebuttal system, it comes across as somewhat sinister. Sheikh Abdullah proved to be less successful in power than he had been in mobilising Kashmiris to oppose princely rule. He was not an instinctive pluralist and while large spirited and sincere in his wish to improve the lot of poor Kashmiris in particular, he was also impulsive and intolerant of criticism. Some of his one-time allies ended up in his jails.

Once working for Sheikh Abdullah, B.P.L. Bedi put his political loyalties aside. He was an insider, a confidante of the Kashmiri leadership, and by his own account a coordinator of government policy and occasional author of key speeches. The small band of Kashmiri communists were in any case sharply divided about whether, and how actively, they should support Sheikh Abdullah's administration. Bedi was also out of tune with the new direction of the Communist Party of India, which had swung sharply to the left, abandoning working with what were termed 'bourgeois' parties for support for peasant insurrections, notably in Telangana in southern India. Bedi's advocacy and implementation of the most radical measures in the 'New Kashmir' manifesto, the redistribution of land which turned hundreds of thousands of labourers into peasant cultivators and greatly alleviated rural indebtedness, was seen within the CPI as promoting reformism over revolution.

Now this was the one act which earned me the severest condemnation from the Communist Party, as to why all these measures were not brought about in the Telangana manner: that is by murder of officials, murder of landlords, and then taking over lands and all that. To that I said, 'I have never come across a more stupid approach than this. When the entire national movement was adopting the programme, which I myself had drafted, and then the entire national movement plus the government ... without a single mishap the whole thing was implemented. You don't realize than [sic] in Kashmir it was not just a mere handing over of power to the national movement ... It was virtually, if you look at it realistically, a seizure of power. ... Telangana means that you are too set and rigid in your pattern; that because Kashmir has not followed the bloody path of killing and murder, it is the wrong way.'[16]

This sharp (though unpublicised) difference, Bedi said, led to what amounted to his expulsion from the Communist Party. Retelling this episode more than a decade later, he was still deeply aggrieved by the manner in which the party repudiated him. 'To be frank, I was a very vain man,' he recalled. 'I am no less now. I knew that my expulsion from the party was more a reflection on the party itself than upon myself. So I said, "Don't bother. Leave it."'[17] His sense of grievance must have been sharpened by knowing that it was his fellow detainees (and at the time political allies) in Deoli who had pushed the CPI towards ultra-leftism. The breach was too wide to be made good.

Bedi was caught between the Communist Party which no longer supported him and a Kashmiri government which was determined to bring its left-wing supporters to heel. Sheikh Abdullah, in his memoirs, suggested that the implementation of the land reforms outlined in the 'New Kashmir' manifesto was not so much an indication of communist influence as a means of restricting their role. 'Not that we were not progressive in our outlook,' Abdullah recorded, 'yet we had no desire to pawn our mind and conscience with the communist party. Actually, we were anathema to them, as we had purged our region of germs of communism by implementing the land reforms and waiving off the farmers' agricultural loans. By these measures we had, if you like, pulled off the carpet from beneath the feet of the communists in the state, leaving them with no excuse to incite the people and create a space for themselves.'[18] This was a self-serving argument—Sheikh Abdullah's real grievance with the CPI was that some communists were organising against him, and rallying behind one of his rivals within the National Conference.

Nehru also pressed Sheikh Abdullah to keep communists at a distance, with Bedi the main target of his displeasure. In May 1949, after a brief visit to Kashmir, Nehru wrote to 'Shaikh Saheb' with a gentle warning:

Quite a number of our embassies here are greatly worried at, what they say, the communist infiltration into Kashmir. ... Most of them have heard about Bedi and they enquire about him. I understand that Bedi is editing the newspaper there and is drawing a substantial salary plus free car etc. I have no personal grievance against Bedi, but in view of the trouble we are having with the

Communist Party in India, naturally Bedi's name is constantly coming up before people here.[19]

Sheikh Abdullah's reply isn't available—but Nehru wouldn't let the matter rest. He wrote again to the Kashmiri leader:

You referred to the Bedis. I rather like them and especially Freda. I know that Freda left the Communist Party some years ago. What she has done since, I do not know. But so far as I know, Bedi has continued in the Party, and the Party, especially today, does not tolerate any lukewarm people or those who do not fall in line with their present policy.

I do not want you to push out the Bedis and cause immediate distress to them. But I do think that no responsible work should be given to them and they should be kept completely in the background. Yesterday I saw a little book on you written by the Bedis. This kind of thing immediately makes people think that the Bedis are playing a prominent role in Kashmir and are closely associated with you. These create reactions in their minds against you and your Government.[20]

The publication which had attracted Nehru's attention was a twenty-page pamphlet in praise of Sheikh Abdullah. This unsophisticated piece of propaganda written jointly by the Bedis sought to portray the Kashmiri leader as one of 'the Great Three' figures of India's independence era alongside Nehru and Gandhi—a theatrical over-statement which should have brought a blush to the authors' cheeks.[21]

B.P.L. Bedi was aware of Nehru's antipathy and of the attempts to marginalise him. He said there was 'very great pressure ... exerted by the Government of India for my being sent away from Kashmir, because they felt leftist policies would be going on more and more adamantly if I stayed on there.'[22] His influence and access started to diminish. Bedi was removed from his counter-propaganda role and deputed to Kashmir's education ministry to revise school textbooks. Freda was also involved (and probably more active) in drafting new textbooks and both husband and wife were nominated to Jammu and Kashmir's Central Advisory Board on Education. 'Over 90 books were rewritten and printed ...' Freda commented, 'and Kashmir was the first part of India to reorganise its teaching material so that the books fitted in with the new world and the new free India that our children now live in.'[23] These were important tasks but at some remove from the most sensitive political decision making. Nehru's advice, it seems, was being heeded. For Bedi, this sidelining must have added to a sense of anguish. After almost twenty years of incessant political activity, both the main political forces to which he had owed allegiance—the Communist Party and the Kashmiri nationalists—were cutting him loose. He had seen himself as a key and perhaps indispensable figure; that's not quite how others viewed him.

The waning of the activism which accompanied the National Conference's advent to power also entailed a retreat in the public role of women. The brief moment of women's political empowerment appeared to be over, and the disbanding of the Women's Self-Defence Corps reflected a return to what might be described as business as normal. There was, however, an abiding achievement. In the autumn of 1950, several of those who had been active in the women's militia were prominent in establishing the Government College for Women, which took over a large property in central Srinagar built as a home for the widows of the royal family. Freda returned to her old role as a lecturer in English and told friends that the college would produce its first graduates within two years of its foundation. 'There are 160 girls studying in the college, which is quite a good number for a part of the world where in the old days everything was done to discourage rather than encourage higher education for women.'[24] This was another aspect of 'New Kashmir' in action, a real measure of social transformation, allowing the women of Kashmir more choices about their lives and livelihoods. The college retained a keenly political edge. Freda kept the single sheet programme to a college cultural event at the start of its second year of operation, which included a song by the sixteenth-century Kashmiri woman poet and mystic Haba Khatoon 'when the sceptre of foreign invasion was hovering over the beautiful hills and dales of Kashmir'. It also carried the text of an anonymously written new poem entitled 'Inqilab Zindabad', or long live revolution, which declared: 'I shall go out with a machine gun, I will not surrender this land my garden in to alien hands'. Not the normal fare at a women's college—and a sharp reminder of how the conflict over Kashmir, and the militarisation of the valley, moulded attitudes there.

In spite of the deeply unsettled military and political situation, the Bedi family remember their years in Srinagar as a time of stability. The family had money and status, indeed this was the only time when Bedi had a regular job and salary. Their home was comfortable and well situated. Binder Dewan rejoined the household. He had imbibed Bedi's leftism and as a student at Allahabad University was active in the students' communist movement—but when a crackdown loomed, he made his way quickly to Srinagar. He enrolled at Kashmir University making friends with several Kashmiris who were later to be prominent journalists and politicians and so ensuring a lasting bond with the Kashmir Valley. Ranga attended Srinagar's most prestigious school, founded by Anglicans and situated close to Lal Chowk in the heart of the city. He was head boy and a close friend of a pupil a year his junior, Farooq Abdullah, Sheikh Abdullah's son and political heir. Ranga was determined to be an army officer, but was turned down twice for the Indian Military Academy at Dehra Dun. He recalls going with his parents to see General K.S. Thimayya, then in charge of operations in Kashmir, who said he would make inquiries. The general got in touch a few months later to say that having a father who had been involved in 'criminal activity' (probably a nod both to Bedi's communism and the court convictions he had been given while in Lahore) was an insuperable bar. In 1950, Ranga moved to Delhi to study at one of its most prestigious colleges, the Christian-foundation St Stephen's. In the first of what became a tradition of Christmas newsletters at the close of 1951, Freda gave a pen portrait of her three children. Ranga was 'still the out-of-door boy, happiest among a gang of friends'. She described Kabir as 'perhaps the most English looking, having honey eyes and brown hair' and 'something of a dreamer'. Guli was 'rather a tomboy … She combines golden hair with black eyes and rosy cheeks'.

The Bedis also had a more active social life during their years in Srinagar than probably at any other time of their marriage. They enjoyed their status and the attention that surrounded it—which stemmed both from their association with Sheikh Abdullah and Freda's exceptional position as a white woman who entirely identified with India and with Kashmiri nationalism. Michael Brecher, a Canadian academic, spent three months in Srinagar with his wife in the summer of 1951 and saw a lot of the Bedis. He found them both compelling but 'very different in almost every respect'. B.P.L. was clearly well connected, though a touch arrogant—'someone who could be very jovial and charming' but also 'a very serious committed ideologue'. He took more to Freda, 'a striking looking person, a very handsome lady … most impressive as a human being: bright, engaged, caring'. He considered her a 'dual character—being very British, it seemed to us' but totally immersed in her environment. Brecher came across a constant stream of visitors to the Bedis' home, including a woman he met in their garden who was 'very quiet, demure, almost inconspicuous'. This was Indira Gandhi, Nehru's only child, then in her mid-thirties. 'My sense from Freda was they were good friends.'[25] The friendship nurtured in Kashmir between Indira and Freda, both Oxford graduates, strengthened over the following decade.

The Bedis left Kashmir rather precipitately early in 1953. B.P.L.

had been pondering about leaving since the previous summer but he recalled that he finally felt impelled to move to Delhi seeing the plight of Punjabi refugees in the city. 'I told Sheikh Sahib about this, I said, "I have done my bit for Kashmir, my humble bit; now I must come down."'[26] That's part of the story. As Bedi also acknowledged, the growing influence of Sheikh Abdullah's deputy, Bakshi Ghulam Mohammad, was accompanied by the marginalisation of Bedi and others seen as on the left. And with the convening of the Jammu and Kashmir Constituent Assembly in November 1951, Bedi also felt that the key task of seeing the former princely state through the turbulence which accompanied accession to India had been completed. 'So there was really no political job for me and I had started to search my heart, whether now for the sake of the apples and pears of Kashmir it was justified for me to stay.'[27]

There were other currents circulating. In his opening address to the Constituent Assembly, Sheikh Abdullah—while reviewing all the options—clearly supported the state's enduring accession to India and warned that 'practical considerations' made untenable the option of an independent Kashmir. But in private, and in conversations with foreign diplomats, he was warming to the idea of independence, and Delhi was becoming increasingly anxious that Kashmir might slip from India's grip. Bedi apparently counselled against advocacy of independence and would have understood India's imperative to hold on to Kashmir and avoid it falling into Pakistan's sphere of influence. That storm broke in August 1953, when Sheikh Abdullah was arrested and replaced as prime minister by Bakshi, who was seen as more tractable and pro-India. By then the Bedi family had embarked on a new life in the Indian capital—and Freda had also found the spiritual path she had been seeking, during a posting with the United Nations Social Services Commission for Burma.

12

Buddha and Baba

Burma was Freda Bedi's gateway to Buddhism—her assignment there changed her life utterly. She found a teacher, a faith, a form of meditation, and had a moment of awakening which marked a personal turning point. When she returned to India she not only regarded herself as a Buddhist but had decided that her life had a new purpose. Her encounter with Buddhism was more by chance than design. She had for some years been a spiritual seeker—persisting with her regular meditation sessions and taking up yoga as well. But of the world's four major faiths, Buddhism was the one to which she had been least exposed. She had reviewed a children's storybook based on the Jataka—an early Buddhist work about the birth tales of the Buddha—and read from it to Ranga. It stayed with her. Several years later, she wrote about the Buddha's various incarnations, weaving this into her reflections on war, famine and death.[1] She had read Buddhist texts along with other spiritual classics which she found so rewarding. But her visit to Burma was, in so many ways, a revelation. It was her first time immersed in a Buddhist culture and she felt instinctively 'that was my home. Then I knew that in some former life, I think in many former lives, I'd been in the Buddhist way. That's what I feel,' she told a California radio station, while adding 'of course it may be wrong.'[2]

It was money more than spiritual considerations that attracted Freda to Burma. Towards the close of the Bedis' time in Kashmir,

she accepted a six months' United Nations posting to Burma, which
had won its independence from Britain a year after India. She could
probably sense that her husband wouldn't continue for much longer
at Sheikh Abdullah's side, and the family needed an income. Her
family also needed a home, and before taking up the post Freda
had to ensure that her children were cared for. Freda had travelled
a great deal but usually with one or other of her children in tow.
This was the first time that she had made a long trip leaving all her
family behind. Ranga was eighteen and at college in Delhi; Kabir
and Guli were much younger, seven and three. She decided against
leaving them in the care of her husband, and arranged for them to
stay in Delhi with a Czechoslovak friend, Jana Obersal.

Freda's new role with the United Nations was to help in the
planning of Burma's social services: 'A job after my own heart,'
she told Olive Chandler, 'but it's hard not to be with the family.
However, in their interest, I can't throw opportunities away + this
opens new fields for us all.'[3] She was restless by nature and relished
the opportunity of working somewhere new. 'Burma is like India
enough to be homely,' she wrote, 'unlike enough to be beguiling.'
Without family responsibilities, she had more time to devote to her
own interests, and above all to meditate. She met a Buddhist teacher
in Rangoon, U Titthila, who had spent the war years in London
where he had on occasions abandoned his monk's robes to serve as
an air raid warden and, during the Blitz when London came under
sustained German air attack, as a stretcher bearer. Freda found
him 'very saintly'; she asked him to teach her Vipassana (insight)
meditation techniques. 'And it was then ... I got my first flash of
understanding—can't call it more than that. But it changed my
whole life. I felt that, really, this meditation had shown me what
I was trying to find ... and I got great, great happiness—a feeling
that I had found the path.'[4]

While Vipassana meditation dates back many centuries, the
Vipassana movement—which developed particularly in Burma in

the mid-twentieth century—was an adaptation of earlier teaching. It was innovative and linked broadly to rising anti-colonial sentiment. The meditation technique was intended mainly for lay people and offered quick results (some see it as shaping the more recent mindfulness movement) but because of its intensity, it could on occasions overwhelm new practitioners. For Freda, it brought an early moment of illumination—one which was life-changing but also destabilising.

For two months, she had a weekly session with U Titthila. 'And I remember him saying when the eight weeks was coming to an end: if you get a realisation or a flash of realisation, it may not be sitting in your room in meditation, in pose in front of a picture of the Buddha or something, it will probably be somewhere where you don't expect it.' That's exactly what happened. 'I was actually walking with the [UN] commission through the streets of Akyab in the north of Burma—[it was] as though some gates in my mind had just opened and suddenly I was seeing the flow of things, meaning, connections. And when I went back to Delhi, well, I told my husband I'd been searching all my life, it's the Buddhist monks who have been able to show me something I could not find and I'm a Buddhist from now on. Then I began to learn Buddhism after that.'[5] Her family's recollection is that this 'flash' of spiritual awakening was accompanied by a breakdown. According to Ranga, his mother fainted and was taken to hospital. Bedi managed to get emergency travel documents, headed out to Burma and brought his wife home. 'When she came back, she didn't recognise B.P.L. or anybody. She didn't recognise her children. She would sit on her cot doing nothing—completely blank. You couldn't make eye contact with her,' Ranga recalls. 'There was no speech, no recognition—though she could eat and bathe. That lasted for about two months when she gradually started reacting to things. All she recalled was that when walking down the street ... she saw a huge flash of light in the sky and she lost consciousness.'

This was a moment of epiphany—an incident which redefined her life and purpose. From then on, she regarded herself as a Buddhist. And this was much more than simply a religious allegiance. It quickly became the most important aspect of her life. On her return to Delhi, she set up an organisation that she called the Friends of Buddhism. She took a personal vow of brahmacharya, a commitment to virtuous living which implies a decision to become celibate. Her engagement with the faith radically refashioned her links with her family and set her on the course which defined the last quarter-of-a-century of her life.

The household faced several concurrent crises. Freda's collapse not only raised concerns about her health; it also brought an end to any prospect of a longer-term UN role in Burma or indeed anywhere else. Bedi's hasty exit from Kashmir had closed the door on the only regular, decently paid job he ever secured, and plunged him into the much more uncertain arena of small-scale publishing and writing and translating on commission. 'That was a very traumatic move,' Kabir recalls, 'suddenly overnight we arrived in Delhi.' Their reduced circumstances were reflected in the family's accommodation in the Indian capital. From the relative grandeur of a house close to Dal Lake, they took a flat—a 'grotty' apartment, in Kabir's words—in the crowded Karol Bagh area of central Delhi. It was quite a come-down.

Once she was fully recovered, Freda again had to take on the responsibility of being the family's primary earner. She got a helping hand from a well-placed friend. Among her papers is a handwritten note from 'Indu', Indira Gandhi, on the headed paper of the Prime Minister's House: 'Durgabai Deshmukh wants to see you at 11 a.m. tomorrow … in her office in the Planning Commission, Rashtrapati Bhawan. I shall send the car at 10.30.'[6] Deshmukh was an influential figure in the Congress Party and had been a member of India's Constituent Assembly. She had just been appointed as the initial chairperson of the Planning Commission, which in Nehruvian India with its faith in the state to engineer social and economic progress was an important post. She was adamant on the need to champion the interests and promote the welfare of women, children and the disabled. Her meeting with Freda clearly went well. The following month, in January 1954, Freda began working for the government's Central Social Welfare Board establishing and editing a monthly journal, *Social Welfare*. Although she was not a natural civil servant, she embraced the social agenda and the opportunity to travel across India and throw a spotlight on women's concerns and on projects which successfully addressed them. She remained in the job for eight years.

Freda's government employment wasn't particularly well paid, but it allowed the family a measure of financial security. They moved from Karol Bagh and by the close of 1954 were living in the more comfortable locality of Nizamuddin East: 'a nice house (for Delhi) in the shadow of a Mogul wall, near the beautiful Humayun's Tomb,' she told her old friend Olive Chandler.[7] It was only a temporary respite. For a while the family lived under canvas at a Buddhist centre at Mehrauli just outside Delhi but eventually Freda was allocated government accommodation in the middle-class district of Moti Bagh. She described it as 'one of those nicely tailored modern flats complete with fans and shower-baths. To be frank, it doesn't suit us at all even though it has got its points in terms of comfort. We are a nice sprawly joint family, equipped on the male side with booming Punjabi voices, and hardly fit into a flat at all.'[8] Money was tight. Freda travelled to work by bus or—for a while—on a scooter. She was responsible not only for earning but also for managing the household's finances. She was provident, as you might expect of someone brought up in a non-conformist, north of England household. Bedi was the opposite—earning infrequently, and splashing out when he did. He was a writer for hire, Kabir says, but his earnings were irregular. 'Papa's style was whenever he got money he would then splurge, buy baskets of mangos for everybody in the family and take us on big treats. That was his way of showing his caring.'

Bedi faced his own moment of revelation which, uncannily, also involved a breakdown and a dramatic change in his life. It was as if husband and wife were mirroring each other at just the moment their marriage was unravelling. He started taking part in seances—perhaps, Ranga believes, to try to contact his brother who had recently died. He started writing wildly, sometimes apparently in languages of which he had no knowledge. One day, Ranga returned home to find his father motionless and with his eyes closed. He eventually arose, came out on a terrace and held his hands outstretched 'like a Muslim prayer'. Ranga's recollection is that his father remained as if in a trance for days. He was motionless and without speech. A doctor repeatedly administered injections, which failed to have any obvious effect. 'About eleven o'clock on the third day, he came down the stairs, went into the loo, had a bath, put on his kurta and went to sleep. He woke up that evening and ate something. But for two months, he was exactly the same as mother had been—no recognition, no eye contact. His eyes looked totally stoned, though he never took drugs,' Ranga says. 'It was so similar to mother's breakdown. And he also came out of it.'

As with Freda, Bedi's crisis had a lasting spiritual aspect. He developed a keen interest in the occult, establishing the Occult Circle of India; he became attracted to the mystical Sufi tradition within Islam and—re-engaging with the religion he was born into—in Sikh mysticism; he believed he had acquired special powers, and took to hands-on spiritual healing. He dressed in a smock and carried a staff; as his hair became increasingly unkempt, he looked like a latter-day Moses. He chose to be known as Baba, which carried with it an echo of a mystical or spiritual identity. It was a reinvention almost as complete as those that marked out the phases in Freda's life; he had gone from gilded youth, to communist and peasants' rights activist, to political apparatchik, to prophet and visionary. Bedi had largely broken links with the organised left and although he remained active in a Delhi-based Kashmir support group, he moved decisively away from active politics.[9] 'I had been under an impulsion to take to spiritual life,' he recalled a decade later. 'I resigned at once from all organisations. ... It was like a realization that now [the] time had come to quit all this work and take to a new form of life.'[10] Bedi insisted, not altogether convincingly, that his embrace of a spiritual purpose did not involve any repudiation of his socialist beliefs. 'The statue of Lenin I loved still lies on my mantelpiece, and not a dent on [my] Marxist convictions exists.'[11] But several of his old associates felt uncomfortable with Bedi's new look and message and kept their distance. Ranbir Vohra, who had known the Bedis in Lahore and Srinagar as well as Delhi, recalled that his old friend offered to help him communicate with anyone who had passed on: 'He suggested that I talk to Marx. I declined the generous offer.'[12] Among the constants in his life were the heavy smoking and use of paan masala, and a more occasional appetite for alcohol.

The death of Bedi's brother also provoked another far-reaching change for the family. T.D. Bedi had a mistress, Raj Narindra. Before his death, he asked his younger brother to keep an eye out for her. Bedi saw through that obligation—and helped Raj complete the building of a house in Jangpura in south Delhi. 'At first this posed only a financial problem,' Kabir commented, 'later it became emotional. As Freda moved closer to the spiritual path, through Buddhism and meditation, Baba's relationship with the mistress grew closer. It was a time of testing.'[13] Bedi's increasingly intimate relationship with Raj was an open secret. 'It was clear to me, absolutely, that there was more than just friendship,' Guli recalls. 'He would tell me not to tell mother about my visits to Jangpura Extension with him.' And there were other women in his life. Guli describes her father—in the demotic language of modern-day America—as a chick magnet. 'My mother never spoke about it, but he did have a wandering eye. ... He was very charming and

charismatic and women came to him like moths to a flame,' Guli
says. 'It wasn't exclusive; my father was a free spirit. It was his
Achilles heel. He just enjoyed women. He loved my mother—but
that was his Achilles heel. She must have suffered with that. She
was a woman, after all.' Whether Freda's celibacy encouraged her
husband to be less circumspect about his extra-marital liaisons, or
whether his affairs made it easier for Freda to adopt this form of
renunciation, it's difficult to say. Her husband's affairs certainly
weren't the impetus behind Freda's turn to Buddhism, but it may
have made her pursuit of a religious life easier. Her husband had
disavowed his marriage through his infidelity. It perhaps allowed
her to forsake sex without feeling she was being selfish.

The emotional bond between Freda and Bedi remained strong.
They were loving and respectful to each other. They appear not
to have given serious consideration to ending their marriage. But
behind the facade of a happy and contented partnership, the distance
between the couple widened. In 1957, Berinder Dewan—by now
an accomplished Urdu language journalist and short-story writer
using the pseudonym Zafar Payami—married Manorma Das, the
daughter of veterans of the Independence movement who were
good friends of the Bedis. Manorma, known within the family as
Moma, spent the first few months of her married life living with
the Bedis in Moti Bagh. She remembers it as a three-bedroom flat:
Bedi had one bedroom; his mother Bhabooji was in another; and
Moma and Binder took the third. Freda slept on the floor in the
drawing room and kept her clothes there too. Moma was aware
of, and uncomfortable about, Bedi's infidelities. When Freda was
out of town for work, Bedi would occasionally bring women home.
'They were not educated but they were quite beautiful. They would
cook for him and take care of him,' Moma remembers. 'When
Freda came back, I told her—such and such a woman was here
… She thought marriage was being comrades together, thinking
together—not all the time this sex business. I used to have a lot of

fights with Berinder about Bedi sahib having other women.'[14] She saw it as demonstrating an exploitative attitude to women. It didn't change Bedi's behaviour.

The heaviest burden of this fractured household was borne by the youngest child. Gulhima was packed off to an Anglican boarding school in the north Indian hills at the age of six. She spent eleven years there. Although Guli liked the school, she did wonder why she was sent as a boarder so young, and she never got a straight answer until she became a mother herself. 'When I had my first child, my mother said to me: "I never told you why I sent you to boarding school—I did it to keep you safe." She was travelling a lot and didn't want me to be left with the servants because as a social worker she was aware of the danger of sexual abuse. Father was happy-go-lucky and not very responsible, though a wonderfully positive man. My mother couldn't trust him not to leave me with the servants.' Kabir too went to boarding school, though only at the age of thirteen when his progress at school was slipping.

In the years when Freda was becoming immersed in Buddhism, Kabir was the only child routinely living at home. He was close to his mother and intrigued by her spiritual journey. In the summer of 1955, she returned to Burma to study meditation. She found a new teacher—the most prominent of those pioneering the Vipassana movement, Mahasi Sayadaw—and when a few months later she next made the journey, Kabir travelled with her. Remarkable photographs taken on that visit depict Kabir in the dress of a novice monk. 'I ordained myself as a Buddhist monk at the age of ten: head shaved, robed,' Kabir recalls. 'I was living in the same Buddhist centre, Mahasi Sayadaw's centre, where Mummy was, so I'd get to see her once a day maybe. But the rest of the day, we'd rise early in the morning, have our bath, get our robes on, take our begging bowls and head in a crocodile down the streets of Rangoon, with people coming out early in the morning with portions of food. They put the food in the bowls of the monks, these wonderful black lacquer bowls. And being the youngest, I was always at the end of the line, so they would start filling up the bowls of the monks in front and when they had enough they would cover the bowl and the monks behind them would get the offerings. And by the time they came to me, if I had enough in my bowl, they had no one else to give it to. So they were very upset if I closed my bowl and I would always return with this overflowing bowl.'

'There's something in the atmosphere of Buddhism, Buddhist monks, the way of life based on meditation which attracted me,' Freda reflected twenty years later. 'When I saw the stupas and the monks with their begging bowls—just simply going out in the morning, taking enough food and managing for the day—the golden robes, and my first gurus ... then I knew that in some former life, I think in many former lives, I'd been in the Buddhist way.'[15] On a subsequent visit to Rangoon (now Yangon), she took Upasika vows from Mahasi Sayadaw, reflecting a devout lay commitment to a spiritual path. Her vows had eight precepts, activities from which to refrain: killing or injuring any living being; taking that which is not given; excessive sensuality; false and harmful speech; fault finding; harsh and abusive speech; meaningless conversation; and wrong means of livelihood.

Although her faith loomed increasingly large in her life, she had a demanding job too. At the Central Social Welfare Board, Freda had a free hand in devising the new monthly publication. *Social Welfare* launched in April 1954 with Freda named as executive editor and promising to be 'the beginning of a new experience in co-ordinating social welfare in India.' It was conspicuously well produced and made effective use of black-and-white photos and on occasions bore striking modernist-style covers. The journal's purpose was to support the Board's endeavour to develop 'services for women, children, the delinquent and handicapped and the family as a unit'. Freda occasionally wrote under her own by-line, reporting on projects and initiatives she had visited in different parts of India.

Both Binder and his wife Manorma were roped in as occasional contributors. She was able to reprise some of the themes she had introduced in *Contemporary India* twenty years earlier—prevailing on Devendra Satyarthi to write on Indian cradle songs, traditional dance, and women's life as reflected in folk song. But the hallmark of the magazine was the focus which it placed on women's issues, including many which rarely appeared in the mainstream press.

In the first year of publication, *Social Welfare*'s agenda was cautious. Once established, it became more adventurous, tackling such themes as deserted wives, family planning, unmarried mothers, trafficking of women and children, and prostitution. It also prompted discussion of the widening career opportunities for women, and published exercises for expectant mothers. Freda enjoyed the opportunity to see something of village life in different parts of India. She described herself as 'somebody who loves the village old and new, and finds happiness there'.[16] Her conviction that the village was the essence of India, and village women the backbone of the nation, remained undimmed. The monthly had the advantage over commercial magazines that it was not vulnerable to dips in circulation or revenue, and the frustration that as a government publication its impact was limited. It was the job that Freda stuck to longer than any other. She saw herself as a social worker as much as an editor and journalist and welcomed the prospect of contributing to independent India's social development.

Some of the missions on behalf of the Social Welfare Board took her to corners of the country which were rarely seen by outsiders. In 1958 she accompanied Indira Gandhi to north-east India, visiting areas which are now in the Indian states of Mizoram, Nagaland, Meghalaya and Arunachal Pradesh. 'Indu' remained a close friend, and perhaps a confidante—her marriage had also hit problems. Freda's children remember going to eat at Auntie Indu's and attending the birthday parties of Indira's sons, Rajiv and Sanjay. 'Sometimes we would go privately and play with their remarkable collection of trains,' Kabir says. 'They had a wonderful room in the prime minister's house that had these trains around tracks, gifts of foreign dignitaries. ... As we got older, we'd go out on the president's estate and ride horses and see movies there or go to the swimming pool or go on car rides together. So it was that kind of fairly close relationship with the Gandhi family.'

Freda's government role allowed plenty of opportunity for the networking at which she excelled. Among her new friends was Tara Ali Baig, a prominent social worker from a privileged background who became the president of the Indian Council of Child Welfare. Baig first met her at a United Nations Youth Conference at Simla, and was struck by both her appearance and personality:

> Instead of the learned academic I subconsciously expected, I was confronted with a tall motherly woman in Punjabi salwar kamiz, with merry blue eyes, hair pulled back in a tight, unfeminine bun, and a warm, slightly buck-toothed smile. Almost immediately we started talking about our children, a preoccupation that dominated both our lives. Immediately a bond of close friendship sparked into being. Freda was one of those radiant people who to the end of her days could believe ill of no one. This was no mushy sentimentality, but an almost saintly reverence for the individual and a total absence of the kind of judgement people instinctively make about each other. In some extraordinary way she could only see the good and never the evil in anyone. ... What she constantly sought was an absolute faith.

All through her various metamorphoses, she remained consistently herself, conscientious, hard working and self-denying. Her husband who resembled Henry VIII, with his beard and regal robes, was more a thinker and philosopher than a wage earner. While he toyed with publishing and other esoteric activities, Freda reared her children with the help of their generous godparents

... [17]

Freda's involvement with Buddhism introduced her to several rich and influential Punjabi women who shared her interest. Goodie Oberoi had married into the family that ran one of India's leading chains of luxury hotels. The Maharani of Patiala was part of a Sikh royal family which retained its political influence after the dissolution of the princely states. In 1957, Freda travelled to Britain at the maharani's request—her first visit for a decade—to accompany her two daughters to their new boarding school. She took the opportunity to visit her mother and brother in Derby and see old friends. Freda saw no inconsistency in championing the interests of poor village women and accepting the patronage of the moneyed elite.

The late 1950s were a period of transition for the Bedi family. Bhabooji, Baba's mother and a constant in Freda's life ever since she had arrived in India, died in August 1958. She was told just before her death that Ranga had got engaged. He had spent a year or two with friends farming on 600 acres of remote land near the border with Nepal—and, for a second time in his life, living in huts without electricity or running water. That hadn't worked out, and he secured a job as an assistant manager on a tea estate in the far reaches of Assam, one of the first Indians to break into the hitherto 'ex pat' domain of tea planting. He and Urmila Paul, known universally as Umi, married in November. She was from a Christian family and they had a Christian wedding at her uncle's home in the Lodhi Estate in Delhi. Indira Gandhi attended and brought a note from her father, Jawaharlal Nehru, bestowing his blessings. Freda told friends approvingly that Ranga's bride 'comes from a Punjabi family like ours'. Amarantha, the first of Freda and Bedi's grandchildren, was born the following October. Ranga and his family lived at a vast distance from Delhi. Binder and Moma were closer to hand. Binder at times felt insecure about his place in the household. He was regarded as a member of the family but he was keenly aware that he wasn't a Bedi. Both he and Moma were writers and instinctively on the left and so had much in common with

Freda and Baba—Freda described them as 'our adopted children'. But they left Delhi to undertake a long trip through the Middle East. When Kabir went to boarding school at Nainital, the house emptied out. Bedi continued to put on weight, as Freda teasingly mentioned in her Christmas newsletters. Both enjoyed rich Punjabi food as well as the cakes and trifles which Freda made a point of making, a culinary legacy of her English upbringing.

Towards the close of 1956, Delhi hosted a major international Buddhist gathering that was Freda's introduction to the Tibetan schools of Buddhism, which are in the Mahayana tradition as distinct from the Theravada school which is predominant in Burma. This Buddha Jayanti was to celebrate the 2,500th anniversary of the Buddha's life. The Indian government wanted Tibet's Buddhist leaders to attend, particularly the Dalai Lama, who was that rare combination of temporal ruler and spiritual leader of his people. The Chinese authorities initially said no but at the last minute relented. Jawaharlal Nehru was at Delhi airport to welcome the twenty-one year old Dalai Lama on his first visit to India; the young Tibetan leader had at this stage not made up his mind whether he would return to his Chinese-occupied homeland or lead a Tibetan independence movement in exile. Freda played a role in welcoming the Tibetan delegation to the Indian capital. 'The radiance and good humour of the Dalai Lama was something we shall never forget,' she told Olive Chandler. 'I also got a chance of shepherding the official tour of the International delegates to India's Buddhist shrines and made many new friends.'[18] A snatch of newsreel footage shows Freda Bedi at the side of the Dalai Lama at Ashoka Vihar, the Buddhist centre outside Delhi where the Bedi family had camped out a few years earlier. Both Kabir and Guli were also there, the latter peering out nervously between a heavily garlanded Dalai Lama and her sari-clad mother.[19] Freda also received the Dalai Lama's blessing.

In the following year, when she made a brief visit to Britain, Freda made a point of visiting the main Buddhist centres in London and meeting Christmas Humphreys, a judge who was the most prominent of the tiny band of converts to Buddhism in Britain. She was becoming well-known and well-connected as a practitioner of Buddhism. What prompted her to become not simply a devotee but an activist once more was the Dalai Lama's second visit to India—in circumstances hugely different from his first. Nehru had dissuaded the Dalai Lama from staying in India after the Buddha Jayanti celebrations. Early in 1959, Tibet rose up against Chinese rule, an insurrection which provoked a steely response. The Dalai Lama and his retinue, fearing for their lives and for Tibet's Buddhist traditions and learning, fled across the Himalayas, crossing into India at the end of March and reaching the town of Tezpur in Assam on 18th April 1959. Tens of thousands of Tibetans followed the Dalai Lama, undergoing immense hardships as they traversed across the mountains and sought to evade the Chinese army. Freda felt impelled to get involved.

13

Brave and Wonderful People

'Technically, I was Welfare Adviser to the Ministry,' Freda wrote
of her time at the Tibetan refugee camps in north-east India;
'actually I was Mother to a camp full of soldiers, lamas, peasants
and families.'[1] It was a role she found fulfilling. Freda was able to
use the skills and contacts she had developed as a social worker and
civil servant and at the same time to be nourished by the spirituality
evident among those who congregated in the camps. The needs
of the refugees were profound. For many, the journeys had been
harrowing—avoiding Chinese troops, travelling on foot across the
world's most daunting mountain range and sometimes reduced to
eating yak leather to stave off starvation. Many failed to complete
the journey. And while the Indian camps offered sanctuary, they
were insanitary, overcrowded and badly organised. For hundreds of
those who arrived tattered, malnourished and vulnerable to disease,
the camps were places to die.

In October 1959, six months after the camps were set up,
Jawaharlal Nehru, India's prime minister, asked Freda to visit them
and report back—though it may be more accurate to say that Freda
badgered her old friend into giving her this role. Among Delhi's
Buddhists, who had welcomed the Dalai Lama so reverently three
years earlier, the plight of those who had followed in his footsteps
over the mountains would have been of pressing concern. For Freda,

it offered her a cause in which to immerse herself as well as an opportunity to deepen her spiritual engagement.

As soon as she reached the camps, Freda realised the urgent and profound humanitarian crisis that was engulfing the thousands of Tibetans who had made it into India. Within a matter of weeks, she had persuaded the government to keep her in the camps for six months as welfare adviser for Tibetan refugees. She took on this role as a secondment to the Ministry of External Affairs—the refugees and their camps were on Indian soil, but given the intense diplomatic sensitivities of offering refuge to such large numbers of Tibetans, the foreign ministry led on the response to the influx. 'I stayed 6 months in a bamboo hut rehabilitating + looking after refugees,' Freda wrote to her old friend Olive Chandler at the close of the assignment. 'It is an experience too deep to translate into an Air Letter. The Tibetans are honest, brave + wonderful people; the 5000 Lamas we have inherited contain some of the most remarkable spiritually advanced monks + teachers it has been my privilege to meet.'[2] She became entirely absorbed in the lives and welfare of the refugees, and of the Buddhist practice of the monks, nuns and lamas among them. 'I am going back to the [Social Welfare] Board tomorrow—' she told Olive, 'but my heart is in this work.'

Freda's home when working with the refugees was at Misamari camp in Assam, where a former military base—the American air force had been stationed there during the Second World War—was hastily expanded by the construction of rows of large bamboo huts. Misamari was near the town of Tezpur which the Dalai Lama had reached in mid-April 1959 at the end of his flight across the mountains. By mid-May, the Indian authorities had built shelters at Misamari sufficient for 5,000 refugees—and it was already clear that would not be sufficient.[3] It was a remote corner of the country—though not too far as the crow flies from Borhat, still further up the Brahmaputra but on the southern bank, where Ranga and Umi and their young family were living on a tea estate.

For the Tibetans, reaching Misamari was a refuge of sorts at the end of one of the most gruelling journeys imaginable. Lama Yeshe Losal Rinpoche, now abbot of the Samye Ling Buddhist monastery in Scotland, was a teenager when he escaped from Tibet with his two older brothers. They were part of a group led by a twenty-year-old abbot who was to achieve renown in the west, Trungpa Rinpoche. Of the 200 or so Tibetans in the entourage, fifteen completed the mammoth trek across the mountains and into India. For weeks, they went without food, and were reduced to boiling their leather shoes and chewing the soles. They were frozen—and terrified of the Chinese troops believed to be pursuing them. By the time these young religious leaders reached Misamari, they were—in the words of Lama Yeshe—'totally lost human beings. In Tibet, we used to have everything. Each one of them had their own monastery, attendants. And then when we escaped, we lost not only our wealth, power, possessions, but also our attendants.'[4] The abbots, lamas and tulkus were not simply the religious elite of Tibet, they were also the intellectuals and men of power and influence. By the time they reached the camps, they were in rags. Many were gravely ill. Lama Yeshe had TB and required a major operation; his oldest brother died of TB.

The camp may have been safe, but for many Tibetans it was not hospitable. This was alien terrain—much lower in altitude, stiflingly hot and humid, with a different culture and cuisine. 'Tibetan people don't know [the] language [or] how to make Indian food,' recalled Ayang Rinpoche later one of the most respected Buddhist spiritual teachers in India. He was about sixteen when he arrived at Misamari shortly after the camp opened. 'That place [was] very hot, and underground water [was] very uncomfortable. By this way, Tibetans [were] much suffering and many people died. My mother also died at that place, Misamari.' Another widely revered Buddhist spiritual figure, Ringu Tulku, also reached Misamari in 1959 after a long and arduous journey, 'sometimes fighting, sometimes running, sometimes hiding', from Kham in eastern Tibet. He was about seven years old, and recalls the long bamboo sheds at the camp, each providing shelter to scores of people. 'And very, very hot, so we couldn't usually sleep at night. So we sang and danced all night—and then we had a little bit of shower. And then we didn't know how to cook dal; we didn't know how to cook all these vegetables.' He too has vivid recollections of the large numbers who died at Misamari from fever and disease.[5]

Lama Yeshe came across Freda Bedi in his first few weeks at the camp. 'Before that I [had] never seen any white woman in my whole life. But she is a very caring, motherly human being.' Ayang Rinpoche also met Freda for the first time at Misamari; he remembers her as 'an English lady with Indian dress, very active, she work[ed] a lot'. Indeed, she kept herself furiously busy—arranging, organising, improving the health facilities and the water and food supply and ensuring that there was sufficient baby food and vitamins for the newborn and nursing mothers. This became her life. When she decided to dedicate herself to an issue or a cause, it consumed her. The plight of the women among the refugees was a particular concern as they were so central to the Tibetan family groups and tended to avoid attention even when they desperately needed it. Both Kabir and Gulhima spent several weeks of their school holidays with their mother at Misamari—not quite what they would have expected to be doing once liberated from their boarding schools in the north Indian hills. 'It was an amazing experience,' Kabir says. 'I remember her telling me that when these refugees arrived from Tibet … the men would be absolutely shattered, probably fit to be carried. And the women would always be standing. And within days of their arrival, there would be women who would collapse and the men would stand. So it's the women who held them together in that long trek across the Himalayas.'

'Looking after 4,000 refugees, daybreak to dark, for months in Misamari Camp … is something I can't forget,' she told friends and family in her end-of-year newsletter.

Women and children were barely 1,300 but how precious they are, for on them the continuance of the old, Tibetan Buddhist culture depends. We struggled with GLAXO and barley to save babies, whose mother's milk had dried up on the journey, or out of their suffering; others with worms and diseases contracted on the long journey down. There were no office hours. Sunrise was the signal for the first visitors.

We had no electricity, so work slowed down when the dark came. But even after that, we used to go round the barracks and into the hospitals, with volunteers and interpreters to pick up the sick and solve the day's problems. Every morning and night, the chanting of incredibly soothing and rhythmical prayers of the lamas filled the air. Each home group had its private shrine— butter lamps were burned even if rations had to be sacrificed—their piety and devotion meant more than bread.

I can't begin to tell you of the tragic stories all carried in their hearts. We even avoided enquiring so that old wounds would not be torn open, and gave instead positive hopes of work and resettlement. Much of my time was spent in keeping friends and family groups together when the dispersal to work sites … and centres was taking place. For those who have lost home, country, almost every possession, family and village ties are all that is left and they assume tremendous importance and significance.[6]

Her most immediate task was to remedy the shortcomings in the running of these hastily set-up camps. She used the privileged access she had to India's decision makers. She went straight to the top—to Nehru. And he listened. In early December, Nehru sent a note to India's foreign secretary, the country's most senior career diplomat, asking for a response to concerns that Freda had brought to the prime minister's notice. He endorsed one of Freda's suggestions, 'the absolute necessity of social workers being attached to the camps'.

> The normal official machinery (Nehru wrote) is not adequate for this purpose, however good it might be. The lack of even such ordinary things as soap and the inadequacy of clothing etc. should not occur if a person can get out of official routines. But more than the lack of things is the social approach.[7]

What concerned Nehru even more was Freda's complaint of endemic corruption. 'She says that "I am convinced that there is very bad corruption among the lower clerical staff in Missamari [sic]". Heavy bribery is referred to. She suggested in her note on corruption that an immediate secret investigation should take place in this matter.' Nehru ordered action to investigate, and if necessary to remove, corrupt officials. 'It is not enough for the local police to be asked to do it,' he instructed. It's not clear what remedial measures were taken but the interest in the running of the Tibetan camps shown by the prime minister and by his daughter, Indira Gandhi, will have helped to redress the most acute of the problems facing the refugees there.

Freda sought to raise awareness of and money for the Tibetan refugees in other ways. At the end of January 1960, just ahead of the Tibetan New Year, she wrote from Misamari to the *Times of India*, seeking donations from readers to allow the thousands of refugees on Indian soil to celebrate this religious festival. 'The vast majority of the Tibetan refugees are in Government refugee camps and are living on refugee rations,' she wrote. 'With very few exceptions they are penniless. If they light sacred lamps (deepa), they will do it by sacrificing their ghee rations for some days together. They need money for ceremonial tea and food, for incense and for community utensils ... The Tibetans are separated from country and often from family. Let us give them a feeling of welcome and belonging. Friendliness is as important as rations.'[8] This was very much part of her approach to refugee welfare and reflected her own personality. For Freda, compassion and concern was as essential in aiding the refugees as food and medicine. The Tibetans needed to be reassured that the bonds of shared humanity embraced them too after the ordeal so many had suffered.

'Misamari was a bamboo village, made up of hefty bamboo huts, over a hundred of them, capable of housing eighty or ninety people,' Freda wrote in her only published account of her time in the Tibetan camps. This was titled 'With the Tibetan Refugees', which was as much a declaration of personal allegiance as a description of her role. She recounted that there had been as many as 12,000 refugees in the camp in mid-1959, but it was always intended to be a transit centre and many moved on after a few weeks. 'By the time I reached Misamari, with its fluttering prayer flags and its Camp Hospital of eighty beds, there were about four thousand still to be rehabilitated before the Camp could be closed.'[9] She was writing for the government magazine she also edited, and this was not the place to raise complaints of corruption and maladministration. But she expressed sensitivity to Tibetan customs and needs.

> Two main feelings united all the Tibetans. The first was a deep devotion to the Dalai Lama, and some of the big Lamas who had escaped with them. Every group had its small shrine on the barrack wall. In the case of monks and lamas their shrines were carefully set up, improvised out of wood and paper, and decorated with brass or clay images and the chased silver caskets of the kind they used as protection against the terrors of the way. ...
>
> The second feeling was the feeling for family. To a man or woman who has left everything ... home, livelihood, land, friends, all that life meant, a family member or a relative, even an uncle or a cousin, assumed tremendous importance. Many had come from the battlefield, direct, and these soldier groups found their substitute family among their fellow soldiers, and developed a

deep, almost mystic affection for the Commander of the Khampa Army. The monks and Lamas were divided into four main groups ... For these monks, the monastery group was supreme, and they showed a sense of discipline and a certain cleanliness and orderliness of living and programme that reminded me often of more mundane groups, like the crew of a big ship or a sports team. They had the same loyalty to the group, and the same cheerful spirit. If they took decisions they took them together, and not individually.

Freda wrote about the efforts made to educate the young Tibetans and provide vocational training. She made only glancing reference to the deployment of many thousands of Tibetans in road building gangs at a paltry daily rate, and none at all to the most unjust aspect of this close-to forced labour, the separation of large numbers of Tibetan children from their parents.[10] Freda would have instinctively rebelled against such callousness, and her article with its emphasis on keeping families and groups together can be construed as advocacy of a more sensitive approach to the refugees. She was adamant that they were 'India's new responsibility'—and they also became her new responsibility.

While based at Misamari, Freda also visited the other principal Tibetan camp, at Buxa just across the state border in West Bengal. This was both more substantial than Misamari and more forbidding. It was initially a fort built of bamboo and wood, but had been rebuilt in stone by the British and used as a detention camp—and as it was so remote, it housed some of what were seen as the more menacing political detainees. When the buildings were made available to the Tibetans, they were in poor repair. All the same, these were allocated for Tibetan Buddhist monks and spiritual teachers. Freda referred to it rather grandly as a monastic college. And unlike Misamari, which was open for little more than a year, Buxa was intended as a long-term camp. It's estimated that at one time as many as 1,500 Tibetans lived there. Conditions were so poor that many monks contracted tuberculosis but it remained in operation for a decade.[11]

Towards the close of her six months in the camps, Freda Bedi again sought out Nehru, and this time was more insistent about the measures the Indian government needed to take to meet its responsibilities towards the refugees. She wrote to the prime minister to pass on the representations of 'the representatives of the Venerable Lamas and monks of the famous monasteries … living in Misamari', though the vigour with which she expressed herself—this was not the temperately worded letter that India's prime minister would be more accustomed to receive—underlines her own anger at what she saw as the harsh treatment of the Tibetan clerics in particular. Her main concern was the enrolling of Tibetan refugees on road building projects.

> Roadwork is heaving, exhausting, and nomadic, it is utterly unsuited to monks who have lived for long years in settled monastic communities. They can't 'take it', any more than could our lecturers, or officials, or Ashramites, or university faculties and students. Let us face that fact, and make more determined efforts to rehabilitate them in their own groups on land.[12]

She insisted that those who did not offer to do roadwork were not lazy, and that almost all those in the camps were 'eager and willing to work on land in a settled Community'. And she sought lenience for some of those involved in roadwork who were penalised as 'deserters' when they were forced to leave their duties because rain washed away the roads or had made shelter and food supplies precarious. 'I feel it is not worthy of Gov[ernmen]t to be vindictive when the refugees have already suffered as much in Tibet,' she told Nehru. 'We should be big hearted.'

She warned Nehru that the Indian government's responsibility for Tibetan monks wasn't limited to the 700 or so in Dalhousie in the north Indian hills and the 1,500 which at this date—March

1960—were at Buxa. There were a further 1,200 monks in Misamari and new arrivals expected for some months more, and another 1,500 refugees outside the government camps living in and around the Indian border towns of Kalimpong and Darjeeling and 'in a pitiable condition'. Freda was speaking from personal observation. Her letter concluded with an appeal and a warning, again couched in language that only a personal friend could use to address a prime minister:

> Panditji, I am specially asking your help as I do not want a residue of over one thousand unhappy lamas and monks to be left on our hands when Misamari closed. Nor do I want to hear totally unfair statements that 'they won't work'. I am sure you will help to clarify matters in Delhi.

Nehru asked his foreign secretary to investigate, who replied with a robust defence of the use of refugees in road-building projects. They were not acting under compulsion, he insisted, and this was a temporary measure while more permanent arrangements were made for accommodation and rehabilitation. And he suggested that some at least of the refugees were work shy, expressing just the sort of view that Freda had insisted was so unjust and uncaring. 'Mrs Bedi complains that we have been hard on the Lamas,' the foreign secretary wrote in a note to Nehru. 'There are various grades of Lamas, from the highly spiritual ones—the incarnate Lamas—to those who merely serve as attendents [sic]. Our information now is that having found life relatively easy … many ordinary people who would otherwise have to earn their living by work, are taking to beads and putting forward claims as Lamas. I feel that some pressure should be brought to bear on this kind of people to do some useful work.'[13]

In her letter to the prime minister, Freda had mused that if Nehru could see the Buxa and Misamari camps, 'I feel you would instinctively realise the major unsolved policy problems here on the spot.'[14] In a testament to her personal sway with India's leader, the following month Nehru did indeed visit Misamari. He spent two hours at the camp, looking round the hospital and seeing Tibetan girls who were being trained in handloom weaving. He addressed a crowd which consisted of almost all the 2,800 Tibetans then at Misamari, assuring them that he would act on an appeal he had received from the Dalai Lama to extend arrangements for educating both the young and adults.[15] There was no greater spur to official attention to the Tibetans' welfare than the prime minister's personal oversight of the issue. And if any had doubted just how much influence Freda held with the prime minister, persuading him to travel across the country to one of its most difficult-to-reach corners demonstrated just how influential and effective she was.

Freda did not let the matter drop. On her return to Delhi in June, she called on the prime minister and in a remarkable demonstration of her moral authority and personal influence, cajoled Nehru to write to one of his top civil servants that same evening to express his disquiet about what he had heard concerning recent ministry instructions.

One is the order that all the new refugees, without any screening, should be sent on somewhere for road-making, etc. This seems to me unwise and impracticable. These refugees differ greatly, and to treat them as if they were all alike, is not at all wise. There are, I suppose, senior Lamas, junior Lamas, people totally unused to any physical work etc. ...

Sending people for road-making when they are entirely opposed to it, will probably create dis-affection in the road-making groups which have now settled down more-or-less. I was also told that the mortality rate increases.[16]

It reads almost as if Freda was dictating the prime minister's note. She also prompted Nehru to question a reduction in rations for those in the camps, and to urge the provision of wheat, a much more familiar part of the Tibetan diet, rather than rice. Freda Bedi was, Nehru warned, going to call on the ministry the following day—and civil servants were urged to take immediate action on these and any other pressing issues she raised. 'I do not want the fairly good record we have set up in our treatment of these refugees,' the prime minister asserted, 'to be spoiled now by attempts at economy or lack of care.'

Nehru's more persistent concern was the impact of providing refuge to the Dalai Lama and so many of his followers on relations with India's powerful eastern neighbour. A steady deterioration in relations eventually led to a short border war in 1962 which—to Nehru's shock and distress—China won. In the immediate aftermath of that military setback, Nehru came to address troops at Misamari camp, which had reverted to serving as a military base. Nevertheless, India persisted with its open-door policy for Tibetans, and somewhere between 50,000 and 100,000 refugees followed the Dalai Lama into India. The Dalai Lama and his immediate entourage were settled in the hill town of Dharamsala in north India, which became the headquarters of Tibet's government-in-exile. One of Freda's more quixotic interventions with Nehru was to argue that the Dalai Lama and his entourage should remain in their temporary home in the hill resort of Mussoorie rather than relocated to Dharamsala. Nehru replied that he found her arguments 'singularly feeble'.[17]

Freda found her time in the Assam camps both physically and emotionally draining. On her return to Delhi she was admitted to hospital suffering from heat stroke and exhaustion. It was sufficiently serious for Kabir and Gulhima to be brought down from their boarding school in the hills. The doctors said their presence might lift her spirits. 'She responded well to our being there,' Guli says. 'Initially when we went in to see her she did not respond. But the next day she was sitting up and spoke.' Once recovered, she was determined to have a continuing role promoting the welfare of Tibetan refugees even though she was returning to her government job editing *Social Welfare*. Reading between the lines of Nehru's missives, Freda seems to have lobbied him on this point. 'If possible,

I should like to take advantage of her work in future,' Nehru noted. 'She knows these refugees and they have got to know her. Could we arrange with the Central Social Welfare Board to give her to us for two or three weeks at a time after suitable intervals?'[18]

When Freda confided to her friend Olive Chandler that her heart was in working with the Tibetans, she was saying what was becoming increasingly evident to her colleagues in the Social Welfare Board. 'Freda went to these camps and her heart bled,' according to her friend and colleague Tara Ali Baig. 'She neglected her work with the Board more and more, travelling to the centres especially in Bengal and Dehra Dun where distress was greatest.'[19] Her boss, the formidable Durgabai Deshmukh, got fed up with Freda's preoccupation with the Tibetan issue to the exclusion of other aspects of her work. She was determined to sack Freda, and only Baig's personal intervention saved her job. 'I was lashed by Durgabai's best legal arguments against retaining her. But Freda had children and needed her job. I weathered the storm and was rewarded with Freda's reinstatement.'[20] She survived in her government post for another couple of years, by which time the pull of working more fully and directly with the lamas among the Tibetan refugees had become compelling.

In her letters and representations to Nehru about conditions in the Tibetan camps, Freda raised an issue about the treatment of the monks and lamas which became for her a mission. 'We are not trying seriously or systematically to send them to educational institutions to teach them English or Hindi or the provincial regional languages, without which they cannot be suitably rehabilitated,' she lamented. 'A small number should be sent now so that they can, after about 1-2 years, return to their monasteries/farms and teach the others.'[21] Nehru, once again, endorsed Freda's suggestion and passed it on to civil servants, insisting that 'some priority' must be give to arranging teaching of languages in the camps, and to adults as well as children.[22] Freda understood that there would be no early return to Tibet for the refugees and if the spiritual tradition which she and the Tibetans so greatly valued was to survive, then it would need to adapt to its new surroundings. She also wanted the world to appreciate Tibetan Buddhism and to have access to its richness—to share her discovery and the joy that it brought. And for both these goals, that meant educating the coming generation of spiritual leaders—not simply ensuring that their religious instruction and guidance continued in their new home, but that they gained proficiency in English and Hindi.

Freda's agenda in helping the Tibetan refugees, and in particular the tulkus, the young incarnate lamas, was spiritual and humanitarian. It was not at all political. In Freda's letters and reminiscences, there is a striking absence of anti-communist comment or polemic. Freda had been sympathetic to communism and her husband an active and prominent party member and there must have been moments when she reflected that the misery imposed on Tibet was in the name of an ideology she had once supported. She gave no public expression to any such sentiment, and neither sought to extenuate or denounce the Chinese government directly. It is as if, through the course of the 1950s and her turn to Buddhism, her old political interests leached away. For many Indian nationalists, the achievement of nationhood—diminished by the trauma of Partition—was not quite the bright new dawn they had envisaged. For Freda, the eclipse of the radical Kashmiri nationalism espoused by Sheikh Abdullah—who from 1953 spent long years under Indian detention—would also have soured her appetite for politics. Her background in political activism gave her a good understanding of how politics worked as well as a network of friends and contacts which she was wonderfully effective in sustaining. But by the mid-1950s, she no longer saw herself as politically engaged. She was certainly no fellow traveller of communism but nor did she speak out against Chinese actions in Tibet beyond offering and organising friendship and support for Tibetan refugees. The school of Tibetan Buddhism to which she became attached was one of the more reluctant to enter the political fray, even in advocacy of the Tibetan national cause. Those who came across Freda when she was a Tibetan Buddhist got no sense that she had once been engaged in radical, and indeed revolutionary, politics.

While on her initial mission at the Tibetan camps in 1959-60, Freda also visited Sikkim where a number of Tibetan monks and refugees had settled. It seems to have been then that she first met the head of the Kagyu lineage, one of the four principal schools within Tibetan Buddhism. The 16th Karmapa Lama had escaped from Tibet through Bhutan in the wake of the Dalai Lama's departure and had moved into his order's long established but near derelict monastery at Rumtek in Sikkim. Apa Pant, a senior Indian official, told Freda that she really couldn't come to Sikkim without calling on the Karmapa. Pant was an Oxford contemporary of the Bedis. He was from a princely family and had an inquiring mind about faith and religion; he went on to be one of India's most senior diplomats. At this stage of his career, Pant was India's political officer covering Sikkim and Bhutan, two small largely Buddhist kingdoms which lay on the hugely sensitive border with China, and also in charge of the four Indian missions in Tibet.[23] Freda was keen to act on her friend's suggestion:

[Apa Pant] sent me on horseback—there was no road at that point up to the monastery. And I remember the journey through the forest and it was most beautiful. As we neared the monastery, His Holiness sent people and a picnic basket full of Tibetan tea and cakes and things to refresh us. It's about twenty miles, the path up to the monastery. And when I went to see him, there he was with a great smile on the top floor of a small country monastery surrounded by birds, he just loves birds. ... There he was with his birds, sitting in his room, not on a great throne but on a carpet with a cushion on it. And just at that time, the Burmese changeover took place and the gates of Burma were shut. And I was feeling a great sense of loss that I can't see my Burmese gurus and so I asked the question that was in my mind that I was saving up to ask my guru when I met him. I asked it of His Holiness. And he gave me just the perfect answer.[24]

There is perhaps an allegoric aspect to much of Freda's shared memories of her relationship with her guru, as the 16th Karmapa became. But at this time political storm clouds were gathering over Burma, leading up to the military coup in March 1962 which sealed the country off from the rest of the world for a generation. The Kagyu school traced its lineage back to the eleventh century and alongside a monastic structure it emphasised meditative training and solitary retreats.[25] That suited Freda. And above all she was impressed by the spirituality and personality of the 16th Karmapa, by his 'deep roaring laughter' and by a personal conduct and indeed appearance which put her in mind of the Buddha.

At the Misamari camp, Freda got to know two tulkus, reincarnations of venerated spiritual leaders, to whom she became particularly attached: Trungpa Rinpoche had led across the Himalayas the large contingent of Tibetans of which Lama Yeshe was part; Akong Rinpoche was his spiritual colleague and close friend, and Lama Yeshe's brother.[26] Both were part of the Kagyu order. Trungpa, Akong and the small band of refugees who managed to complete their journey reached Misamari at the end of January 1960. Freda was the first Westerner that Trungpa had got to know. They had no common language but they established a firm bond. Freda recognised in Trungpa an exceptional spiritual presence and authority and a willingness to adapt to his new circumstances. Trungpa saw in Freda a woman of integrity and influence who could help him make that journey. 'She extended herself to me as a sort of destined mother and saviour,' he said. Within a short time, Freda was helping Trungpa to learn basic English, the first Tibetan she taught, and he was acting

as Freda's informal assistant at the camp, a role which helped to
spare him from the prospect of being enlisted in a road building
gang.[27] Trungpa and his colleagues were transferred to Buxa camp.
Not long after, Trungpa managed to get out of Buxa—the inmates
were not free to come and go as they pleased—to visit the 16th
Karmapa Lama at Rumtek. The Karmapa invited Trungpa to stay
and join him in rebuilding both the monastery and establishing the
Kagyu tradition in new territory; Trungpa declined and moved on,
an unorthodox and almost rebellious act in the deeply hierarchical
and deferential culture of Tibetan Buddhism.

Shortly after Freda returned to Delhi and her job editing *Social
Welfare*, Trungpa and Akong turned up at the door of her flat.
Trungpa had travelled on from Rumtek to Kalimpong, and sent a
message back to Akong in Buxa camp suggesting that they head
to Delhi. Trungpa and Akong spoke no Hindi and had nothing to
guide them to Freda's home beyond an address written on a slip
of paper. They turned up, it seems, unannounced, confident that
Mummy-La, the name by which Freda was known to the younger
lamas and tulkus, would not turn them away. She didn't.[28] 'This
winter finds us in our modern flat in New Delhi to which we have
had to attach an overflow summer hut,' Freda told Olive Chandler.
'Two young Lamas (age 20) Tulku Major and Tulku Minor share
our home this winter, and spend the time getting adjusted to modern
life and learning English. It is a joy to have them with us. We are
sure they will get ahead quicker with conversation as soon as the
children take them in hand.'[29]

Two young men joining the household put quite a strain on the
already cramped government accommodation, and the temporary
shelter on the veranda which housed Akong and Trungpa would
have been pretty miserable during the monsoon rains and through
the chilly, if brief, Delhi winter. They stayed at the Moti Bagh flat
for the best part of a year. Kabir Bedi recalls an initial feeling of
'great resentment' at this intrusion on the family home.[30] Some of

the induction they received into the 'modern world' was not quite what Freda had in mind. Ranga remembers his father giving the two Tibetans both money and men's shorts, so they could buy treats from the market wearing something less conspicuous than their robes. Trungpa and Akong also acted as a beacon for others—Akong's younger brother, then known as Jamdrak, moved to Delhi to join them. 'Freda's humble home ...' her friend Tara Ali Baig recalled, 'was soon full to overflowing with young incarnate Lamas. Whatever simple Indian food there was, was shared ... Regardless of their present plight, these cheerfully robed young people warmed to the affection Freda lavished on them.'[31]

Freda was concerned that the Indian authorities simply didn't understand the tradition of incarnate lamas, and their critical place in Tibetan society and spiritual practice. Little was done to identify these young lamas, some little more than infants. 'Nobody knew quite what to do with them,' Freda lamented to Olive Shapley. 'In the lamas we have inherited a tradition that dates back to the seventh century—spiritual richness we can only as yet partially realise,' she wrote to friends. 'I am sure the whole world will ultimately be enriched.'

> There are perhaps 200 high 'incarnate' lamas in the country now headed by His Holiness [the Dalai Lama] (including 40-60 child or adolescent incarnations: many of them young people of extraordinary intelligence and physical beauty) ... dedicated monks and lamas of a high standard of learning and spirituality number perhaps 2,500; in addition we have junior and simpler country monks, over 1,500 of whom have volunteered for roadwork. We all pray ultimately we may be able to settle the bulk of the refugees in big land settlements.[32]

Nehru had taken a diplomatic risk by hosting the Dalai Lama and tens of thousands of those who followed in his wake. But there was a limit to the amount of official support and funding that could be expected for the refugees' welfare, with the most urgent and unmet need being the upkeep and education of the young lamas.

Freda was entirely comfortable soliciting money and support from the rich and well connected. She had also established links with Buddhist and similar groups in London and elsewhere. Within weeks of returning to Delhi from the camps, she sought to turn her extensive network to the Tibetans' advantage. In mid-August 1960, she wrote a long letter to Muriel Lewis, a California-based Theosophist with whom she had corresponded for several years. Muriel ran the Mothers Research Group principally for American and Western Theosophists, a network which had an interest both in eastern religions and in parenting issues.

> I should like to feel that the 'Mothers' Group' was in touch with all I do (Freda wrote). Do you think it would be possible for some of your members to 'Adopt' in a small way—write to, send parcels to—these junior lamas? Friendships, even by post, could mean a great deal. We could work out a little scheme, if you are interested. The language barrier is there, but we can overcome it, with the help of friends.[33]

Freda's family had, she recounted, already taken a young lama under their wing.

> Last year my son [Kabir] 'adopted' one small lama of 12, sent him a parcel of woollen (yellow) clothes, sweets and picture books, soap and cotton cloth. This time when I went to Buxa, Jayong gave me such an excited and dazzling smile. He was brimming over with joy at seeing me again! It is very quiet away from your own country and relations for a small lama with a LOT TO LEARN. It was of course most touching to see the 'Mother-Love' in the faces of the tutor-lamas and servant lamas who look after the young ones. They are very tender with them.

Freda's letter was included in Muriel's research group newsletter and subsequently reprinted by the Buddhist Society in London. This was the founding act of the Tibetan Friendship Group, which quickly established a presence in eight western countries and was the conduit by which modest private funds were raised for the refugees.[34] It outlasted Freda and while the group's purpose was not political, it helped give prominence to the Tibet issue as well as the well-being of the Tibetan diaspora.

At the close of the year, Freda sought to enlist her personal friends in this enterprise. 'Do you think you would like to "adopt" a young Tibetan in a small way ...' she appealed. 'Which would you choose—and of what age? The English learning groups include not only junior lamas, young monks and young soldiers (almost all without families) but schoolboys and schoolgirls, some with no father, some with both parents far away on the roads, almost all very keen to make friends and contacts.'[35] Misamari was by now closed and its former inmates dispersed. Some Tibetans eventually settled in Karnataka in south India, others congregated close to Dharamsala in what was then the Punjab hills and small Tibetan communities took root in many of India's cities. This dispersal added to the urgency of ensuring that the young lamas were not simply herded with the rest of the refugees, but identified and offered spiritual guidance and—the point which Freda emphasised—a wider education to ensure that their Buddhist practice could be nurtured outside Tibet in a manner which would allow the wider world access to the spiritual richness that the lamas both represented and bestowed.

14

The Young Lamas' Home School

Of all the ventures that Freda Bedi embarked upon in her varied life, the Young Lamas' Home School has borne the biggest legacy. This was entirely her initiative and although it wasn't either a large or a long-lasting venture, and was never intended to be, it was a crucial step towards enabling Tibetan spirituality to find a resonance in the west. 'Over a hundred incarnate lamas and monks have taken training in English,' she told Olive Shapley when looking back on the school's achievements. 'Many of them now are in different parts of the world.' Among the pioneering generation of Tibetan lamas to teach in Europe and North America, a large proportion were pupils at or associated with the Home School. The language skills they gained there, as well as the confidence and breadth of vision and the personal example that Freda offered of outside reverence for Tibetan spirituality, propelled many of the more adventurous among the tulkus to seek new fields of endeavour.

The idea of reincarnation or rebirth is common to several religions, particularly those with their roots in South Asia. In Tibetan Buddhism, this extends to the identification as a child of the reincarnation of the towering figures in the religion. The current Dalai Lama, the fourteenth in a line that stretches back 500 years, was formally recognised as the reincarnation at the age of four, about six years after his predecessor had died. There is elaborate protocol and tradition which guides the finding of tulkus, the incarnate lamas, as there is with many aspects of Tibetan Buddhism. For a revered lama to choose reincarnation and so another life of suffering in the world is regarded as an act of great compassion. When her old Oxford friend Olive Shapley came to visit at Rumtek monastery in Sikkim, Freda sought to explain this aspect of Tibetan practice which is so alien to conventional western thinking.

> An incarnate lama is a special lama—a child who the Tibetans believe has in his former life been a big lama. And you see, the Tibetans are highly evolved spiritually and a rather extraordinary people. Really I do believe that they can find these children. They know the signs of a special child. Of course, in the west we also think about ... educating specially gifted children. They've been doing that with the incarnate lamas in Tibet for hundreds of years. There has to be a special way [to] bring up such children with special gifts. ... And I also feel having worked among them for some time that there's something very special about these children.[1]

She described the lamas as the intelligentsia of Tibet, and she was determined to help them keep the tradition alive 'because it's very deep and very beautiful'. Tibetan society prior to the 1950s was built around Buddhism. The Dalai Lama was a rare, almost unique, institution in the modern world which combined spiritual leadership and temporal authority. Although Tibet's high altitude and unforgiving climate did not deliver much in the way of agricultural surplus, the country supported a huge monastic community. Of Tibet's 6 million population, it's estimated that prior to the Chinese takeover about 200,000 were monks—or approaching 10% of the adult male population.[2]

The Theravada Buddhism that Freda had encountered in Burma emphasised the human nature of the Buddha while the Mahayana school that prevailed in Tibet portrayed the Buddha as a transcendent force not limited to the human domain. It was an approach which,

Freda said, 'fits me like a glove. It brings in all the compassion for all sentient beings and the great cosmic Mahayana point of view which attracts me very much. And of course I do feel a very great nearness to Tibetan culture and the incarnates.'[3] Freda had been enriched by her encounter with Tibetan Buddhism. She wanted others to benefit in the same way, to share in her spiritual discovery. And once she had a cause or a quest, there was an impulsive aspect to her—she just got on and did it, believing that if you got things started they could grow, while too much time planning and preparing was sometimes a drain on energy and enthusiasm.

With the support of the Dalai Lama, Freda's solution to meeting the educational needs of the young lamas was to do it herself. She was throughout her life a 'doer'. She didn't simply comment and diagnose—she rolled up her sleeves and got involved. As a civil liberties campaigner in Lahore, she had made a point of travelling to villages to identify cases of police high-handedness. In Kashmir, she had become involved both in the women's militia and in providing practical support to Partition refugees. In Misamari, she hadn't just compiled a report for the Indian government but had sought personally to provide redress for the problems she identified. She had teaching experience—in both Lahore and Srinagar—and was trusted both at the top ranks of the Indian government and among senior figures in India's Tibetan community. Her lodgers in Delhi, Trungpa and Akong, were potential collaborators who stood to gain from classes and could help in the running of the school. Trungpa in particular was keen to broaden his horizons. 'By contrast to the medieval world of Tibet, India was a very modern place,' he wrote in his memoirs. 'Here for the first time I had contact with Westerners, and I realized that it was absolutely necessary for me to study their language in order to spread the Dharma.'[4] Their involvement also made the enterprise feel less like external do-gooding and more an initiative that Tibetans themselves were shaping—though it was always very much Freda's show.

The Young Lamas' Home School opened in a large, detached house in Green Park in south Delhi in October 1961. It was, as the name suggests, home and school combined. A measure of support was provided by the Indian government while the Dalai Lama nominated the young lamas to be enrolled, who came from all four principal traditions within Tibetan Buddhism. They ranged in age from seven to twenty-one. 'I have 17 young Tibetan incarnate lamas in my latest effort for the refugees—an English-Hindi language school, combined with their Tibetan studies,' Freda told Olive Chandler. 'Such a joy to have them here; to see their own happiness reflected in their faces.'[5] Lama Yeshe, still a teenager, was associated with the school from the start. 'All the young lamas from all four schools were able to learn English and spread Buddhism in the world,' he says. 'It's her vision—otherwise we could not have achieved it.' And as well as the educational and spiritual development, Freda also provided emotional support to young men who were, for the most part, without parents or separated from them. 'We all [had] to call her Mummy. She really like[d] everybody calling her Mummy. And she treated everybody like Mummy.'[6]

Through the Tibetan Friendship Group and the network of western well-wishers, Freda was able to attract independent funding for and interest in her new venture. Lois Lang-Sims arrived in Delhi just a few days before the school opened. She was a few years younger than Freda, a spiritual seeker who had helped to establish the Tibet Society in London and had 'adopted' a young lama as part of Freda's scheme. She wanted to see for herself whether the Home School was worthy of further financial support. Lang-Sims described Freda as a 'tall, fair-haired Englishwoman, with a face that was both soft and strong, looking remarkably Anglo-Saxon despite the rumpled sari which she wore as if she had never known any other kind of dress.' But she also delved beyond first appearances and was keen to get the measure of Freda. 'Her personality was disturbingly potent; but I learnt to shake off its slightly hypnotic

effect ...' Lang-Sims recorded. 'When I got behind the barrier
of her total self-dedication, her blind indifference to her own and
other people's comfort and convenience, I discovered a humanity
and a kind of pathos which drew me towards her in affection and
friendship. Moreover I perceived that she was entirely sincere; and
this was more than could be said for the majority of those persons
who were concerning themselves with Tibetan refugee relief.'[7]

Lois Lang-Sims' passing reference to others' comfort, or the
lack of it, was an elliptical reference to her own astonishment in
discovering that the Bedis' flat, where she had arranged to stay, was
full to overflowing.

> There seemed to be a great many people in the room in which I
> found myself. They were all seated round a low table on the floor,
> with the exception of an elderly Tibetan monk who was dining
> apart from the rest on a raised seat. Two of those on the floor
> were young monks, and there were several other Tibetans, another
> fair-haired woman in a sari, [and] an Indian whom I guessed to
> be Freda Bedi's husband.

The old monk, Lois discovered, was not an incarnate but a geshe
or teacher, and as such treated with particular respect. The young
men were probably Trungpa and Akong, destined to be 'the senior
pupils' in the new school.

> I took a place in the circle and was handed a plateful of dahl and
> rice. The time was half-past ten in the evening but I could see
> that the working day had only just finished. I began to look round
> the room which had a dingy beauty of its own ... There were no
> chairs in this room, only cushions and mats and the hard bed-seat,
> covered by a Tibetan rug, which was occupied by the old monk. In
> the corner of the room was a Tibetan shrine glowing with lighted
> butter-lamps. As my eyes turned to the level of the ground I saw
> a large brown rat sidling along by the wall on soft feet.[8]

She was startled to find that the room where she was to sleep was both a passageway and in use day and night for meditation classes.

Lang-Sims saw at close quarters the setting up of the Home School. The house was newly built with stone floors, standing on raised ground on an 'exceptionally pleasant' site amid an expanse of scrubland. She was invited to stay there but demurred because the plumbing didn't seem to be up-and-running, but she was on hand when the first pupils moved in.

Immediately before the opening of the school two contingents of young Lamas arrived at the [Bedis'] flat. All were refugees and in sore need of the robes with which Freda intended to provide each one as a welcome-present. Several were no more than children; but the behaviour even of these was strangely adult. They sat smiling and talking quietly in Tibetan, accepting everything that was done for them with perfect courtesy and no trace of anxiety or fuss. When the time came for the move they piled into the taxis together with all the furniture, crates, boxes, bedding-rolls and miscellaneous oddments, their gentle gaiety as undisturbed as if they were off on a picnic.[9]

Two days later, Lang-Sims—feeling guilty that she had abandoned Freda and the young lamas for a hotel—returned to see how they were settling in. 'I followed Freda into the house and gazed about me in astonishment. The disorder was cleared away; everything was in its place even to the t'ankas [religious paintings] on the walls; there was an atmosphere of peace. I remembered the plumbing and glanced at a large pool of water in the vicinity of the wash-place. Something had overflowed but at least there was water to flow.'[10] Still more impressive was the shrine that had been constructed in one of the two principal rooms, taking up the whole of a wall, 'a thing of wonder and yet made out of nothing but the simplest oddments, an ordered profusion of colours and shapes seeming as if

it had fallen into a pattern of itself. There were a few small images;
a number of crude prints and tinted photographs; scarves; ribbons;
bits of coloured materials; rows of offering cakes (called 'tormas');
bowls containing water and offerings of seeds, sweets and rice; and,
of course, the lighted butter-lamps.' Seated on floor mats, the pupils
were chanting their morning office each one crouched over a sacred
book and rocking to and fro. 'The boys, on Freda's instructions but
left entirely to themselves, had produced this shrine in a day by their
own unaided imagination and efforts. They were all working hard;
although, of course, they did not expect to be asked to perform
"menial" tasks: the actual work of the house was done entirely by
Freda's servants and the servant-monks.'

Freda's energy, drive and organisation had established the school
and marshalled the young lamas. She was every bit as effective at
developing the profile of the new school, which was so important
in ensuring continued government support and private fundraising.
With an eye perhaps on both goals, Freda took Lois Lang-Sims to
meet Nehru, then in his early seventies and increasingly worn-out
after fourteen years in office. 'Freda expressed her gratitude for his
encouragement and assistance in her school project: suddenly he
really smiled, seeming to wake out of his dream, and said teasingly,
in a very low, quiet voice: "It was not for *you* I did it." Then he half
closed his eyes and appeared almost to go to sleep.'[11] The encounter
gave every indication that it was precisely for Freda that Nehru had
put his weight behind establishing the school.

Within a few weeks of the founding of the school, the *New York
Times* came calling—though they weren't allowed inside. '"We're
sorry, but one of our young lamas is in bed with chicken pox,"' their
reporter was told. 'Mrs. Bedi treats the seventeen boys at the school
as members of her family. She listens patiently to their problems of
growing up. "Even lamas have them," she says.'[12] Freda explained
that the purpose of the school was to impart traditional education
in the context of the modern world. '"It aims," Mrs Bedi said, "at

constructing a bridge of understanding between the young lamas and the changing young people of their own generation. It will make them aware of the new world into which they have found their way after the tragic fate of Tibet.'" She estimated that there were in total about seventy-five incarnate lamas under the age of twenty-five in India. Each group would study for six months, then a new intake would take their place. Four such intakes would cover all the tulkus, then the initial group would return. The plan was to give three semesters of instruction to each group of lamas in rotation—a six-year project. And the school was hoping for financial contributions from abroad, towards which goal sympathetic coverage in one of America's leading daily papers was as good as gold dust.

The school initiative was extempore all the same—and as the *New York Times* pointed out, Freda was still a civil servant and supervising the lamas' school was supposedly a spare-time activity. Apart from the spiritual studies, most of the teaching was done by volunteers—mainly young westerners who happened to be passing through. Anita Morris, an English woman in her mid-twenties who by her own admission had been 'bumming around' Asia, was introduced to Freda and promptly started working at Green Park, teaching English and assisting more generally. She was not a Buddhist, had no Tibetan or Hindi, and her teaching experience was as a dance instructor. She liked Freda and the young Tibetans and relished being part of such a worthwhile project, but there were uncomfortable moments. 'I was going down with a couple of the tulkus to get to Green Park,' she recalls. 'I think Freda must have said: can you take them because they don't know the way. These were more adult people than children. And I can remember one of them suddenly rushing off and disappearing behind a tree. I was not quite sure whether he's going to be sick or he was going to shit. But he came out with a stick with a worm over the stick which had come out of him.'[13]

The school got off to a sound start but Delhi was not the ideal location. Even the more comfortable southern suburbs offered a lot of distractions and—more crucially—little respite from the often oppressive heat. As spring approached the young Tibetans were overwhelmed by the relentlessly rising temperature. Freda's plan had always been to move the school for the summer months to Dalhousie, an old colonial hill resort a day or two's travel by road to the north of Delhi and, at an altitude of 7,000 feet, a lot cooler. A large house overlooking the town was made available on rent. It bore the name 'Kailash', after one of Tibet's most commanding and sacred peaks. Several hundred Tibetan refugees had been encouraged to make their home in and around Dalhousie and the lamas felt less isolated here. When Freda, her volunteers and pupils departed from Green Park in the spring of 1961, it was a final farewell to the school's initial home. 'Dalhousie air is crisp + fresh as new pine needles. Such a heavenly view across the snows!' Freda said in a letter to Olive Chandler in England. And she added: 'To work for the Lamas is blessing unlimited.'[14]

Chime Rinpoche, then about twenty and a friend of Trungpa and Akong from their days in monasteries in eastern Tibet, remembers meeting Freda Bedi initially in Kalimpong and then being nominated by the 16th Karmapa for a place at the Home School. 'She [was] wearing saris,' he recalls, 'and she tried to look like [an] Indian—she's not, she's very very English'. Freda clearly traded on her dual identity. She may sometimes have resented being regarded as an outsider after decades of living in India, but she was adroit in taking advantage of the profile her English pedigree allowed. She almost certainly got more attention, support and funding because potential donors and supporters were more comfortable with a westerner in charge. In a curious way, the English aspect of Freda became more prominent again as she became immersed in a new religion and culture. While others may have been curious about the clash of identities which Freda embodied, it wasn't something she dwelt on herself. She never regarded herself as constrained by the boundaries of race, religion, language or culture—indeed these were barriers to be surmounted to gain access to wider sources of knowledge and stimulation.

Freda encouraged the idea that she had a maternal role towards the young lamas. Ringu Tulku Rinpoche was about ten when he arrived in Dalhousie shortly after the school moved there, and believes he was for a while the youngest pupil. He recalls Freda as 'a very kind and compassionate lady. Like a mother. We all used to call her Mummy. She was running this school. The teaching was done by volunteers. We had different kind of Tibetan and Buddhist classes, and we also had prayers together. But then we also had English classes, maths classes, and these were taught by these other volunteer teachers.' For the more vulnerable lamas, Freda's love and attention was a big support. 'She was especially kind to the younger ones,' Ringu Tulku recalls. 'In the evenings sometimes, she would call us and give hot chocolate, and that was really very nice. So sometimes I used to walk in front of her window, making some noise to remind her that I'm there. Not every day, but sometimes she would call me and then give me hot chocolate and I was very happy with that.' He describes Freda as kind hearted, clear minded and 'a very, very strong lady'. If young lamas didn't write back to the pen friend 'adoptees' Freda had arranged, or send thank you letters, she would reprimand them.

Chime Rinpoche also recalls Freda as a disciplinarian. At Dalhousie, he says, there were strict rules against any socialising outside the classroom between the lamas and the women volunteer teachers. And he admits to being afraid of Freda. He wasn't the only one. 'Freda was tall and, by this time, heavily-built. She wore a maroon sari and kept her well-oiled gray hair tied back in a bun. She had piercing blue eyes and was the quintessential memsahib whose imperious manner quelled even high lamas,' according to Tenzin Palmo, who as Diane Perry went out from England to volunteer at the Home School in Dalhousie. 'Indeed most lamas

were somewhat in awe of her. She was not accustomed to being
subservient and usually gave the orders! Of course, by this time
she was already an older woman which made her dominance more
socially acceptable. She was also great fun and a wonderful source
of Tibetan lama gossip.'[15]

The move to Dalhousie obliged Freda finally to forsake the role
of editor of *Social Welfare* which she had occupied since before the
monthly started publication in 1954. The Central Social Welfare
Board held a farewell party for her, recording that she had resigned
'to devote herself completely to the cause of the Young Lamas'
Home School'.[16] She was no longer a civil servant but alongside
the greater freedom was the loss of her salary and her government
accommodation. The ground-floor flat in Moti Bagh had been
cramped but it was the focus of the family. Ranga was well established
in the tea business and with a family of his own; Kabir was sixteen
and on the cusp of admission to St Stephen's College in Delhi; Guli
was just twelve and increasingly spent time in her holidays with her
older brothers. 'My brothers and Ranga's wife Umi cushioned me
from my insecurities,' she says. Kabir and Guli visited Dalhousie, and
indeed Kabir taught there—one renowned Buddhist lama insists with
a broad smile that whatever the limitations of his spoken English,
Kabir Bedi is to blame.

Baba Bedi moved from the government flat into Raj Narindra's
house in Jangpura Extension in south Delhi where he had been
a regular, if surreptitious, visitor for some years. He continued to
write, if irregularly and without conspicuous success, and to embrace
the occult and forms of mysticism. In June 1963, he sent Margaret
Bourke-White an inscribed copy of his latest pamphlet—'Unity of
Man & World Peace, by BABA, Grand Master of the Celestial
Order of the White Lion, Master of the Occult Circle of India,
Director, Institute for Inquiry into the Unknown'. Although Freda
and Bedi lived apart, they remained close. When in Delhi, Freda
would on occasions come to stay in Jangpura Extension, often with

Freda, her mother,
Nellie, and brother,
Jack, after her father's
death in 1918.

Left: Freda aged about seventeen.

Bottom: Freda while a student at Oxford.

Freda and BPL's engagement photograph, 1933.

Left: The Bedis—probably taken on their honeymoon.

Bottom: Freda and her mother with two-week-old Ranga in Berlin, 1934.

Freda while expecting Tilak, probably in Model Town, Lahore, 1935.

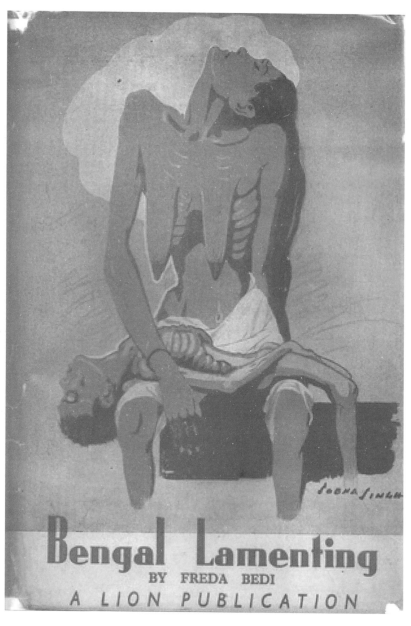

Sobha Singh's arresting cover design for Freda's 1944 book
about the Bengal famine.

A remarkable galaxy of political talent gathered at the annual session
of the National Conference in Kashmir in 1945. From the left:
Mridula Sarabhai; Abdul Samad Khan Achakzai; Bakshi Ghulam Mohammad;
Jawaharlal Nehru; Abdul Ghaffar Khan (the 'Frontier Gandhi') holding
Rajiv Gandhi; Indira Gandhi; Sheikh Abdullah; an unidentified couple; B.P.L.
Bedi; Freda Bedi. Freda is clearly pregnant—Kabir was born in January 1946.

(Photo courtesy of Ramesh Tamiri.)

Left: Freda and eighteen-month-old Kabir during a visit back to Britain.

Bottom: Freda, Kabir and Ranga (astride the family's Great Dane, Rufus) in Kashmir.

Freda as a member of the Women's Self Defence Corps in Kashmir, 1948.
(Photo courtesy of India Picture.)

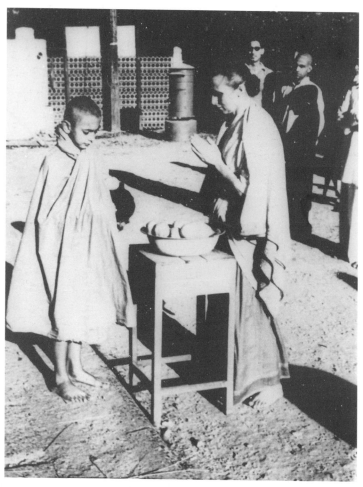

Freda with Kabir, then a novice monk, in Rangoon, mid-1950s.

At Misamari camp in Assam, 1960. The three young men in the centre carrying books or documents are, from the left: Akong Rinpoche; Akong's younger brother, Jamdrak, now Lama Yeshe Losal Rinpoche; Chogyam Trungpa Rinpoche.

The Young Lamas' Home School in Delhi, 1961.

(Photo courtesy of Alethea Ato.)

Freda and the tulkus from the Young Lamas' Home School calling on the
Dalai Lama in Dharamsala, 1962.

(Photo courtesy of Cherry Armstrong, who is standing next to Freda.)

Above: Freda with her two 'adopted' tulkus, Trungpa Rinpoche (left) and Akong Rinpoche, 1962.

Left: The front page of 'Current' in September 1963 which caused Freda great distress.

rday, September 28, 1963

GOD SAVE THE MOTHERLAND

Copy

THE CURRENT

VOL. XV, NO. 3   All India Edition   30 N.P. **WEEKLY**

On Govt. of India notepaper...

... Noted Communist appeals to unwary Americans for funds for

YOUNG LAMAS

By D. F. Karaka

According to an All India Radio news bulletin, MR. GHULAM MOHAMMED BAKSHI recently stated in Srinagar that Communism was infiltrating into Kashmir through Buddhism. This statement was later confirmed by MR. KUSHO BAKULA, Minister of State for Ladakh Affairs, who is himself a Ladakhi and a Buddhist monk.

Information reaching CURRENT through reliable sources indicates that an Englishwoman, married to an Indian, is attempting to express a great deal of anxiety to help the Buddhist cause as a screen for her Communist activities.

✱✱ This Englishwoman, whose name is FREDA BEDI, and her husband, BABA P. L. BEDI, have been most active workers for Communism for nearly 30 years.

Freda has dabbled with Communism ever since my student

Freda Bedi (right) with young Lama.

days in Oxford. She was, in fact, at Oxford at the same time as myself. Later, she married Bedi, a well known Indian Communist. They both came out to India and plunged themselves into the Communist movement.

They were at one time said to be card-holding Communists, and their police records in this country would certainly testify that before Partition they were not mere sympathisers but active workers of the C.P.I.

✱✱ Comrade Bedi was the leader of the Communist Party in Lahore, where in pre-Indepen-

Top: Freda Bedi once ordained as a Buddhist nun, when she took the name Sister Palmo.

(Photo courtesy of Anderson Bakewell.)

Right: The Bedis together, mid-1960s or a little later.

Sister Palmo with her guru, the sixteenth Karmapa Lama,
at Rumtek monastery in Sikkim.

Sister Palmo and her attendant nun, Anila Pema Zangmo, with Indira Gandhi.

The Bedi family together in Delhi, 1968-9: From the left: Guli; Umi, Ranga's wife; Kabir; BPL; Ranga; Freda; Dewan Berindernath, known in the family as Binder; Manorma, Binder's wife. In the front from the left: Saba, Binder and Manorma's daughter; Sohni, Ranga and Umi's daughter; Samira, Binder and Manorma's daughter.

a small retinue of monks and assistants. Some in the extended family described these visitations as 'Freda's revenge'.

Freda was exhaustive in seeking funds for the school. In April 1963, seventeen-year-old Kabir Bedi wrote a letter to 'Aunty Margaret', Margaret Bourke-White, acknowledging a donation which she wished to keep anonymous. 'Here in Dalhousie, the school has almost doubled its numbers and is expected to reach seventy-two Tibetans,' Kabir wrote, with a touch of exaggeration. 'We also have a team of volunteers who teach. I am also teaching until I join college in July.'[17] Freda's reach even extended to her old friends in Derby. A historian of Parkfields Cedars school recorded: 'Something a little different in 1963 was a donation to a school for Buddhist lamas, founded by an Old Girl.'[18] The term networking was not then in common use for maintaining and utilising a web of friends and contacts—but that is what Freda was doing, with both determination and success.

The move to a bigger property at Dalhousie also allowed for some modest expansion of the school, requiring more volunteers and a gearing up of the administration. Cherry Armstrong, an eighteen-year-old whose mother was active in the Buddhist Society in London, arrived towards the end of the school's first summer in the hills. Her role was a loosely defined mix of administrative and secretarial, particularly helping with the correspondence generated by the Tibetan Friendship Group and Freda's scheme for pen friends for young Tibetan refugees.

The western friend would include a small monetary gift, usually in the form of money orders … In return the Tibetan pen friend would send a little photograph or a prayer written in Tibetan … My job initially was to keep this scheme working and it was often a life-saver for individuals with no financial aid. It was a system that needed no overheads—once the connection was established the money went directly to the person for whom it was intended and usually continued for years.

Freda was good at delegating, and at multitasking. Every
morning she 'held court' with a pile of papers (the morning post)
on her lap. Tibetan matters were handed over to Trungpa Tulku
who acted as her interpreter and scribe (as well as doing his own
religious and language studies). Indian matters were handed to the
Indian administrator of the school, Attar Singh; English letters
were handed to me, while Freda herself would be simultaneously
writing her own more important letters. During this time there
would be frequent Tibetan or Indian visitors asking for help or
for Freda to use her influence on their behalf and everyone was
attended to with care and foresight. Sitting beside her whilst all
this was going on I could see that her method of coping was to
give her undivided attention to the specific matter in hand; a kind
of purposeful concentration to the exclusion of all other matters.
When one matter was dealt with, the next had her exclusive
attention. ... She had an immense capacity for work.[19]

Cherry learnt to type, often with an old typewriter balanced on
her lap or on her bed. It was rudimentary but it worked. Alongside
the daily grind, Freda was also adept at maintaining connections
with those of influence. When a couple of months after the move
to Dalhousie Anita Morris headed home to England, she carried
a package for Christmas Humphreys, the judge and doyen of the
Buddhist Society in London, and for the renowned violinist Yehudi
Menuhin. Among those who came to visit was the Beat poet Allen
Ginsberg, who turned up 'with an equally scruffy-looking mate,
looking like a couple of beggars'—as Cherry recalls. 'Freda invited
him to our communal supper. I can't say I was impressed.'[20]

Cherry Armstrong's unpublished account of the year she spent at
the Young Lamas' Home School has the freshness and excitement
of a youthful odyssey but one laced with a shrewd eye for how the
operation held together as well as affection for the lamas and her
fellow volunteers. She described Freda as a 'grey-haired English

lady in a dark red sari, looking very much like a lama herself, who greeted her on arrival with a bear-hug and a resounding kiss. 'She talked of England with some nostalgia in spite of the fact that she had completely adopted the Indian way of life, the Buddhist religion, and the oriental way of conducting affairs.' The main room at Kailash, large and shabby, 'could have been the sitting room of an old English farmhouse if it were not for the red-robed figures padding silently over the worn carpet.' She had a room with views over the mountains, heated by a stove, 'a squat black metal cylinder standing with its three legs in a pan of water to prevent the floorboards burning', with a lid into which wood and fir cones were fed.[21]

In the evening the lamas were doing a special puja, or religious chanting ceremony, to which we were all invited. The lamas were already assembled in the shrine room as we seated ourselves cross-legged at the back of the room. As they began chanting the sound which filled the room was completely alien to my ears and at first seemed quite cacophonous. Yet there was a fascination about it and I soon learnt to notice the rhythms and variations in tone. Half way through the ceremony the chanting faded away. Tin mugs were distributed and a monk brought Tibetan tea in a kettle with a yellow marigold stuck into the spout. I had been warned about Tibetan tea made with butter and salt as well as milk, but no one had warned me that unless I hid my mug somewhere out of reach it would be refilled again and again in spite of desperately shaking my head, nor that my pleadings of 'No more, thank you,' would be taken as mere politeness so long as my mug stood unguarded within easy reach of the spout of the kettle.

Cherry was also drawn into the teaching at the school—one of perhaps half-a-dozen young westerners of different nationalities, only a few of whom had a serious interest in Buddhism. She found the atmosphere at the school to be relaxed and convivial. 'It was a place of laughter and joking.'

The yearly rhythm of the school adapted to changing circumstances. The Home School operated in Dalhousie from April to November. During those summer months, as Cherry recalls, the tulkus could learn English, French or German as well as Hindi, general knowledge and simple mathematics, while still keeping mainly to the rules of monastic discipline. One of the aims of the school was to avoid a social rift between the bulk of the Tibetan refugees who were getting educated in Indian schools and the young lamas, the elite of Tibetan society, whose religious vocation required them to be educated separately. The plan was that each winter the pupils would return to their gurus and concentrate on their religious studies.

In the first winter in Dalhousie, that plan was disrupted by a month-long border war between India and China, which ended with the victorious Chinese declaring a ceasefire on 20th November 1962. China crossed into what India held to be its territory both on the western part of the border, in Aksai Chin a remote area of eastern Ladakh, and in the east in what was then known in India as the North East Frontier Agency where many Tibetans had initially sought refuge. The school wasn't in any immediate peril but there was a real sense of alarm. 'Every evening we sat silently attentive round the tiny transistor radio as it crackled and spluttered out the latest reports of fighting and death,' Armstrong wrote. 'Every evening the news became worse. For this reason many of the tulkus' gurus who were living in the frontier area very near to the fighting had begged Freda not to send the tulkus back to them as was customary for the winter months. Freda had of course agreed and in a manner typical of her ways she decided to turn this into something positive for everyone.'[22] She decided to move the entire school for the winter months to a Buddhist centre in Delhi, the Ladakh Buddhist Vihar, in one of the older and more central districts of the city close to the Yamuna river. And she arranged two coaches to transport both young lamas and volunteers. On the way, the entire school visited the Dalai Lama at Dharamsala—where Freda, Cherry and the lamas had their photo taken with the most revered figure within the Tibetan diaspora—and meandered through Punjab on the way to the Indian capital. From there, several of the group went by train on a pilgrimage to the Buddhist sites in north India—as Freda sometimes remarked, the Tibetan refugees were helping to bring Buddhism back to its original home, to the land where the Buddha achieved enlightenment.

The impact of the border fighting followed the school to Delhi. Hundreds of Tibetans displaced by the fighting, and so uprooted for a second time, appeared at the gates of the Buddhist centre. Cherry Armstrong looked on from her balcony as a yellow-robed senior lama strode over to the entrance: 'the gates were flung open and the people poured through, eager but unhurried'.

Many filled the unoccupied dormitories, others crowded into tiny rooms and some made homes under the stairs, while others claimed a little patch of veranda for their belongings. Those at the back of the crowd for whom there was no room sat down with their loads on the river bank. During the next few days more and yet more arrived until they totalled over a thousand. Huge marquees usually reserved for festivals were erected to house them. Even more camped in the open around Delhi—on islands in the middle of roundabouts, in parks, and on the roadside verge.

Their tattered clothes hung on them, thick and heavy in the Delhi heat, yet their grimy faces were cheerful. Lama Lobsang organised those inside the vihara into groups of a dozen or so, and it was not long before food aid and parcels of clothes arrived. I would never have believed that human beings in such desperate straits could have distributed these windfalls with such calm orderliness. I never saw any ill-feeling or someone trying to take more than their share ... The women and girls were shy about wearing short cotton frocks and indeed all their quiet dignity was lost in the new attire. They had lost everything to do with their homeland and now they had to change even the way they looked.[23]

For Freda, it must have reminded her of Misamari: the destitution, the shortage of medicine, and the desperately ill—there were many suffering from TB among the new arrivals—who sought her out for help in getting treatment.

Alongside this new emergency, Freda continued to pursue another hugely ambitious project. 'My two lama "sons" are coming to England in March ... wonderful young lamas,' Freda told Olive Chandler—an indication of the strong emotional as well as spiritual bonds forged with these tulkus.[24] Along with John Driver, a scholar of Tibet who had spent several years in Kalimpong, she managed to secure a Spalding scholarship to allow Trungpa to study at Oxford University. Akong was to accompany him. They were, in Cherry Armstrong's words, Freda's 'golden boys'. She recognised in Trungpa, in particular, an exceptional spiritual presence and an ability to communicate and to inspire those with whom he came into contact. Both had formal roles at the school—Trungpa as co-director (he described himself as the school's spiritual advisor) while Akong made sure that the place ran with tolerable efficiency. Anita Morris, who taught English both at Green Park and at Dalhousie, had mixed opinions of the two. 'Akong was very much taking care of the younger ones—a lot of them were a lot younger. So if they had any pains or any problems, they would go to Akong,' she recalls. 'He'd be going down maybe to a doctor at Dalhousie if necessary or just for ordinary shopping and taking care of things. Whereas Trungpa just did his own thing, his bits of painting and that sort of stuff.'[25] A Tibetan lama who knew both well at Dalhousie comments that Trungpa always wanted attention and prominence, while Akong was solid and reliable. Trungpa was already developing a reputation as something of a wild child. Although it was a well-kept secret, he apparently fathered a child with a Tibetan nun who came to

Dalhousie to visit him. They took a mattress up on the roof of the school—said Trungpa's English wife in her memoirs—and spent the night there. That was not at all typical of the school, but not entirely untypical of Trungpa.[26] He was an enormously important figure in the spread of Tibetan Buddhism in North America and Europe and one of the first to teach westerners in English, but he had lifelong issues about sexual promiscuity and the use of drink and drugs.

At Ladakh Buddhist Vihar, Cherry remembers Trungpa and Akong sitting in their room studying maps of the London Underground and out-of-date bus timetables in preparation for their journey. They travelled by boat. On the day they were due to dock outside London, the pupils at the Home School—by now back in Dalhousie—held a prayer ceremony on an open patch of woodland on the hillside adjoining Kailash. 'They lit a fire of juniper branches and the smoke rose in a blue spire into the branches of the trees and on up into the cloudless sky. We sat on brightly patterned Tibetan rugs spread over the stony ant-infested ground and the lamas began their chanting. It was a happy, picnic-like affair around the scented bonfire, with kettles of hot buttery Tibetan tea.'[27] At Tilbury, Cherry's parents were on hand to welcome the two Tibetans—as were Anita Morris and other well-wishers—and to provide them with an initial berth at the family home in High Wycombe. Once installed at Oxford, Trungpa and Akong were joined by an old friend and another alumnus of the Home School, Chime Rinpoche. They shared a small flat in St Margaret's Road, on the same street as Freda's old college, and Akong took work as a hospital orderly to help support the household. All three became powerful beacons of Tibetan Buddhism in the west.

Alongside this noticeable success, Freda faced some acute disappointments. She made enemies as well as friends, and sometimes these rivalries became vicious. Lois Lang-Sims commented, without saying what prompted the observation, that Freda's enemies 'were not only numerous but of an almost incredible malevolence'.[28] That intense animosity seems to have been behind the most wounding public assault on Freda and her integrity. The stiletto was wielded by D.F. Karaka, an Oxford contemporary of the Bedis. He was a writer and journalist of some distinction, though by the early 1960s he was the editor of a not-so-distinguished Bombay-based tabloid-style weekly, the *Current*. This was awash with brash, sensationalist stories, reflecting Karaka's fiercely polemical style, his crusading anti-communism and his impatience with Nehru, India's prime minister, for his supposed lack of zeal in standing up for the national interest. The weekly paper bore the slogan 'God Save the Motherland' on its front page.

In September 1963, Freda's photograph graced the front-page of the *Current*, accompanying a story which also took up much of the following page. It was a hatchet job. Under his own byline, Karaka asserted that 'an Englishwoman, married to an Indian, is attempting to express a great deal of anxiety to help the Buddhist cause as a screen for her Communist activities'. He insisted that 'Mrs Freda Bedi … will always, in my opinion, be a Communist first, irrespective of her outwardly embraced Buddhism.' This was an absurd accusation. Freda's days as a communist sympathiser had come to a close almost twenty years earlier. Her husband had abandoned communism a decade previously. But the accusation of being a concealed communist was deeply wounding especially when the Tibetan refugees regarded communist China as their arch enemy—the occupiers of their homeland and destroyers of their culture, faith and tradition—and when India had recently been at war with China.

'Freda has dabbled with Communism ever since my student days in Oxford,' Karaka reported. 'She was, in fact, at Oxford at the same time as myself. Later, she married Bedi, a well known Indian Communist. They both came out to India and plunged themselves into the Communist movement.'[29] The article resorted to innuendo, suggesting that 'the alleged indoctrination of Sheikh Abdulla [sic] was largely to be traced to his very close association with Freda Bedi'. It suggested that some former associates of the Bedis in Kashmir had 'mysteriously disappeared'. Freda was alleged to have been caught up in controversy about Buddhist property and funds before turning, 'with the active encouragement of Shri J. Nehru, the Prime Minister', to the running of the Young Lamas' Home School. The article suggested that Freda was getting money from the Indian government, and using government headed paper to appeal for funds from supporters in America and elsewhere. Karaka suggested that the Tibetan Friendship Group was a 'Communist stunt' and he alleged that 'noted Communists, with the usual "blessings" of Mr. Nehru, are using the excuse of helping Tibetan refugees and Buddhist monks for furthering the cause of Communism in strategic border areas.'

Aside from the venomous smears, the only evidence of inappropriate conduct that the article pointed to was her use of official notepaper to appeal for funds for her school and other Tibetan relief operations. It cited a letter of complaint, sent by an unnamed Buddhist organisation which clearly was antagonistic to Freda, stating that she had been using the headed paper of the Central Social Welfare Board which bore the Government of India's logo. A civil servant's response was also quoted: 'Mrs Bedi is not authorised to use Government of India stationery for correspondence in connection with the affairs of the "Young Lama's Home" or the "Tibetan Friendship Group". This has now been pointed out to Mrs. Bedi.'

Even if Freda has been using government headed paper to help raise money—which those who worked with her say is perfectly possible—it was hardly a major misdemeanour. But detractors were able to use this blemish to damage her reputation. She was, it seems, distraught at this vicious personal attack and took advice about whether to take legal action. She was advised, probably wisely, to do nothing, as any riposte would simply give further life to accusations so insubstantial that they would quickly fade away. 'The accusation was that Freda was a communist in nun's clothing—not that Freda was a nun at that time,' recalls Cherry Armstrong. 'I remember her being particularly distressed and "beyond belief" when she believed she had identified the culprit. Freda was totally dumbfounded about it.'

Freda was convinced that another western convert to Buddhism, Sangharakshita (earlier Dennis Lingwood), was either behind the slur or was abetting it.[30] They had much in common—including a deep antipathy to each other. Lingwood encountered Theosophy and Buddhism as a teenager in England and was ordained before he was twenty by the Burmese monk U Titthila, who later helped Freda towards Buddhism. During the war, he served in the armed forces in South and South-east Asia and from 1950 spent about fourteen years based in Kalimpong in north-east India, where he was influenced by several leading Tibetan Buddhist teachers. In the small world of Indian Buddhism, the two English converts rubbed shoulders. More than sixty years later, Sangharakshita—who established a Buddhist community in England—recalls coming across Freda, then new to Buddhism, living at the Ashoka Vihar Buddhist centre outside Delhi. 'She was tall, thin, and intense and wore Indian dress. She had a very pale complexion, with light fair hair and very pale blue eyes. In other words, she looked very English! I also noticed, especially later on, that she was very much the Memsaheb ... During the time that I knew Freda she knew hardly anything about Buddhism, having never studied it seriously. ... She had however developed what I called her "patter" about the Dalai Lama, compassion, and the poor dear little Tulkus. So far as I could see, Freda had no spiritual awareness or Enlightenment. She may, of course, have developed these later.'[31] His view of the Young Lamas' Home School is also somewhat jaundiced—'some of [the tulkus] developed rather expensive tastes, such as for Rolex watches.'

Sangharakshita's recollection is that he and Freda 'got on quite well, even though I did not take her "Buddhism" very seriously' as they were both English and (in his view) of working-class origin. He was not impressed by her husband: 'he struck me as a bit of a humbug ... I was told (not by Freda) that he was then living with one of his cousins.' In his memoirs, he recycled one of the allegations that featured in *Current*, that an 'Englishwoman married to a well-known Indian communist' was trying to 'wrest' control of Ashoka Vihar outside Delhi from the Cambodian monk who had founded it.[32] Decades later, he continues to recount this and other of the items on the *Current* charge sheet, describing Freda as 'a rather ruthless operator' while in Kashmir. He recalls the furore over the *Current* article, but says that he had no reason to believe that Freda was using the Lamas' School for a political purpose. Freda never tackled him over her suspicions, but he does not deny a tangential involvement. 'It is possible,' he concedes, 'that certain reservations about the Young Lamas' Home School eventually reached the ears of *Current*.'

The incident was a reflection of the intense rivalries within the Tibetan movement and its supporters. 'Strong personalities do seem to draw opposition by their very nature,' Cherry Armstrong comments, 'and there is a lot of personal politics amongst the Tibetan groups—not all light and loveliness as one might like to think.'[33]

15

A Nun's Life

Freda Bedi estimated that of the 20,000 Buddhist nuns in Tibet prior to 1959, only about 150 managed to take refuge in India. In esteem, profile and attention as well as numbers, Tibetan nuns did not fare anything like as well as the monks and male lamas. This was an injustice that Freda sought to redress; the women were heirs to a spiritual legacy that she wished to protect. 'I realised that unless we took a few and tried to keep them as nuns, many of them would go off into a lay life or just live quiet lives here and there and the tradition would be lost. And again there's an oral tradition in the nuns—it's not only a book tradition.'[1]

Nuns were outnumbered ten-to-one by monks and in the Tibetan tradition they were not able to take full ordination. While a small number of women have been accepted as awakened or enlightened, very few have been recognised as reincarnations and positions of authority within Tibetan Buddhism have remained an almost entirely male preserve. Nunneries were often distinctly poorer than monasteries, with a more modest educational level and fewer opportunities for spiritual training and contemplative retreats. There was also a dismissive and hurtful attitude among some Tibetan monks to women religious, regarding them as less committed to a spiritual life and lax in observance of their vows.

In 1963 Freda established a tiny nunnery at Dalhousie close to the Young Lamas' Home School, from which a much more sizeable—and enduring—religious institution developed. It was 'the first Buddhist nunnery for Tibetan women refugees in India', according to Tenzin Palmo, another English woman who championed the nuns' interests. This was twenty years before anyone else thought about the plight of nuns, much less built nunneries for them. Again, Freda demonstrated her prescience and her talent for being ahead of the crowd.'[2] Starting small was part of her approach: get things going because once you can demonstrate that an initiative is up-and-running, it is easier to generate support and funding. She was revered by Tibetan nuns for taking up their cause when so few others paid them much attention. And three years after founding this nunnery, she made a much more profound personal commitment to Tibet's women religious and put on the maroon robes herself.

While establishing the Young Lamas' Home School, Freda was able to do a little to help young women among the refugees. She managed to secure places for two Tibetan girls at the boarding school her daughter attended. But this was a piecemeal approach to a bigger problem. Freda had harboured the ambition of establishing a nunnery—with the support of the head of the Kagyu lineage, the Karmapa Lama—for some time, indeed when Cherry Armstrong came to volunteer, the intention had been that she would concentrate on the opening of the nuns' centre. But fundraising was not easy, as Cherry had good reason to know—she typed out the letters, all individually written, to potential donors.

Of all the Tibetans in India the lot of the nuns must have been the worst. They were a minority group which had been overlooked by the authorities and voluntary organisations dealing with the Tibetan refugees generally. ... Many of them were working as road labourers even though many were elderly. Some were extremely learned and totally unaccustomed to manual labour and there were stories of rape. A few had resorted to begging in the big cities.[3]

Freda along with Cherry and several of the Tibetans at the Home

School went scouting for suitable properties to rent in Dalhousie which would suit their purpose—and they found one, known as Akash, on a hillside high above Dalhousie. 'The house was on the other side of the hill from Kailash, overlooking the plains on one side and distant mountains on the other,' Cherry recalls. 'As well as the main part of the building where the nuns would live, it had a conservatory, a good terraced vegetable garden and a lovely flower garden. The kitchen was a separate building, large but rather dingy though it could be improved. It was just what we wanted with room enough for twelve nuns, the Head Lama, me and one or two other volunteers or visitors.' The Home School volunteers were levied into whitewashing the house and a shrine room was established. Wooden beds were made for the nuns, vegetables planted, and Freda's younger son, Kabir, brought a carload of plates, mugs and kitchen equipment. Over the entrance Sherab Palden, a Tibetan artist who stayed at the Home School, painted a signboard: 'Karma Drubgyu Thargay Ling'. In English, the institution was—and is—known as the Mahayana Buddhist Nunnery.

The building was ready for its first occupants in early May 1963. Although a Kagyu nunnery, nuns were admitted from all schools of Tibetan Buddhism. Karma Thinley was the head lama. He had been in Delhi with the young lamas and volunteers the previous winter. 'I remembered him as always very quiet and swathed in an enormous number of robes. Although always smiling and cheerful and popular with the tulkus, he was also known to be very strict, so Freda considered him a good choice for this role.'[4] The head lama was not required to live permanently at the nunnery. A head nun and another senior nun in charge of discipline were making their way to Dalhousie from Sikkim. The initial complement of nuns on the opening day was three. Cherry Armstrong recalled them 'sitting in a huddle feeling overwhelmed by the number of Europeans and tulkus. Freda introduced me and they grasped my hands warmly and pressed their foreheads to mine in the Tibetan greeting. They were all quite young and until coming here had spent some time in an ashram where they had been taught a little English and a lot of Hindi.'[5]

Some weeks later, a senior religious figure in the Kagyu school came to bless and purify the nunnery—a visit which prompted a frenzy of cleaning and tidying. Shortly afterwards, the two senior nuns from Sikkim arrived with two younger nuns and also two nieces of the Karmapa who were destined for nurses' training in Delhi but were to stay in Dalhousie for a while and improve their English. The nunnery fell into a routine. A breakfast of porridge and Tibetan tea was followed by Cherry's English lessons, often conducted not in the classroom but while walking around the hillside. In the late morning, the nuns turned to religious studies; in the afternoon they copied Tibetan scriptures; each evening they chanted prayers, accompanied by a hand bell and an assortment of drums.

When Diane Perry came out to Dalhousie in 1964 to replace Cherry Armstrong, she was already a Buddhist and, although only twenty, considering becoming a nun herself. She had received some training in meditation before leaving England with Trungpa Rinpoche, who also repeatedly propositioned her and put his hand up her skirt (she responded by stamping her stiletto heel on his sandal-covered foot). Although her main work was at the Home School, Diane stayed at the nunnery, where she found living conditions to be desperately basic. She initially slept on the covered veranda, and then was allocated a tiny room of her own. 'It was cold, freezing cold, and when it rained, it rained outside and in,' she recalled. 'And then there were the rats. They were everywhere. They were also enormous and would eat everything, including cloth and my prayer beads. They used to keep me awake at night by jumping on me.'[6] She had been in touch with Freda by letter explaining her interest in the life of a Tibetan nun and was emboldened by Freda's response: 'Please come, come. Don't worry, just come!' So she did—and she took to Freda. 'She was definitely a character—a strange mixture of

Indian and English county. She never completely shed her roots. Everyone called her Mummy. I loved her very much. ... The thing was she was very good at initiating ideas and excellent at getting money.'[7] Perry was less convinced about the way Freda spent the money, and in particular her failure to buy property in the hills when prices were modest.

Freda may have assumed that she would provide spiritual guidance to the new volunteer, but that's not how it worked out. A few weeks after arriving, on her twenty-first birthday, Diane Perry was introduced by Freda to a visiting high lama, Khamtrul Rinpoche, and immediately felt a strong affinity with him. At that first meeting, she asked to be ordained a nun—the ceremony by which she became a novice nun took place in Khamtrul Rinpoche's nearby monastery just three weeks later. Diane Perry shaved her head, put on the maroon robes and was given the name Tenzin Palmo. She began to work as Khamtrul Rinpoche's secretary and he became her guru. Tenzin Palmo later took a higher ordination and achieved particular renown by living for twelve years in a cave 13,000 feet up in the Indian Himalayas, practising intense meditation.

The nunnery grew steadily. Within two years, there were more than twenty nuns. A larger house in Dalhousie, Geeta, became the main building. The more remote Akash was used as a meditation centre, where a small group of nuns stayed, by rotation, for three months. Funding remained hand-to-mouth, and Freda's write up of the nunnery's progress for the Tibetan Friendship Group's newsletter gave a sense of how precarious the finances were in spite of her talent as a fundraiser. The Lama, Karma Thinley, reports that the meditating nuns are doing very well indeed. One of them is a new nun, who is the sole surviving nun in India of a famous Nunnery of 700 nuns in Tibet. Her name is Kacho. We would like to find a helper for her. Incidentally, four more nuns are without pen friends still. It means a great deal to them to have a friend who sends monthly or occasionally a small amount of money as the nuns live very very simply.'[8] Small donations, a trickle of Indian government money and an even more precarious income from selling handicrafts kept the nunnery and the Home School afloat, just about. Freda expressed her gratitude to all donors: 'may they receive the fruit of their devotion to the Tibetan Sangha in this life and in lives to come.'

The Home School and nunnery suffered double blows in the course of a few months when in May 1965 a cyclone brought down part of the school's wooden roof and stone-built chimney stack making it unusable until repairs were completed, and then in September another war prompted Freda to evacuate most of those in her charge. The conflict was between India and Pakistan and while Dalhousie was not directly in the firing line, it was close to the contested former princely state of Kashmir and no one was sure how the fighting might escalate. While the Indian army had the upper hand, reports that Pakistani commandos had been airlifted to Pathankot, the nearest railway terminus, caused alarm. The volunteers—a couple now Indian but most from Europe and North America—felt particularly vulnerable. 'Due to the war emergency, I am leaving with three nuns and about twenty-three lamas for Andretta,' Freda reported to her sponsors in the Tibetan Friendship Group. 'It is vital for all foreign volunteers to get to the plains.' She added, a touch waspishly: 'Diane Perry (England) intends to stay on with the Kha[m]trul Rinpoche party: I understand her decision. They will take responsibility for her and she hasn't got to take responsibility for other lives, as I have.'

Freda had a small property at Andretta and many friends there, and her charges remained in the Kangra Valley until the school disbanded as usual in November. These were not the final chapters in the Young Lamas' Home School, but they could be seen as portents that the institution was nearing its end. In the summer of 1966 the school was transformed into a Mahayana monastic house, with a veteran of the Home School, Ato Rinpoche, as head lama. He insists that the change of name was more political than a repurposing of the school. But over time the institution did assume a more monastic rather than scholastic purpose and sought to become largely self-financing.[9]

Ato Rinpoche unwittingly provided Freda with one of the dramas besetting her years in Dalhousie. He was a tulku and high lama who had spent three years at the Karmapa's request representing the Kagyu order at the Dalai Lama's religious office at Dharamsala. When Trungpa and Akong headed to England, Ato was keen to replace them—he knew Freda and the set-up at Dalhousie, and he was keen to learn English. So he took over as the senior Tibetan spiritual figure at the school, and Freda provided him with an English tutor, one of her new volunteers, Alethea Martineau, an Oxford Classics graduate in her mid-twenties. The lama and his English teacher fell in love. Ato Rinpoche wrote to the 16th Karmapa saying he intended to renounce his monk's robes. Freda had words with the couple. 'She was certainly upset,' Alethea recalls. 'But I was very grateful to Freda—she never took it out on me. She wanted to know if we were serious. She'd tried carpetting [Ato Rinpoche], and if he doesn't want to talk he doesn't talk. So then she turned her fire on me. She said: "there's something going on, are you serious?" And I said: "yes, we're serious". And after that, as far as I know, she accepted it.' It must have reminded Freda of her own unconventional romance more than thirty years earlier.

The couple married in Delhi in February 1967 and then made their home in England. Trungpa and Akong had already headed to England—both were to marry and so leave formal monastic life, though they remained important Buddhist teachers and heads of influential Buddhist centres. Ato Rinpoche suggests, perhaps a touch impishly, that the 16th Karmapa became concerned that sending senior lamas to Dalhousie was risking the loss of some of the most talented spiritual communicators from monastic life—though the incident doesn't seem to have caused more than a fleeting difficulty between Freda and her guru.[10]

In 1968, the Karmapa Lama decided to move the nunnery from

rented premises in Dalhousie to a six-acre site at Tilokpur, still in the north Indian hills though at a much lower altitude and close to the Dalai Lama's headquarters at Dharamsala. This was deemed to be an auspicious location, overlooking caves which had been the home of Tilopa, an ascetic and practitioner of meditation who was a key figure in the establishment of the Kagyu tradition. The new venture got off to a troubled start: the temporary nunnery constructed at Tilokpur, with its thatched wattle roof, burnt down. When Susan Rowan—now Lama Shenpen Hookham—came out to Tilokpur in 1969, the nuns were living in the grounds of a Sikh temple while they prepared to rebuild. Rowan had been in touch with Trungpa Rinpoche, who had in 1967 established the landmark Samye Ling Buddhist centre in the Scottish Borders. He had advised that she study meditation with Karma Thinley Rinpoche, who remained the abbot of the nunnery. So she arranged with Freda to volunteer with the nuns—though Freda again assumed that she would be providing the spiritual guidance. 'I think she got used to people treating her as a kind of guru figure', in Shenpen Hookham's assessment. She remembers Freda as bright eyed, chatty and open, but at times overpowering. 'She had very strong views, like a mother figure where she feels responsible for telling everybody what they should be doing. … She is somebody who accomplished a lot because she did things very impulsively but didn't really think them through.'[11] Shenpen Hookham spent five years at Tilokpur and found a tremendous sense of gratitude towards Freda—but no clear leadership. 'She would suddenly appear on the scene and tell them that they should all be doing this-that-and-the-other, whereas they didn't really have much connection with what she was saying.'

The nuns had to do much of the building work at Tilokpur themselves. 'We took part in the construction of the different buildings, and we carried sand and building materials from the road and up the steep steps (164 steps) to the nunnery,' recounted a Sikkimese nun, Pema Tsultrim. 'A few porters were hired from the village to help in the construction, otherwise we did the work ourselves. ... We used to eat a paste consisting of radishes and poor flour. We could not afford to buy rice. ... We kept two buffaloes for the milk, and had to take turns herding them, which meant that we had to sleep out in the open. We also grew some of our own vegetables and we took turns gathering firewood for cooking.'[12] Freda's sponsorship scheme remained one of the principal sources of income. The nuns looked on her as their founder and benefactor and some cited remarks supposedly made by the Karmapa Lama suggesting that she was an emanation of White Tara, a female Buddha associated with compassion and long life—though that may have been not so much what he said as what the nuns wanted to hear.

Freda had her own rooms at Tilokpur and when poor health frustrated her active involvement in the running of the nunnery she first identified four among the nuns to share that role and then installed an abbess, a role not unknown within the Tibetan tradition but exceptionally unusual. She also broke down gender barriers by securing her candidate's admission to a degree course at the Central Institute of Higher Tibetan Studies at Sarnath in north India.[13] The Tilokpur nunnery continues to thrive and is the home to more than sixty women religious. It describes itself as the oldest Kagyu nunnery outside Tibet.

While volunteers such as Diane Perry were finding spiritual teachers and seeking enlightenment, Freda too was strengthening her bonds with her guide and instructor. In 1963, she had taken a Bodhisattva vow in Dalhousie from the visiting 16th Karmapa. This is a commitment to strive for awakening—one's own and that of others. These were the first formal and public vows that she had made with the Karmapa. It marked a deepening of her spiritual engagement with him. It was another three years before she took ordination from the Karmapa and became a novice nun in the Kagyu tradition. It is the act that defines her. According to Tibetan lamas who knew Freda well, the Karmapa asked her to secure her husband's consent for the ordination; she told Bedi of her intention, but not her children. It was a step which entailed withdrawal from the world but not, as we've seen in the prologue, withdrawal from her family, a precarious balancing act which she undertook with a large measure of success.

Freda Bedi is often described as the first western woman to become a Tibetan Buddhist nun—that's both true and not true. She was certainly the pioneer in taking the full ordination, six years after her novice vows, but not in going through an initial ordination and wearing the nun's robes. Diane Perry had taken that step two years earlier, and she in turn insists that she wasn't the first. That was probably Sister Vajra, a Scottish woman who was a follower of both the 16th Karmapa and Kalu Rinpoche and who lived in Darjeeling in north-east India; she knew Freda and had visited the Home School. She died when a landslide carried away her small house.[14]

Why exactly Freda Bedi became a nun when she did remains far from clear. Her own much repeated mantra—that her ordination was like an apple falling off a tree, it's simply that the time was ripe—has a poetic truth to it, but glosses over all the other considerations which must have been a part of her decision. Freda had, in her own mind at least, been heading towards the life of a spiritually enlightened Buddhist for some time. Being, in a sense, overtaken on that journey by Diane Perry may have spurred Freda towards ordination. Living most of the year in the hills, she was immersed in Tibetan Buddhism, including the life and devotion of the women who had come to the nunnery she had established. She was already at a distance from her husband and must have been aware of his new relationship. Her children seemed to be coping well without her constant presence. Her work and travel—and their work and education—meant that she had become a less pervasive part of their lives. All the same, she misjudged the intensity of their resentment of her ordination, and—as we have seen—was stung by the forthrightness of Kabir's and

Guli's response. For a woman with such well developed emotional antennae, the manner in which she became a nun, and disclosed this to her children, was curiously maladroit. She may have simply lost sight of how the family would respond in her excitement to embrace a religious life. She might have thought whatever the turbulence, best to get it done with because her wish to become a nun was not subject to negotiation. She believed that she could combine the life of a nun with that of a mother—and she managed that to a degree—but she also made clear by her actions which was now the greater imperative in her life.

The biggest factor is likely to have been the guidance of her guru. The spiritual bonds between the Karmapa and Freda were strong and became over the next decade still more intense. The prospect of being ordained by the Karmapa himself in the order's Dharma Chakra Centre at his newly restored monastery at Rumtek, just twenty miles or so from the Tibetan border, would have been enticing. On 1st August 1966, she took the ten precepts of the Samaneri-Getsulma, the novice nun. The Karmapa gave her the name Karma Tsultim Khechog Palmo. From this moment on, the new nun signed herself as K.K.P. or Sister Palmo, adding Freda in brackets when writing to old friends. In her own mind, she had a new identity—it wasn't a rejection of who she had been earlier, but she now had a new name, status and purpose. When she returned to Dalhousie, Freda's delight in taking her vows was evident to all. 'She was very happy, very pleased about it,' Alethea Ato recalls. 'She was bursting with it.'

The death in Derby of Freda's mother just two weeks before her ordination must have sharpened a sense of casting aside old allegiances—of a new beginning. Freda bore a feeling of guilt that she hadn't been around to care for her mother, or indeed to visit her, in her old age. She didn't travel back for the funeral. Nellie Swan had been a widow for the last four years of her life. She lived with a housekeeper and companion, Renee Webster. 'I'm so deeply grateful for all you've done for her. More than I could have done even if I'd been in England,' Freda told Renee just a few days after the ordination ceremony. 'You have been a real daughter to her. Thank you from the bottom of my heart.'

> So far away it's difficult to keep up personal links, but I believe these ties transcend the body. Since Mother died I have seen her in dreams, with Pop, happy, wearing the colour sacred to the Buddha (maroon). Her own dress, of course. This is between us. It has given me the faith that even if she rejected orthodox Christianity, the innate goodness + kindness in her has had its own reward + she is happy. I can only say that this is a conviction with me as I've seen this happiness. May the Buddha guide her footsteps.[15]

This was not a letter of atonement, but there is an underlying sense of contrition as well as of gratitude. By describing Renee as a 'real' daughter to her mother, Freda was acknowledging a shortcoming in her own fulfilment of filial responsibility. When she wrote again to Renee a few years later—to say that Guli, then approaching twenty-one, was planning a visit to England—her brother was also dead and the family links to her homeland had become increasingly tenuous. 'I feel I must write as Guli is coming over ... and I feel you'd like to meet her. How Mother longed to see her! But it was not to be, and now Jack has gone too. ... I am feeling the loss of Jack so much: we were very close, even if far from one another. And it was such an untimely departure.'[16] Freda had a book of Tibetan prayers in English translation printed in memory of her brother, and sent an inscribed copy to her niece. 'A beautiful Buddhist custom,' she wrote. 'For my mother I also did the same thing.'[17]

On her ordination, Sister Palmo—as we should now call her—received a privilege which reflected the importance the Karmapa attached to her and the work she was undertaking for the Kagyu lineage. He arranged for a young nun, Anila Pema Zangmo, to be her attendant and assistant. Pema Zangmo had been accepted as a novice nun at the age of five, spending the winter at a monastery and joining her family for the summer to help on the land. In her mid-twenties, she came with three other nuns to the new nunnery at Dalhousie. 'We had heard that there we could study English and also could practice the Dharma. When I met the holy mother [Sister Palmo] for the first time, she gave to me and my friends blankets and all other important things for our daily life.'[18]

For the remaining years of Sister Palmo's life, while she was in India she and Ani Pema were inseparable. 'She's very cheerful and uncomplicated,' Sister Palmo confided to Olive Shapley, 'and it's very helpful having her around when I'm meditating. She's racially Tibetan, but she's always lived on the Indian frontier. She knows Hindi and she can cook the sort of food I like, which is Punjabi food.'[19] The relationship was deeper than this casual remark indicated. Ani Pema certainly cared for and looked after Sister Palmo, but they were also a formidable team. Ani Pema was an effective fundraiser in her own right, and a champion of the Tilokpur nunnery and of Tibet's women religious. She was both loyal and reverential to Sister Palmo but not afraid to speak her own mind. Both saw themselves as fortunate to find the other.

Just a few weeks after the ordination ceremony, a nineteen-year-old English woman, Maxine Elvey, came to Dalhousie and wrote a long letter back to her parents about the remarkable and well-connected English woman who talked of 'we Indians' and 'we Punjabis'. 'When I went to see her I was a little nervous,' Maxine explained. 'It seemed she must be such a busy woman. I found out only when I got there that I had come at the right time. She had just got back from three months in Sikkim.' She shared with her parents a vivid account of that encounter. 'I was shown up to her room, small, carpeted, with a Tibetan Buddhist altar with a Milarepa thanka ... a picture of her Guru, and his Guru, and the Dalai Lama, and on the table, covered with a maroon cloth, a small gold Buddha, butter lamps, and incense sticks, which were kindled, giving their sweet smell to the whole room':

> On the bed opposite the altar, which was also draped with a maroon cloth, sat Mrs Bedi. I was a little awe-struck at the sight of her well-filled but not fat body, draped in a maroon nun's robe, which contrasted so strangely with her bright clear blue eyes, the white stubble of her shaved baby-pink scalp, and her very white well-rounded heavy middle-aged arms. It was above all the shaved head that I was constantly tempted to stare at—I had never seen a European woman with one before. She had the general air of a headmistress—I felt I should say the right thing. She immediately ordered tea, and despite the fact that [she was] seated like a Buddha on the bed quite snowed in by letters, she wanted to know all about me. ... I was deeply moved by her extreme compassion. She is a person devoting herself to others.[20]

Elvey was quickly absorbed into Sister Palmo's ventures in Dalhousie. 'Mrs Bedi has the habit of finding jobs for people, and I soon found myself teaching English to two Tibetan boys of my own age for three weeks. Their names were Panjo and Dupa, and they were both very intelligent, though Panjo much more determined and hard-working.'

Two years after her ordination, Sister Palmo returned to Rumtek for a year-long retreat. This was an opportunity to meditate, to work on translating prayers from the Tibetan, and to seek guidance and spiritual initiation from the Karmapa. While there, her old Oxford friend Olive Shapley, accompanied by her two sons, came to visit. Sikkim was a sensitive border region and both difficult to get permission to visit and awkward to reach, but Olive managed to spend five days at the monastery, taking with her a bulky BBC-issue reel-to-reel tape recorder. She recorded her old friend talking about her life, her religion and the routine of being a nun on a retreat.

'The early morning time is very good for meditation,' Sister

Palmo remarked. She rose at four every morning in her bare room at Rumtek, and had a cup of tea as she settled into her daily spiritual regime. At seven, she had breakfast, followed by a further three hours of meditation, a break for lunch, and meditation once more. In the afternoon, she had a three-hour break in which she could write and set down translations from the Tibetan. Then at six in the evening, she returned to meditation and prayer. 'In the deeper meditation, we combine certain prayers and visualisations with the silent meditation—and what we call protector prayers are done, to remove hindrances. It's quite hard to meditate. It's quite an effort. It's not so easy to sit in one room all the time.' In the evening, she usually had an hour free before going to bed at ten.

Sister Palmo and Ani Pema were the only nuns in the masculine environment of Rumtek monastery. For a year, she was largely confined to her room—unless she was taking a lesson from the Karmapa. 'I may go for three or four days without getting a lesson. Or I may ask him if he can teach me after two days. It depends on the stage of the meditation. If I feel the need to ask a question or get his help then I send a message to him. He's very busy but he's very good and he helps in a very wonderful way. To struggle alone for realisation as a lonely meditator is very, very hard. It may be very beautiful in its own way. But a real living teacher helping—somebody to whom you can ask questions—or even without asking questions, just sit in front of him and somehow from that which is beyond the mind, something comes...the main thing about Buddhist meditation is that the Buddha is the greatly compassionate one.'

16

Seeding the West

Taking vows as a nun marked Freda Bedi's withdrawal from the world, yet in the last decade of her life, while she was wearing the maroon robes, she travelled more widely and incessantly than ever before. As Sister Palmo she strove to bring the Dharma—Buddhist teachings—to new audiences, particularly in the west. And she persuaded her guru, the Karmapa Lama, to travel too—accompanying him on a landmark visit to North America and Europe in 1974-5, the first such mission by a figure of his seniority within Tibetan Buddhism. Through the influence she brought to bear on the Karmapa, the work of lamas and tulkus she had helped to educate, and by her own witness, she was, in the words of a senior Tibetan lama, 'the seed for Buddhism in western countries'.[1]

Sister Palmo's closeness to the 16th Karmapa Lama both reflected the spiritual levels she achieved and greatly enhanced her standing and authority. When asked about her guru, she on one occasion replied: 'they say when the pupil is ready, the teacher appears—here was the one who really was to mean so much in terms of the understanding of the Dharma.'[2] She was thirteen years older than the Karmapa. One of the consequences of Tibetan Buddhism's recognition of new incarnations is that many of its most senior figures are young and hold their religious office for a long time. The 16th Karmapa held his first Black Crown ceremony—the theatrical ritual for which his lineage is renowned—at the age of seven and was in his mid-thirties when, in 1959, he led more than a hundred of his followers from Tsurphu monastery near Lhasa, the traditional seat of the Kagyu order, into Bhutan. He is often regarded as displaying foresight among Tibetan leaders in recognising the need to flee and in realising the unlikelihood of return. He had a warm and smiling disposition, a loud laughter and a noted affinity with and affection for birds, both wild and caged. For Sister Palmo, he was a spiritual guide—and also a close friend. She revered him. He was, she told a radio interviewer, 'a living Buddha to my mind, a walking Buddha'.

> When His Holiness moves and walks and deals with people, I can sort of see the Buddha quality. … If the Buddha was on the earth, he would have walked and talked and done things like that. Even physically there is a certain Buddha quality about him. A certain radiance.[3]

She described the Karmapa's 'warm great quality of Buddha-ness' as evident from their first meeting when she posed to him a question she had been wanting to ask her then guru in Rangoon. 'I remember it was on mindfulness. And I said: "How can one combine saying the rosary with mindfulness?" Because in mindfulness you have to give away all concepts and ideas and just sit. His Holiness said: "Oh, just be mindful that you are telling the rosary". Well, of course, it was a deep answer. So simple.'

After her year-long retreat, Sister Palmo was peripatetic. She spent time at the nunnery at Tilokpur, in Delhi, with Ranga and his family in Assam, but the summers and the rainy period that followed she would often spend at Rumtek on a retreat. The monastery was her principal home. Although there was a tradition that some Tibetan monasteries had a small number of nuns attached to them, that hadn't been the case at Rumtek—which had only recently been brought back into monastic use. It was a rare privilege that Sister Palmo and her assistant Anila Pema Zangmo were allowed to stay there. More than that, in the rigidly hierarchical world of Tibetan Buddhism, she was given a room towards the top of the building, close to the Karmapa. There could be no more emphatic demonstration of the confidence the Karmapa placed in her. She offered good counsel and got things done. She was well connected and understood the ways of the world in which the Tibetans were now taking refuge. There was another aspect of their partnership. In India, the Tibetan government-in-exile sought to instil a unity among Tibetans which probably hadn't existed within Tibet, where there were sharp regional as well as doctrinal fault lines. The Karmapa Lama became a figurehead for those Tibetans who, while reverential of the Dalai Lama, wished to maintain some autonomy and were resentful of the dominance of the Dalai Lama's Gelug school within Tibetan Buddhism. Freda was sufficiently attuned to diaspora politics to express a sincere regard for the Dalai Lama but also to help sustain those who wished to ensure continued diversity within Tibetan Buddhism.

The Karmapa's evident regard for Sister Palmo may have disquieted some of the monks at Rumtek, for she was after all an outsider who had almost gatecrashed the community. Few outside converts at this time came to live and worship in the main Tibetan monasteries, and for a foreign woman to be accorded this honour was unheard of. But the Karmapa's wishes were not open to question. 'Lamas, monks, nuns never question Karmapa's judgement,' says Lama Yeshe, who spent two years at Rumtek in the late 1960s as the Karmapa's private secretary. 'He is like the God himself. So if he make[s a] decision, it has to be good.'[4]

A steady trickle of western adventurers and spiritual seekers made their way to the Rumtek monastery—with some difficulty given the additional permissions required to travel to Sikkim—and, either by arrangement or accident, met Sister Palmo. Nancy Cooke was an American socialite and, for want of a better term, spiritual tourist—she stayed with the Beatles at an ashram at Rishikesh on the Ganges and visited Kashmir with her guru, Maharishi Mahesh

Yogi. She was encouraged by a friend to see Rumtek and assembled a small group of wealthy westerners with whom she travelled to Sikkim. Her vivid account of that visit reflects Sister Palmo's openness to outsiders and her exceptional ability to make friends. By chance they arrived just in time to see the monthly Black Crown ceremony—and afterwards were ushered into a small hall:

> As I entered, I gasped in surprise. On a low platform sat an English woman in monk's robes. She appeared to be in her sixties—her large, pale blue eyes looked enormous because of her shaved head.
> 'Come in, I am Sister Palmo. It is a joy to welcome you.' Recovering from our start, we formed a circle around her on the floor. As we gathered confidence, we asked questions about herself and the significance of the ceremony we had just witnessed. 'What good fortune, coming here on this particular day. It was not accidental; every movement of even a grain of sand is planned.'

Sister Palmo suggested that the visitors come again to the monastery—and if they did, could they possibly bring some shopping from the market in the Sikkimese capital, Gangtok, where they were staying. The following day, having called on the chogyal or king of Sikkim and his young American wife, Nancy Cooke and her party came again to Rumtek, laden with bread, butter, cream and the requested fruit and vegetables.

> Anila, Sister Palmo's tiny attendant, took our parcels from us with joy and the quiet, silent movements of a bird. Sister Palmo was sitting as she had been when we left her the day before. 'Good morning, what a treat to get all these lovely foods. Come sit near me—are you sure you wouldn't like chairs brought in?' We assured her not. ...
> We discussed her early years as a nun. ... She even discussed the shaving of her head. 'I guess that is the final commitment

for a woman,' her eyes twinkled. 'You know vanity is gone when you see your hair on the floor.'[5]

Sister Palmo talked to the group about Tibetan Buddhism and the 16th Karmapa, and—in passing—her mission for the Dharma to reach a wider audience. "'Man feels more secure in clinging to tradition. ... He wants to possess and make his knowledge exclusive,'" Sister Palmo reportedly told the group. "'Even the Karmapa once admitted to me, 'It took the Red Chinese to force Tibet into sharing its wisdom with the outside world.' That was our bad karma, trying to keep it to ourselves.'" It was an arresting remark—seeing the positive aspect of extreme adversity, and seizing this as an opportunity. Sister Palmo's guests admired her honesty—though they were a little less sure at first about how to respond to her hospitality.

Soon it was time for lunch. Rik [Cooke's son] and I were hesitant to eat at the monastery, where sanitary conditions were uncertain, so we said we'd had a large breakfast. 'Not at all; that was hours ago,' insisted the nun. 'Anila is cooking our meal in the next room; I have taught her to make crepes.'
     ... The crepes, when served with cream and honey whipped with butter, were delicious. ...
'What a treat for me,' said Sister Palmo. 'Our diet is sparse here. One of the things I miss is toast with my tea—we often go weeks without bread. We raise chickens and goats outside the monastery. So it's an eggs, goats milk and grain menu.' No wonder the foods we'd brought were thought so dazzling.[6]

After the meal, the visitors were received by the Karmapa. At the audience, Nancy saw an old friend, Goodie Oberoi, a Punjabi woman who had married into a family which ran some of India's most prestigious luxury hotels and who was in turn a close friend of Sister Palmo. By the time the group left, they had agreed to carry a wad of bank notes to the nunnery at Tilokpur on the other flank of

India, and had ordered five thankgas, Tibetan Buddhist paintings on fabric. A year or two later, on her first visit to the United States, Sister Palmo stayed with Nancy Cooke in Beverly Hills. Cooke also hosted members of the Karmapa's entourage on their visits to California and even took a group of monks who had come to teach a course on death on an excursion to Disneyland. Sister Palmo had turned a chance encounter into a lasting friend and valuable contact.

During monsoon retreats at Rumtek, Sister Palmo worked on versioning religious works from the Tibetan. She completed her first booklet of Tibetan prayers, translated from old Buddhist texts, in 1970. *A Garland of Morning Prayers* was dedicated to both the Dalai Lama and the Karmapa Lama in an elegant and adroit form of words: to the Dalai Lama 'who first opened for me the door of the Mahayana. Ocean wide / Ocean deep / it is by your Grace / that this humble seeker offers these prayers / in the language of her birthland / to her Guru-Lama', in other words, the Karmapa.[7] This was her most widely circulated prayer booklet but over several years she worked in all on more than thirty devotional texts, many of them published by the Karma Rigdol press in Seattle. Sister Palmo studied Tibetan and gained a basic knowledge of the language but not sufficient to translate. Ato Rinpoche recalls that while she picked up some facility in reading Tibetan, her ability to speak the language was not good. Her reversionings into English were collaborative ventures. Lamas and monks helped her with the basic meaning, and then she fashioned the prayers in English bringing to bear her facility with words honed by many years of writing and journalism. But her standards were not universally admired. Shenpen Hookham, who as Susan Rowan had come out to volunteer at the Tilokpur nunnery and became proficient in Tibetan, harboured reservations about the authority of her renditions. 'She would say: "oh, this translation has to be right because I had it checked by the tulkus". And they were quite badly wrong—and it isn't enough to say they'd been checked by the tulkus. ... I suppose it was overconfidence really about how much she knew.'[8]

Sister Palmo received initiation into some of the more esoteric aspects of Tibetan Buddhism, and still more remarkably, she was awarded the authority to give initiations. Much of this was cloaked in confidentiality. Among the papers Sister Palmo left, for instance, are three typed pages of prayers of penitence she set down. These are marked 'SECRET: FOR INITIATES ONLY'. There was a belief that it is dangerous to introduce devotees to aspects of religious and meditational practice for which they were not prepared. She was not only receiving these privileged aspects of spiritual knowledge; she was imparting them too.

With the Karmapa's support, Sister Palmo started travelling overseas. Towards the close of 1969, she visited Malaysia, Singapore and Thailand, attending the general conference of the Bangkok-based World Fellowship of Buddhists. The following year, she travelled to Britain seeking support for Tibetan refugees, and visited the Samye Ling Centre in the Scottish borders, which described itself as the first Tibetan Buddhist centre in the west and where Akong Rinpoche was in charge. But her first big mission overseas, what she called her 'pioneer visit', came in March 1972—to South Africa. She was invited by Rosemary Vosse, a Cape Town Theosophist who probably also funded the trip. As an Indian resident, travelling to apartheid South Africa was not straightforward. And as a European woman with an Indian passport—and wearing the robes of a Buddhist nun—she did not easily fit in to South Africa's racial categories. The story is told—perhaps parable more than literal truth—that South African immigration staff couldn't decide whether to regard Sister Palmo as white or non-white; she refused to be defined in racial terms, and was admitted as a non-white visitor.

In the course of a month, Sister Palmo visited Cape Town, Durban, Johannesburg and Port Elizabeth (where she was asked to

conduct the funeral rites of a Chinese seaman). She called this her
Dharma tour, giving teachings and meditation classes. She also, on
the authority of the Karmapa Lama, carried out initiations. 'The Sister
Khechog Palmo has been authorised to give the Refuge Ordination,
which is the same in all four Tibetan Sects,' the Karmapa told a
prominent Buddhist in Johannesburg ahead of the visit, 'and also to
give a few special initiations of the Kagyudpa Line to the meditators.
I have given her this special initiation training, and those who receive
such ordination and initiations will be automatically considered to be
my devotees and initiates.'9 This was a rare privilege for any Buddhist
monk or nun, and a remarkable one for a convert.

The small groups of Buddhists and spiritual seekers Sister Palmo
met were overwhelmingly middle class and white. Among them
was the writer Sheila Fugard, who was struck by her 'soft English
accent' and wrote a spiritual memoir of the visitor, and Andre de
Wet, an artist. In Durban, she met members of the large Indian
community and was 'warmly welcomed because she is so very much
Indian despite her Derbyshire origin and an Oxonian accent.' On
her return to India, she recounted how she had 'preached to the
whites, the browns ... [but] regrets that she could hardly meet any
"coloured Africans".'10

Although a very small number of South Africans of Asian descent
practised Buddhism—Sister Palmo gave the Refuge initiation to
an elderly member of the Natal Buddhist Society, which she said
embraced thirty families—the religion was not well established.
The tiny band of Theosophists had helped create an awareness of
Buddhist teachings, but a newspaper feature about Sister Palmo's
visit described Buddhism as 'alien to South Africa'.11 Her visit
achieved its immediate purpose, the founding of the Karma Rigdol
Buddhist Association to give a structure to the provision of Buddhist
teaching and retreats, building on the South African branch of
the Tibetan Friendship Group established a few years earlier. She
attracted attention in the South African press, with articles bearing

headlines such as 'A Woman who blends Western Logic and Eastern Mysticism', and—on the women's page of the *Argus*—'Celibacy and Saffron'.[12] She also developed enduring personal friendships and spiritual bonds. Both Rosemary Vosse and Andre de Wet toured with the Karmapa and Sister Palmo across Europe in 1974-5—Andre was ordained by the Karmapa in Copenhagen, taking the name Samten. Sheila Fugard travelled with Sister Palmo in North America. On a personal, spiritual and institutional level, her 'pioneer' mission had been a success.

Her next trip abroad just a few weeks later took her east again—and this was an even bigger deal. At the prompting of the Karmapa, she travelled to take the full bhiksuni ordination as a nun. This full ordination of women dated back to the early days of Buddhism, when the Buddha's aunt and other women in princely families established a bhiksuni order. However, in Tibetan Buddhism, with its emphasis on direct transmission of religious practices, the full ordination of nuns had been interrupted many centuries earlier—if it ever existed. 'At some point in history, there were either no teachers or no pupils or people died or there was some invasion or what happened, and the line got cut,' Sister Palmo explained to her family. 'That's to say there wasn't a living teacher who could ordain the nuns who wanted to be ordained, or there was a living teacher but there were no nuns to be ordained. So we could not get it after the eighth century in India and the same in Tibet. And for that reason His Holiness Karmapa decided that I must go to Hong Kong when he heard that there was an unbroken Chinese line of the old school.'

One of the most exhaustive academic studies of Tibetan Buddhist nuns asserts that there is 'no evidence in the textual material or from oral sources that the full ordination ever existed in Tibet' and that Tibetan nuns could only 'go forth' as novices.[13] Sister Palmo was certainly the first western Tibetan nun to take the higher, bhiksuni, ordination; she may well have been the first nun in the Tibetan tradition ever to have received this full ordination. Freda Bedi, Sister

Palmo as she had become, had crossed another border—and had taken a huge stride in advancing the recognition of and opportunities for women within Tibetan Buddhism.

When she travelled to Hong Kong in July 1972 to take her vows, she took a new gadget along with her—a cassette recorder. 'I thought I should get a little modern,' she told her family. 'Instead of writing down a letter that never seems to get written because there's too much to say, I thought I'd make this little recording to tell you what happened.' This became a family custom: Sister Palmo's cassettes recorded as she toured the world and then posted back to India. On her way to Hong Kong, she stopped in Rangoon for a couple of days—a return to the land which introduced her to the Dharma. She met both the men who had been so important in leading her to Buddhism and to advanced techniques of meditation. 'I always feel very, very close to my Burmese gurus,' she recorded, and she wanted their blessing before taking higher ordination. Mahasi Sayadaw she said 'was looking just the same, perhaps slightly thinner'. At the Shwedagon pagoda, Rangoon's main Buddhist temple, she met U Titthila, now in his mid-seventies but still with 'that same charming humour and simple way'. The country was isolated by an army-decreed form of socialism which had taken its toll. 'About Burma itself, it looked a little poorer, a little sadder I think. The people didn't give such an impression of light-heartedness as I remember before.'

After a stopover in Bangkok, she arrived in Hong Kong two days before the ceremony. She was one of thirteen Buddhists—four of them women—getting ordination at the same time. A Korean novice nun has been given the task of helping her through the various protocols and procedures. She was disconcerted to find that journalists were among the large numbers in attendance and that the ceremony was broadcast on Hong Kong television. She found the more active ceremonial involvement of devotees, a contrast to the contemplative style she was accustomed to, quite a strain. 'There is a constant bowing and kneeling, which is agonising for old knees like mine. ... I must have lost pounds in this.'

> Well, at the end of this, I was pretty tired—physically tired. But light and happy in a way that I cannot possibly explain. The effect of the whole ceremony is such that no words can express. ... It's like a stream—a stream of history. And I do feel incredibly pure ... and enriched in every way since taking the ordination.[14]

The continuity of the custom was a crucial part of its importance—the person who gives the ordination had received the same ordination in an unbroken line which is regarded as going directly back to the Buddha.

An uncomfortable part of the ritual was the little lumps of incense placed on the ordinands' shaven heads and left to burn—the resulting scar was intended as a lasting reminder of their vows.[15] 'I meditated with great concentration on the Buddha, and believe me I did not feel the burn at all after that,' Sister Palmo reassured her family. 'When they said now that's over, I just was conscious of a little soreness and the scar was not healed until about ten days after in Rumtek.'

The extraordinary achievement of Sister Palmo in achieving full ordination encouraged other western women within Tibetan Buddhism to follow her example. Tenzin Palmo (Diane Perry, as she was known when she first came out to Dalhousie to work with Freda) was ordained in Hong Kong the following year. Tibetan nuns, who faced a more daunting challenge raising the money and arranging the travel, also started making the journey to Hong Kong or Taiwan and taking bhiksuni vows. By the early years of the new century, fifty or more western Tibetan nuns had taken the higher ordination—though most lived outside monasteries and nunneries; of the smaller number of Tibetan women who followed the same path were at least eight of the nuns at Tilokpur.[16] At the time of her ordination, Sister Palmo expressed the hope that the tradition of bhiksuni ordination could be re-established in India bringing with it the prospect of a community of fully ordained Tibetan Buddhist nuns. That has not as yet been realised, but it remains a goal for many of the western women in particular who have been drawn towards Tibetan spirituality.

Before leaving Hong Kong, Sister Palmo had a look around. 'I only got two hours shopping in Hong Kong, believe it or not,' she told her family—long enough to buy a portable typewriter with money she had been given for that purpose. On her return to Rumtek, she made a point of meeting her guru. 'I went to see His Holiness and prostrated at his feet, and he was so delighted that I had been able to take the ordination.' He had just returned from neighbouring Bhutan. While she had been away, the King of Bhutan, Jigme Dirji Wangchuck, had died. This was a personal sadness for Sister Palmo. He was in his early forties and had been a benefactor of the Kagyu lineage; more than that, he had given the money for Sister Palmo's air ticket to Hong Kong.

Emboldened both by her ordination and the success of her trip to South Africa, Sister Palmo took up a new challenge—to encourage her guru to travel to the west to teach and spread the word. He was open to the prospect of travel with a religious purpose. She was convinced that there was a receptive audience; she believed that the Karmapa's warm personality would charm and engage Americans and Europeans; and she considered that she had a responsibility to promote more widely a faith which had brought her such comfort. When the spiritual tradition was under such peril inside Tibet, then the more extensively it could take root, the better the chances of its survival. Ayang Rinpoche, who was then based at Rumtek (and had been provided with a pen friend by Sister Palmo, a dentist from Santa Barbara), was present when she tried to persuade the Karmapa. She insisted that it was vital to establish Buddhist centres in western countries. He was eventually won over to the idea. 'I know this very well,' Ayang Rinpoche recalls, 'as I was a translator.'

In the autumn of 1973, the year after her full ordination, Sister

Palmo made a trip back to Britain and again stayed at the Samye Ling Buddhist centre in Scotland, which under Akong Rinpoche's leadership was developing as an outstandingly successful Tibetan Buddhist centre. And she met up with another alumni of the Young Lamas' Home School, Chime Rinpoche, who had just established the first Tibetan Buddhist centre in England near Saffron Walden, north-east of London. Alongside the impact Trungpa Rinpoche was achieving in the United States, she must have had cause to reflect with satisfaction of the achievement of those connected with her school in bringing the Dharma to the west. She lectured on Buddhism and taught meditation, and was able to renew acquaintance with old friends and make new contacts among British Buddhists. David Stott, then an undergraduate at Manchester (and now the meditation master Lama Jampa Thaye), went to a meeting that Olive Shapley held at her home at which Sister Palmo was to talk about the plight of Tibetan refugees. It didn't go quite as he'd expected. Stott was already a Buddhist—most of those present weren't, and were surprised when Sister Palmo played a tape of Tibetan Buddhist chants and offered a blessing with a reliquary she had been given by the Karmapa. Sister Palmo didn't see any boundary between her help for Tibetans in India and her promotion of Tibetan Buddhism—and she couldn't see why anyone else should be uncomfortable about the elision of the two.

On this visit, Sister Palmo was able to travel to Scandinavia and Switzerland, and called on Baba Bedi, then living and teaching in Italy. Her intention was to stimulate interest in the prospect of a visit by the Karmapa. But plans for him to come to the west remained simply an aspiration until, in November 1973, the Dharma Centre of Canada extended a formal invitation. They wanted him particularly to inaugurate a Buddhist retreat and meditation centre in Ontario. And they offered to pay for return airfares for the Karmapa 'and a full complement of attendants suitable to Your Holiness's rank, to and from Canada, including stopovers in Europe'. This was quite a commitment for an organisation which, as its treasurer lamented, had just 159 paid-up members—not all of whom responded promptly to the levy of C$100 each for the 'Karmapa Fund' to meet the cost of the visit.

The Karmapa intended to travel across the United States as well as visiting Canada and stopping over in Europe. To prepare the way, Sister Palmo made her own visit to the U.S. in the spring of 1974. She arrived in New York and flew on to Syracuse to speak at the University there, where she fell and twisted her ankle badly. Within a couple of days of arriving in the U.S. for the first time, she was on crutches. 'Perhaps I needed to be slowed down a bit,' she mused in a cassette recording posted back to India. Her tickets had been paid for by American friends and well-wishers. 'Everybody is so excited that His Holiness the Karmapa may be coming to the States in September.' She travelled relentlessly across the country, giving talks and occasional initiations and meeting up again with the poet Allen Ginsberg. In Arizona, she spent time with leaders of the Hopi community, whose spiritual beliefs and traditions were attracting wider interest and attention. She recorded on cassette a conversation with White Bear which makes uncomfortable listening, with the Hopi leader expressing stridently anti-Catholic (the Pope is 'the most wicked man') and anti-semitic views. In California, she was the guest on a New Age radio programme, 'Frontiers of Consciousness', where she spoke at length about herself, her initial engagement with Buddhism and urged wider teaching of meditation because it would 'lead to a saner people who don't crack up and go to the mental hospital and take sleeping tablets', which given her personal history is a revealing statement. It was one of the very few occasions when she sought to make a connection between her political activity decades earlier and her embrace of Buddhist teachings.

Although outwardly I was a social activist, a follower of Mahatma Gandhi and so on, inwardly this meditation idea was within me, and I was sitting alone and I used to feel that. I don't think I could have borne those years with all their difficulties and strains unless I had done so ... I think the basis of a Buddhist life, of a Dharma life as you call it, is non-violence. That was the message from Mahatma Gandhi too. The basis is not to harm others. If you harm others the law of karma comes and you yourself are harmed.[17]

Most of those who came across Sister Palmo when she was fully ordained got no sense at all of her previous political activities, and no whiff of a onetime communist allegiance, but in the narrative she rehearsed to herself her political and spiritual existences dovetailed.

The highlight of her first visit to the U.S. was a reunion with Trungpa Rinpoche. He had been through a turbulent few years since they had last met. Under his guidance, the Samye Ling centre in the Scottish Borders had developed a reputation in its early years for sex, drugs and drink ('crazy wisdom' in the indulgent view of some Buddhists) as much as pursuit of the Dharma. Trungpa gave up his monastic status and—after a bitter falling out with the more sober and sedate Akong Rinpoche—left Samye Ling, took up with a star-struck young English woman, suffered severe and lasting injuries in a car accident, emigrated to Canada with his new wife and once able to enter the U.S. established a Buddhist centre in Boulder, Colorado, in the foothills of the Rockies. His abilities as an inspiring guru and teacher were unimpaired, and he must count as the most influential Tibetan Buddhist spiritual figure to settle in North America. 'Trungpa evolved a style of teaching Buddhism that broke with the dry vocabulary of academia by employing colloquial terms and idioms with a poet's gift for metaphor,' in the judgement of a prominent historian of western Buddhism. 'He was the first Asian Buddhist teacher to plunge into the existential plight of a Western culture and to articulate a way out of that dilemma in the language of those undergoing it.'[18]

By the time Sister Palmo reunited with Trungpa Rinpoche, he had published perhaps his most influential writing, *Cutting Through Spiritual Materialism*. He was in the process of setting up an educational institute. In that summer of 1974, in the period between Sister Palmo's visit and that of the Karmapa, gatherings in an old bus depot in Boulder attracted some of the biggest names in the counter-culture. It was the founding moment of what is now Naropa University (and of the linked Jack Kerouac School of Disembodied Poetics), a liberal arts college which while not explicitly Buddhist proclaims a commitment to 'contemplative education' and enjoys a high reputation. Trungpa and his followers also established meditation centres and rural retreats in several American states and in Europe.

'This tour of America is an amazing human experience ...' Sister Palmo wrote to her husband. 'Trungpa Rinpoche has given me a great welcome. ... Trungpa in his suit and tie is different from our Tulku floating about in robes, but in essence the same.' In a cassette recorded at Boulder, she shared with her family in India a sense of her excitement at the reunion.

Of course the great interest of this tour has been to meet Trungpa Rinpoche again and all our family know he's been a lama brother of Ranga, Kabir and Guli and we've had—with Akong and Trungpa—many happy days in Moti Bagh in New Dehi when the lamas were learning English. Now Trungpa Rinpoche is a truly famous Dharma teacher in the States and he has an enormous network and projects going ... astounding when you think he's only been here for four years.[19]

At a public meeting, she was touched that Trungpa spoke about their first meeting at the Misamari refugee camp. She went to his home and met Diana, his wife, then twenty-one—'a lovely healthy English girl very like ... my niece in England'—and their two children. She reported that Trunpga 'looks well, a little heavy of course now he's in his middle thirties ... He's dressed in American dress and neat, modern, well-made dress, not at all the hippy type—in fact rather the business man variety, and still retains his great feeling for colour and texture in all he does. We had [a] long, long talk, and it really was an amazing feeling.'

Trungpa Rinpoche had been excused his 'crazy wisdom', not that his hedonism was quite as much in the past as Sister Palmo imagined. Initially, the Karmapa—communicating through Sister Palmo—had insisted that his North American tour should be planned by Namgyal Rinpoche, a Canadian convert to Buddhism, while the European leg was to be coordinated by Akong Rinpoche in Scotland. After Sister Palmo's visit, Trungpa too was brought more fully on board. He acted as American sponsor for the visit as well as helping to finance it. From Rumtek, Sister Palmo sent a series of handwritten airletters conveying the Karmapa's wishes about the itinerary. She was the lynchpin at the Karmapa's side, though the burden of making and coordinating the detailed arrangements fell mainly to Buddhist groups in the countries to be visited. In August, Sister Palmo wrote yet another letter of instructions and suggestions to Colorado. She began endearingly: 'Dear Trungpa Son'. By then, she was heading from Sikkim to Delhi to finalise visas and the Karmapa's world tour was about to start. Over the ten months between the invitation being proferred and the Karmapa's travels beginning, the scope of the trip grew incessantly. His first visit to the west became a 'world tour' on a scale more associated with rock bands than religious leaders, taking in twelve countries in North America and Europe and extending over four-and-a-half months. The Karmapa travelled with a retinue of eleven, including Sister Palmo. She was the only member of the entourage with an Indian passport; all the others used Bhutanese travel documents. Of the four first-class tickets, one was to allow a seat close to the Karmapa for the Vajra Crown, the revered, ruby-adorned, fifteenth-century artefact which took centre stage in the Black Crown ceremony. The total cost of the flight tickets exceeded C$30,000—to the relief of the Canadian Buddhists, Trungpa Rinpoche's Buddhist centre in Colorado met almost half the travel bill.

On 17th September 1974, the 16th Karmapa Lama and his entourage flew out of Calcutta en route to New York. He was beginning his tour in the country where the opportunities to reach a sympathetic audience were greatest, not least because Buddhism had already attracted a small but influential following. It was Sri Lankan Buddhism that had most influenced the American pioneers of Theosophy in the closing years of the nineteenth century. The Zen school of Buddhism was most evident in the beats' spiritual quest: three of the most important writers associated with the beat movement, Gary Snyder, Allen Ginsberg and Jack Kerouac, had come across Buddhism at the very end of the 1940s and in the 1950s, and Kerouac's 1958 classic *The Dharma Bums* is in part about his and Snyder's pursuit of Buddhist awakening and idiosyncratic practice of Buddhist ritual.

Buddhism, and Oriental spirituality more generally, became an important strand in the two US-based social movements which derived from the beats: the hippy movement, and its successor the New Age movement. It's an awkward and imprecise ancestry, but all these amorphous counter-cultural movements offered an opening for Buddhist teachings. Tibetan Buddhism was at first a minor strand within western Buddhism. *The Tibetan Book of the Dead*—a translation (with a title which Tibetans would not have recognised) of a discussion of consciousness in the period between death and rebirth—became something of a cult classic in the mid-1960s, when it was much talked about by the LSD-taking gurus of psychedelia. Trungpa Rinpoche was involved in a new translation of this work which appeared in 1975. Indeed Trungpa's own remarkable success as a Buddhist teacher and inspirational force from the start of his sojourn in North America, perhaps as much because as in spite of his own rebellious hedonism, also helped pave the way for the Karmapa.

Within days of his arrival in New York, the Karmapa performed the Black Crown ceremony 'for the first time in the Western world'. A *New York Times* reporter was among the audience at the Manhattan Center.

> The Karmapa sat on an elevated throne which was heavily decorated in colorful brocade.
>
> He was flanked by chanting monks who intoned what in effect became a plea for his blessing and an acknowledgement of misguidedness and imperfection.
>
> The ceremony reached its climax when the Karmapa placed a black crown on his head thus completing a spiritual link with his audience. After the service, he blessed those who moved forward. ...
>
> Many of the 1,000 people attending were young couples informally dressed in jeans and Indian print shirts and dresses. But the ceremony attracted an older age group as well. ... In fact the gathering in some ways resembled a congregation of New England churchgoers. A sense of community and reverence seemed to characterize the crowd, and for many it was a family affair.[20]

The attendance and level of interest was exceptional. The newspaper cited the estimate of organisers that about half those attending were Buddhists with the remainder having a definite interest in the religion's teachings. It quoted Trungpa as saying, with customary immodesty, that he had 'done the plowing' and the Karmapa was now allowing his efforts to 'blossom'.

Wherever the Karmapa travelled, 'by far the greatest impact he made on the public' was his twenty-minute performance of the Black Crown ceremony.[21] Trungpa wrote a pamphlet explaining to those new to this religious performance its meaning and ancestry. 'There is such a vital new movement in the States,' Sister Palmo wrote to Baba Bedi in Italy, 'that old religions in their Christian form have no meaning (which many of the Church people themselves recognise), there is a great deal of inter-religious fellowship among the discerning. Looking at it from the Buddhist point of view, it's fertile for the perenially new Dharma, ... not too tied to Tibetan, Japanese or any national idiom.'[22] The Karmapa delivered more than thirty lectures in North America, including three at leading Universities. In San Francisco, an array of the big figures in the beat movement came to hear him. It was another five years before the Dalai Lama came to the United States, though given his political role that was accompanied by much greater diplomatic sensitivity and importance. The more decidedly spiritual purpose of the Karmapa had been achieved. Sheila Fugard recalled that Sister Palmo emanated great happiness at the reception given to her guru; she was 'fulfilled'.[23]

After weeks of incessant travel across the United States and Canada, the Karmapa and his entourage came to Europe. Chime Rinpoche was given the task by Sister Palmo of organising a Black Crown ceremony in London for the Karmapa. 'And she was speechless with me: "my goodness, Chime, you [have] done so well. Eleven-hundred people [have] come to [the] hat ceremony, that's so good."'[24] He has no doubt about the magnitude of Sister Palmo's achievement. 'For the westerners, Dharma coming into the west, it's fantastic, extraordinary, outstanding.' The Karmapa was shown round Westminster Abbey by the Dean and attended receptions in his honour hosted by the Buddhist Society and the Tibet Society. He lectured at Cambridge and at Birmingham—Sister Palmo described this to her family as 'homeland country', not too far from Derby—and stayed at Samye Ling in Scotland. 'His Holiness has had a really triumphal progression through the west and at Samye Ling he had a quiet, rather meditative time ...' Sister Palmo reported back to India. 'Akong has managed to install a yak and the yak's wife known as the bri. Of course, the great joke among the Tibetans is the Europeans calling the Tibetan butter yak butter ... as it's really bri butter.' She took time off to visit old friends and family, including her sister-in-law. She visited her niece Pauline and family in East Kilbride. Steve Watson, Pauline's husband, recalls that she caused quite a stir with her shaven head and brown robe—'a star among the local Glaswegian children ... she had a troupe following her wherever she went.'[25] The couple travelled with Sister Palmo to Samye Ling where they were blessed by the Karmapa.

By Christmas, the Karmapa and his group were in Scandinavia—and the logistics were proving tricky. He travelled with a menagerie, including three dogs and eight huge bird-cages, which required special arrangements for their heat and light. They came south through Germany and the Netherlands, France and Switzerland to Italy, where the Karmapa and a small group of associates, Sister Palmo among them, had an audience with Pope Paul. 'It was a very memorable day. The Pope presented us all with specially inscribed medals to show that we had received a blessing.' But the pace was punishing—the Karmapa was unwell at one stage, and towards the end of the tour Sister Palmo had a bad spell of flu. She was able to stop for three days in Milan to catch up with her husband, and then after a few quiet days in Switzerland, the entourage flew back to India in early February to be in Rumtek in good time for the Tibetan New Year. There is, in Sister Palmo's recordings for her family, an exhausted exhilaration that this hugely complex and ambitious spiritual tour had been such a success.

The Karmapa clearly believed his visit had been worthwhile and had succeeded in attracting interest in and devotees to Tibetan Buddhism. He carried out two later world tours—in 1976-7, when he travelled even more extensively around Europe, and in 1980-81, which took him to South-east Asia as well as Europe and the United States. Sister Palmo did not accompany her guru on his next big tour—she probably did not have the stamina for another gruelling schedule. But after a retreat at Rumtek, she again started planning how best to promote the Dharma in the west. She had got a taste for travel and in 1976 she returned to the United States, celebrating the tenth anniversary of her initial ordination in some splendour at the Californian home of her close friend, Barbara Pettee, in San Mateo. 'Many come to the anniversary celebrations,' Sheila Fugard wrote. 'Musicians play in the garden. There is an anniversary cake with ten burning candles, one for each year of your saga as a nun. Old friends in America, new young students, Allen Ginsberg, and Lama Karma Thinley of Toronto, come to wish you well and great happiness.'[26] After brief stays in New York and London, Sister Palmo was back home by September 1976 at the close of what would prove to be her last foreign trip.

Shortly after her return to India, Sister Palmo got a letter out of the blue from the government. She was one of forty-six 'foreign women' being given an award for their outstanding services to India. It was to mark International Women's Year. The committee which conferred the award was chaired by the prime minister, Indira Gandhi. And no doubt it was meant by her as an affectionate and appropriate tribute to an old friend. Nevertheless, for Sister Palmo, to be described as 'foreign' was a kick in the teeth. She had lived in India for more than forty years; she had married an Indian and given birth to children who were unambiguously Indian; she had been jailed as an Indian nationalist; she had worked as an Indian civil servant; she travelled on an Indian passport. Kabir Bedi, sensing that his mother would feel offended, got in touch with her promptly to persuade her not to make a fuss. 'Mummy felt Indian, saw herself as Indian, and when she was offered a Distinguished Foreigner award, she was very upset,' Kabir recalls. 'She didn't see herself as a foreigner.' His intervention worked. On the back of a Tibetan prayer slip, Sister Palmo wrote a note to her son easing his concern. 'Thank you for the Cable. I am not refusing the Award, as I realise the inevitability of Govt. "categories" as I have a white skin and was born in England.'

As she mused on the award, she came to relish the idea of government recognition for her work in and for India. She shared the news with her husband, writing from Rumtek to Baba Bedi's new home in Italy.

I was frankly surprised that after my fourteen years in the mountains they had remembered me and touched too. Also delighted that FREDA BEDI has slipped so naturally into SISTER PALMO on the Indian 'scene' too, as the anomaly is that Sister Palmo is now fairly well known in the Buddhist world of the West but she has not yet settled into the consciousness of the Indian plains.

Mountains and plains are not just different terrains: they constitute two different cultures and ways of life here. Coming together of course in the New Age Crucible.[27]

She also passed on the news with some pride to Olive Chandler, though she was a touch dismissive of the citation, silver box and four volumes of Indira Gandhi's *The Spirit of India* that constituted the award. 'Something for the grandchildren,' she quipped.[28] And she dropped a line to the editor of the journal at her old Oxford college, to ensure that her old friends and contemporaries would hear of her recognition. After all, she said, 'the honour also goes to St. Hugh's!'

17

Sister and Mother

Once back in Calcutta, at her eldest son Ranga's new home, Sister Palmo embarked on telling her life story. She had become comfortable with talking into a cassette recorder, and wanted to set down on tape the story of her life in England and then in Lahore. She took the task seriously. Although she was simply speaking into the microphone, and the listener might imagine that she was ad-libbing, she prepared detailed handwritten notes stretching over dozens of sheets of paper. She didn't, however, spell out her motivation. It was perhaps prompted by her children, and with her grandchildren in mind; the recordings don't seem to have been intended for a wider audience. The Karmapa was travelling, so she had a little time. And her awareness of her age and at times failing health may also have impelled her to tell her story before it was too late. The tapes run to about three hours and cover simply the first half of her life, more-or-less up to India's independence. They are more sugar coated than the historian or biographer would wish, but they amount nevertheless to a hugely valuable resource in understanding their subject.

The cassette recordings are also a reminder that while Freda Bedi now styled herself as Sister Palmo, she was still also a mother, grandmother and—nominally at least—a wife. She had struggled at times to sustain familial bonds while becoming more immersed in spiritual life. She loved and was loved by her family, and she didn't want her renunciation of the world implicit in her vows to be seen as a repudiation of them. That was not an easy line to walk.

For ten years or so after Freda left her job with the Indian government and moved to Dalhousie, Baba Bedi lived with Raj Narindra at her home in Jangpura in south Delhi. For Raj's adopted daughter, Seerat—she was the daughter of Raj's nephew and adopted informally within the extended family—Baba was a father figure. While growing up, she was closer to him than to her mother. 'For me as a girl, everything Mummy would say no to, he would say yes. He used to play with me, all the fun things. If Mummy was strict he would give leeway, saying: "Go on—don't tell Mummy!" Baba-ji was like my guardian. He looked after my interests with my school, with any problems I had with teachers. He gave me strength to be vocal when I needed to.'[1] It was in some ways an unconventional household. Seerat recalls that Bedi would on occasion bring over Sufi qawwali singers from the Nizamuddin shrine to perform. Saba Dewan, Binder's daughter, got the impression that 'Bedi had a court, a durbar, an open house. I remember as a young girl seeing my first set of nautch [dancing] girls in the Jangpura house.'[2] Baba Bedi had no regular work or income and would often spend the summers in the hills, occasionally visiting Freda in Dalhousie and on at least one occasion returning to Kashmir. There was a self-aggrandising aspect to his promotion of the occult and the mystical, but he still had personal warmth and a convincing way with words.

In 1972, Baba Bedi headed to Italy where he believed there might be more interest in his healing and psychic powers. Raj and Seerat went to visit him, spending two months in Rome and Milan. Bedi liked Italy, made friends there and found a receptive audience for his idiosyncratic style of spirituality. In style and appearance, he was what many in the west expected of an Indian guru. Freda, now Sister Palmo, stayed in touch, sending letters and other tokens of friendship. 'HAPPY BIRTHDAY Ever respected and dear Babaji,' she said in birthday wishes posted from Johannesburg, where she was on her first Dharma tour. In a later letter, she concluded: 'Love to Seerat and Raj too.' Seerat Narindra spent three years as a college

student in Italy. Raj visited on occasions too. The affinity between
Baba and Freda, husband and wife, remained. Freda visited Milan
several times, staying with Baba on at least one occasion. It was at
times perplexing to hear a nun speak of her husband, and perhaps
that—as much as a growing gap between them—explains the one
time Sister Palmo talked of 'my former husband' in a radio interview
a year before she died.[3]

Kabir recalls that even when, after his mother's death, Baba
married again, 'there was a huge photograph, of my mother in the
sitting room right opposite where he sat … I feel that the bond
was more than physical, there was a kind of spiritual bond that they
had, and each had enormous respect for the journey of the other.'
Baba Bedi's second wife, Antonia Chiappini, was much younger
than him. They collaborated together on spiritual ventures, notably
in establishing the Istituto di Pedagogica Acquariana which still
exists in Cittadella in Padua. Seerat spent some time there though
she found some of the adherents to be 'strange and weird'. Although
Baba became increasingly frail, aggravating an old back injury which
meant that he was often confined to a wheelchair, he wrote tracts
and spiritual guides which were published by the Centre in Italian.
He was styled 'Baba Bedi XVI' somewhat in the Papal fashion, as
the sixteenth generation of descendants of the founder of the Sikh
religion. Baba's marriage to Antonia didn't go down too well with his
children and it was even more negatively received by Raj. 'When my
father married my step-mother, Auntie Raj was livid,' Guli recalls.
'I had to tell Raj my father had married Antonia. I stopped seeing
Raj, because it was verbal diarrhoea.' Baba visited India for the last
time in 1993 and died shortly after returning to Italy—prompting
an acrimonious dispute between his widow and his children about
the disposal of his ashes.

Ranga Bedi was well established in his career as a tea planter,
married and with children by the time his mother took her vows as
a nun. She came to visit at the estate in Upper Assam, sometimes

with an entourage of monks. Labour relations on the tea gardens were at times menacingly turbulent. Ranga's first spell as an acting estate manager came when his English boss, having survived an assassination attempt, understandably took leave at short notice. Ranga got a message early one morning that his mother, in her robes, was at the nearby railway station. Ranga drove there to discover that she was accompanied by four monks. She said that her son's life was in danger and she had come to purify the site. For two days, she and the monks—much to Ranga's embarrassment—prayed in the home and the estate's tea factory, scattering rice as part of the purification.

Sister Palmo sought to be an attentive grandmother, as much as her spiritual life allowed. In her cassettes posted home, she included endearing messages for Ranga's daughters and word of the books and presents she was bringing back for them. 'Sohni darling,' she recorded in a message to her granddaughter, 'I've bought a beautiful book for you which your father used to love and we used to read it out loud as a family when we were in Kashmir. It's called *Wind in the Willows*.'⁴ For Sohni's sister, Ami, she had bought a book by Tolkein. And on the same cassette, she recounted how she had gone into a music shop in London to buy something for Kabir and found 'a very pleasant looking record … by Van Morrison called "Veedon Fleece", and this is it … it's a change from Christmas carols'—and then she recorded several minutes of the album.

In the letters that she wrote to British family and friends in particular, her pride in her children is evident. She recited all the landmarks and achievements of their lives, and particularly of Kabir's movie career. 'Keep your eyes open for Indian films in Derby or East Kilbride—', she told her niece, Pauline Watson, 'Kabir is a leading film star now!' She also touched on her anxieties, but at no time was there any hint that she found her religious vocation a hindrance to being there for her family. There were clearly occasions when her children faced crises in their lives without their mother to hand. If they resented her absence, they did so silently; if she at moments regretted the distance from her children, she didn't openly acknowledge it.

Kabir Bedi was still a college-going teenager when his mother put on the nun's robes. As a student, he broke a bone in his back which extended his college education by a year and gave him an opportunity to get involved in modelling, drama and moonlighting as an announcer on All India Radio. This was his way in to a career as an actor, indeed a star of film and TV. He has always seen himself unequivocally as Indian, but he owes his striking good looks in generous measure to his English mother. And he has succeeded not simply in Bollywood but in what might be described as 'crossover' roles, including as the villain Gobinda in the 1983 James Bond movie 'Octopussy', and achieving particular acclaim—by coincidence—in his father's adopted country of Italy, in the lead role of the pirate Sandokan in the TV series of that name.

In late 1960s India, Kabir Bedi raised eyebrows by living openly with his girlfriend, the model (and later a distinguished Odissi dancer) Protima Gupta, then a tempestuous teenager. He had broken off another romance to take up with Protima; his mother was anguished. 'You are a man now and it is hard for me to sit in judgement and tell you what to do,' she wrote, before offering the sort of parental advice that she could have received from her own mother a generation earlier. 'Marriage is for the procreation of children and their care in the years before they grow up. Just that …' she counselled.

A girl's great treasure is her virginity: a man's his pure body which can father perfect children. The companionship of a wife who has spiritual understanding is another treasure which can bring life through its varying phases. Love has got other meanings, as you know, than the love of those beginning life. Companionship grows with the years. Papa and I can say that.[5]

Kabir and Protima married in October 1969 in a fashion that borrowed something from his mother's influence—Buddhist monks performed the ceremony and she gave a blessing. 'It was a simple Buddhist ceremony: just chanting and incense,' the couple said in a printed card announcing their marriage. 'There will be no reception, no presents, no damn dowry. Just register your shock / disapproval / joy the next time you see us.' It's difficult to be sure where on that scale Freda stood. She once mentioned in a letter to her niece in Britain, in words capable of more than one meaning, that she was in Bombay and 'staying with Kabir and his modern little wife Protima. She's such a frank, lively girl and there's a very pleasant atmosphere in the flat.'[6]

The first of the couple's two children, Pooja, was born the year after their marriage. In June 1971, Protima—now pregnant again—took the baby with her to visit Sister Palmo at the Rumtek monastery, who followed up with a long, mildly admonishing, letter to her son.

> Protima has been telling me of your mental conflicts, and the wish to stop too many children in the modern way. Kabir dear, that's not the Buddhist way, or the Bedi way, or the Guru way, or the spontaneous way. … I have said a lot of things verbally to Protima that I do not wish to write down: the yogic way of control will give you beautiful children, but not too many …[7]

She clearly relished the visit and regretted that Kabir didn't accompany his wife and daughter. 'Getting to know that beautiful being called Puja, and getting to know Protima in a relaxed way has been infinitely worthwhile,' she wrote. 'I only hope this will only be the first of many family visits.' And she sent Kabir what could be described as a relic or amulet, ascribed with medicinal properties.

> I am sending you a tiny bit of the robe of the last Karmapa … Keep it near you. In case of any bad headache or mind suffering, you can take out a few strands and burn it, and inhale the smoke.

No one could accuse Sister Palmo of inattentiveness to her family's needs. Kabir and Protima's marriage broke up in 1974. That same year Protima Bedi had attracted huge attention by streaking naked along Juhu beach, apparently to promote the launch of a new movie magazine. 'There's a limit to what any man can stand,' Sister Palmo wrote to her husband about the break-up. 'I think the Bedi family can't stand it too.'[8] Kabir says that he had his mother's strong support in leaving his wife as 'she knew how upset I'd been by Protima's behaviour for years.'

The loyalty which Sister Palmo showed to Kabir and the pride in his film career was reciprocated. Kabir says he felt closer to his mother than to his father, and while all three children have gone some way along their mother's spiritual path, Kabir has perhaps pursued it furthest. 'She shared a lot with me, more than with the rest of the family,' Kabir recalls. He lived for fifteen years in California, which was in part a spiritual quest. 'I explored various belief systems, from American Indian retreats, to Sufi masters, to J. Krishnamurti in his Ojai centre, to the New Age prophets like SETH (Jane Roberts channelled him), RAMTHA, another channelling, plus many of the Zen masters like Alan Watts, and many of the off shoots of New Age movements like EST and the PRIMAL SCREAM.'[9] Both Kabir and Ranga kept in touch with several of the Tibetan lamas who had been associates of their mother.

Gulhima was hit hardest by her mother's ordination and the break-up of the family home. She had been at boarding school from a tender age, and while she had spent long holidays with the family in Delhi, she had much less experience of the Bedis as a family. Guli was just twelve when her mother headed to Dalhousie (she had the chance of moving to a school there but declined) and sixteen when she became a nun. Her father, who was generous, impulsive and reckless, was living with another woman—and while Guli was welcome at their home, there was another girl there, a few years younger, who also had a claim on her father's attention. And there were other women. Guli recalls the awkward occasion when her father brought an unfamiliar woman to visit—'an attractive Italian woman, and he brought her up to my school. I felt embarrassed.' But Guli believes that the mutual esteem between her parents persisted. 'My father never flaunted the women in front of my mother. He respected her deeply and I do believe he loved her dearly and she him. It was what it was.'

When not at school or college, Guli increasingly spent time with Ranga and his wife Umi and with Kabir. Her older brothers had at times to navigate a path between a teenage girl keen on more independence and a conservative-minded mother who was not at hand but who did not intend to relinquish her parental role. At one point, Kabir, who was only three years his sister's senior, got a note in which his mother unburdened herself about the freedoms her daughter was seeking and more generally the path that her own life had taken.

> Strictly between us.
>
> I still think I was right in refusing to let Guli go to the school social. In fact I think the school is wrong in getting 14-year-olds interested in such things. Even by Western standards it is too young. ... It is bound to lead, in such immature minds, not to immorality but to silly or rather premature emotional 'crushes' and attachments which may again lead to a lot of frustration and unhappiness. ...

'Guli has developed a certain stubborn way,' she complained, without any apparent awareness of her own strong sense of resolve. Sister Palmo's letter was written a couple of years before her ordination, but when she had already moved to Dalhousie. She pleaded for Kabir's understanding, sharing with him a narrative of how her absorption in Buddhism necessarily changed her style of life and engagement with her children.

You more than any other member of the family understand what my life is now. For years, it has been slowly growing into a life where the spiritual side is dominant ... it began when I too was a teenager and used to slip away into the Church to sit quietly for hours (the beginning of meditation); later during all my busy public life I would meditate (a sort of yoga), and concentrate, even when outwardly leading a different life, even in jail. With the finding of the Buddhist path in this life (although I know I have followed it for countless lives) there was side by side with my Gov[ernmen]t work and responsibilities, an unswerving effort to learn more of the inner path. Visits to Burma, the meetings with great Maha Theras [long-serving monks] and Lamas, including His Holiness. Now these seeds have flowered, and this life in a series of stages, has reached the 'point of no return'. I cannot take up work and responsibilities in Delhi, be an ordinary and normal housewife and mother to Guli ... in any case, I had been living like a lay nun for so many years now (over 10 years).

That does not mean I can no longer love Guli and work for her as a Mother—only that deep though she is in this heart, it has opened to include all beings.[10]

A dispute about an issue which was almost trivial prompted Sister Palmo to set down in writing the tension she felt between her life as a Sister and a mother.

Sister Palmo's renunciation of the world, and resignation from her government job, brought about another problem for Guli in particular. The family had no money. Baba Bedi was hardly in a position to make good the shortfall. This meant another call on Ranga's income in particular and in some ways he became the head of the family. Their mother called in all the favours she could. Indira Gandhi paid the fairly modest fees for Guli to attend Miranda House, one of the more prestigious of Delhi's women's colleges. In 1971, Guli married Shakti Maira, an artist. Their second child was born in Bombay just three days before Sister Palmo's death. 'My mother was adamant about being with me, so my mother and I got to see a lot of each other in those days before her death,' Guli recalls. 'As it turned out it was a complicated birth and my mother was in meditation outside the delivery room.'

Alongside her family, Sister Palmo attracted the loyalty and devotion of those embarked on a spiritual quest who were won over by her personal example and generosity and the deep faith that she was so keen to share. Most, but by no means all, of these men and women who came to regard Sister Palmo as their guru were westerners. Several came across her by chance. Anderson Bakewell, an American-born musicologist and entrepreneur, got to know Ranga and Kabir while working on Carnatic music and occasionally as an extra on films and TV. He travelled to Rumtek to meet their mother. 'Her eyes were the most remarkable thing. Her eyes were like they were turned on their side—so wide and brilliant and blue just like an ocean. You could look at them forever. ... I saw for the first time in my life someone who was awake—everybody else was sleepwalking. ... It was a bit like falling in love, to be in her presence.'[11] He was impressed by her elevated position in the monastery. 'They are very hierarchical, the Tibetans—and she was at the top of the monastery, and only the Karmapa was above her. ... The room was very simple; small, simple, with very few personal possessions. Books were piled all over.' In the weeks Bakewell spent at Rumtek, he was struck by the spiritual affinity between Sister Palmo and the Karmapa. 'She was in a way the Karmapa's consort—the two were very very close. I suspect that might be a bit difficult for Tibetans.' A year later, Bakewell met Sister Palmo again—in California. 'That was a real opportunity to be close to her all the time. She had given me a lot of things to study—prayers and pujas. Her teachings and initiations were very important. She was given some very high initiations.' He's clear about Sister Palmo's central role in introducing Tibetan belief to new audiences. 'She wasn't a missionary, more of an architect. She was the architect of Tibetan Buddhism in the west—she put into place all the components. It wasn't a mission; it was her devotion and enthusiasm.'

Jim Robinson first came across Sister Palmo as a teenager in Assam. His family were tea planters and good friends of Ranga Bedi and his wife, Umi. He recalls meeting Sister Palmo for the first time at Ranga's bungalow—and indeed knew her by the family nickname, Ooggee. 'She was bald, obviously, with saffron robes, with lunette glasses—and she was reading *Vogue* magazine, which I thought was a bit odd.' It was one of Umi's magazines—and her mother-in-law, who after all once was involved with a women's magazine largely about lifestyle, was intrigued. Robinson was still at school and developing an interest in Hinduism. 'She gave me *Jonathan Livingston Seagull*. She literally had it with her and gave it to me as: you will read this because it will help you understand Buddhism—and maybe will turn you away from Hinduism. It was like trying to direct me in a certain way.'[12] She took an interest in his academic as well as spiritual potential, giving him the confidence to strive and eventually pursue research into Indian religions. She peppered him with notes about people he must meet at Oxford and prayers and pamphlets that he should sell to raise money for Tibetan religious institutions. Robinson was involved, a few years after Sister Palmo's death, in the re-establishing of the Oxford University Buddhist Society, an important step in Oxford's engagement with Buddhist practice and research—he sees this as part of her indirect legacy. If she was insistent in her manner, it was—Robinson says—because of the certainty of her conviction and belief. 'I've met very few what I would call "holy" people and she definitely fitted that category. And I don't know how one can explain that, but being in the presence you did feel that you were very special. She made you feel special pretty much instantly.'

Not all those who came across Sister Palmo, who liked her and shared her faith, are as fulsome in their assessment. Lama

Shenpen Hookham, another English woman who had taken ordination within Tibetan Buddhism, did not regard Sister Palmo as particularly enlightened. 'She would come out with statements very authoritatively that were clearly wrong. ... It just felt to me that she didn't have those qualities I was looking for, like a real openness and a real lack of egocentricity.'[13] Hookham was not convinced that Sister Palmo had sufficient spiritual understanding for some of the exacting teaching she undertook. 'I remember one time, she said she was going to South Africa: "and I'm going to be teaching." And I said: "oh, what are you teaching?" And she said "maha mudra." Now the way I've been trained, you don't just teach maha mudra, that is something you would have to realise. And I made some comment to that effect, I think, and she said: "oh, you just do your best" ... in this very, I suppose, mem-sahiby way ... I didn't feel she was very rigorous.' Lama Jampa Thaye, another English convert who came across Sister Palmo and who has become an eminent Buddhist and teacher of meditation, also has reservations about her spiritual authority. 'She was not a great scholar and never very learned,' he says. 'She was in the lowly foothills of western Buddhism—and that's no criticism. Her goodness of heart, and the goodness she did for the Tibetans, that's impossible to deny.'[14]

Among Tibetan lamas, particularly those in the Kagyu lineage with their intense loyalty to the 16th Karmapa Lama, any criticism is muted. The main misgiving, though often recounted with a smile, is about her bossiness, which made her at times a scary and forbidding figure for erring young tulkus. More generally, there is a deep gratitude for the personal support she gave to Tibetan spirituality, and to the lamas and nuns who practised it; for the advocacy and fundraising she undertook with such success; and for the clear-headed way she cajoled and encouraged the Sangha, Buddhist clerics, to adapt to exile and to reach out to the west. They express respect more than reverence.

18

Postscript

Sister Palmo had—in a phrase widely used by her fellow Buddhists—a 'good' death. She died suddenly in Delhi in March 1977 at the age of sixty-six. 'She was fully prepared,' says Anderson Bakewell, one of her devotees. She had been guided by a Tibetan lama considered a master of phowa, a meditative practice intended to aid the transference of consciousness at the time of death. Sister Palmo had entered her sixties in generally good health and had suffered no life-threatening illnesses since her childhood bout of diptheria. But there were warning signs. As a nun, her lifestyle was sedentary. She had shared with her husband a healthy appetite. Even in nun's robes, when she had the chance, she ate with a determination which astonished some of those accompanying her. For much of her life, she had been on the lean side; not any longer. Early in 1976, she wrote to Baba Bedi in Milan in the aftermath of what clearly had been a spell of poor health: 'Since I came to Rumtek the healing "vibes" of [His Holiness Karmapa] have completed the healing process and I am 90% back to normal—about 10% of stamina missing, but at 65 … you can't altogether expect to be the same as at 25.'[1]

There was a serious underlying health condition. She had a heart problem. Sheila Fugard met up with Sister Palmo in California in 1976 and could tell at a glance that she was ill.[2] Sister Palmo made light of the condition, writing to Olive Chandler on her return to India: 'My bronchial heart complaint seems very very much better with good Californian medicine.'[3] She looked forward to returning to California—'as long as health and strength lasts, this could be a yearly routine'—but she never made it there again and within a few months her weak heart had killed her.

In March 1977, Sister Palmo came to Delhi for an international Buddhist symposium. She stayed in a suite at the Intercontinental as a guest of her friend Goodie Oberoi, whose family ran the hotel. On the evening of 26th March, a Saturday, she had guests until about 9:30 in the evening and then went to bed, according to an account Ranga Bedi put together and sent as a cassette to his father. A few minutes later, Anila Pema Zangmo, who was staying in the same room, heard what she described as hiccups. Sister Palmo was rubbing her chest and complaining of a pain. Pema Zangmo left the room to get help and returned with two hotel guests. She found Sister Palmo sitting in the lotus position with her face glowing. Pema Zangmo saw this as a sign that Sister Palmo was in samadhi, in limbo as an awakened Buddhist making the transition away from this world. She was adamant that the nun's body should be left undisturbed, while the guests were determined to give a chest massage to see if Sister Palmo could be revived. Pema Zangmo started screaming that the samadhi must not be interrupted; the guests didn't understand—and it seems that the attendant nun was bundled out of the way. When a doctor reached the room, at about 10:30, he confirmed that Sister Palmo was dead.

The body was taken to Binder Dewan's home in Nizamuddin East, just a few minutes' drive from the hotel. Binder's daughter Saba says that Sister Palmo had been to their home earlier that day. 'The morning she died, she had visited the house and brought a polka dot halter top for me, I thought it was very daring. I remember that very vividly.'[4] On that same day an old friend, Tara Ali Baig, had called on her at the hotel. 'She looked wan and tired that day, but talked of friends and associates with such intensity, it was as though, in the brief span of an hour, she had to encompass a lifetime.'[5] Nathan

Katz, an American academic who was speaking at the symposium, had a long talk with Sister Palmo during the day. 'We had made plans to have lunch the next day. I gave my talk, and when I showed up at the conference the next day, I learned that she had died overnight. ... I went to a viewing and she was lying on a block of ice to prevent decay, and then the monks chanted "anicca, anicca, anicca" ("impermanence, impermanence, impermanence").'[6]

Many people from different stages of her life were at hand for a final meeting, or to mourn her passing. Olive Shapley had been in Delhi a few days earlier. Som Anand, a colleague from Lahore days, came round to Binder's home to pay his respects. It was, he reflected sadly, 'as if another link with the Lahore of pre-partition days had been snapped'.[7] He was astonished to see there another of the old Lahore circle, the poet Hafeez Jullundhri, who happened to be visiting from Pakistan; he was 'sitting there with sorrow writ large on his face and talking of the old days'.

Early on Sunday morning, Ranga flew in to Delhi from Calcutta and Kabir and his partner Parveen Babi took a flight from Bombay. They went straight to Binder's home to say their farewells. 'We saw her in utter tranquillity with lots of flowers and fragrance all around,' Ranga reported to his father. Kabir went to the symposium venue to share the news. Those attending rose in prayer and then adjourned. Many came to pray alongside the body. The family was faced with an urgent decision: where to have the cremation. The Karmapa Lama, who was visiting Canada, asked that the body be taken to his monastery at Rumtek in Sikkim. That was an arduous journey by air and road at a time of year when the weather was getting hot. What's more, the monks insisted that the body should not be embalmed. Ranga and Kabir decided to take up Goodie Oberoi's offer to hold the cremation in the grounds of her farmhouse on the outskirts of Delhi.

On Monday morning, Ranga recorded, 'we adorned Ooggee in the finest of her robes, the robe of the Gelongma [fully ordained nun], the ordination she brought to His Holiness Karmapa's monastery.' Buddhist monks from several countries chanted as Sister Palmo's body was consigned to the flames. With hindsight, Ranga regretted the decision not to take the body to Rumtek. 'One makes mistakes in life,' he told his father, 'and I know realising the ignorance of mortal beings, material beings, like us, His Holiness will forgive us for what we have done in cremating Ooggee's mortal remains at Delhi.' Kabir, accompanied by Anila Pema Zangmo, carried the ashes to Rumtek, where forty-nine days of prayers requested by the Karmapa were already underway.

Pema Zangmo was convinced that Sister Palmo knew the date of her death three months ahead of time. In an account that she set down a couple of years after the death, she told a story fitting the stylised account of the passing of a spiritually realised Buddhist. 'Many persons saw together with me the rainbows which were around her.'[8] Some other accounts suggest phenomena at the time of her death and cremation which defy conventional explanation. Whether or not these are literal, verifiable accounts, they were believed by those who recounted them, and seen as a reflection of the great faith of the woman whose death was the occasion of such signs of holiness.

Of the reflections and reminiscences prompted by Sister Palmo's death those of the veteran leftist Som Anand stand out, because of his evident disappointment at the turn her life took. As he looked on at Freda Bedi's body, 'her voice kept ringing in my ears, the voice which gave hope to so many troubled souls'—yet her turn towards religion, he believed, gave 'an impression that salvation could be obtained only by running away from one's real work in life.'

But it was not Freda Bedi's body which was lying there; it was Sister Palmo who had died. Freda Bedi had in fact taken leave of us many years earlier when she shaved off her head [sic], donned a monk's cloak and went to a Buddhist monastery ...

Despite all this, I could only remember her as a writer, social worker, an eminent public figure and, above all, a Communist intellectual. It may be odd to remember a person as a Marxist who had distinguished herself in the field of spiritual pursuits. She, in fact, did not want to be reminded about her association with the Communists. But the past cannot be erased and no one who knew her in the pre-partition days can forget that she was a prominent figure in the leftist circles of Lahore.[9]

He saw Freda's 'drift towards spiritualism' as an 'escape from the disappointments' she faced in her life and as 'a total loss for the good work she could have done for the welfare of the underprivileged.'

Som Anand's resentment that his old friend turned away from her youthful political certainties was clearly heartfelt, but unwarranted. She did 'good work' in greater measure as a Buddhist than as a leftist. Her involvement in Tibetan Buddhism was much longer and deeper than her embrace of communism. From her youth, her anger at social injustice and quest for spiritual enlightenment went hand-in-hand, though the balance between the two changed markedly in different phases of her life. Her own writings offer little to suggest an intellectual commitment to Marxism, and given her devotion to Tibetan Buddhism, a spiritual tradition which China's communists had tried brutally to erase, it's not hard to see why towards the end of her life any suggestion that she had been a fellow traveller would be so toxic.

Among her children and grandchildren, there is an evident pride in Freda, and her rich and transgressive life as well as the spiritual path she pursued in her last two decades. Ranga keeps an ecumenical prayer room in his home in Bangalore, which is akin to a shrine to both his parents. Kabir and Guli keep their mother's memory alive in other ways. All talk of their mother as a continuing presence in their lives. Kabir has at various times toyed with the idea of making a film about his mother's life. In the 1980s, he drew up a proposal to produce 'Lady of the Lotus'. Rumer Godden, a British novelist who knew Freda in Kashmir, was interested in writing the screenplay. The idea hasn't entirely gone away.

As someone who straddled so many of the fault lines which define identity, there is always a suspicion that the 'real' Freda Bedi may not have been the one on public display. The repeated description of her as a mem-sahib—the privileged English woman transplanting her values, customs and authority to India—poses a question about Freda's centre of gravity. It's not one that would have worried her much. She had something of the haughtiness, the imperiousness and the establishment accent, which were markers of the mem-sahib. She also relished some residual aspects of the culture she had left behind. 'She revelled in her English heritage and celebrated Christmas every year, though not as a religious festival,' her daughter recalls. 'She was a wonderful baker and we always had a Christmas tree. We had English trifle every Christmas.' Her imperfect grasp of Hindi, colloquial but with an accent Guli describes as 'awful', fitted the same mould. 'I once said to her: "Why do you say Ka-bee-yar when it's Ka-beer?" She replied: "Why didn't anyone tell me, dear?" She pronounced words incorrectly, but nobody ever told her.' Yet in contrast to the typical mem-sahib, Freda made a life-long commitment to India, embraced its religions, culture and language, and far from being an apologist for Empire, she was a loud and brave critic. Everyone was clear where her loyalities lay. 'My mother had a very profound sense of her English roots and she was proud of them,' Guli says. 'But she adopted India. My mother always revelled in the fact that she married an Indian and totally immersed herself in another culture. She made it her own. I think it must have been very difficult at times—but she never complained about it as far as I remember.'

All of Freda and Baba's children—except of course Tilak, who died so young—were able to mark the fortieth anniversary of their mother's death. None of her adopted children could do so. Berinder 'Binder' Dewan died in 1989 aged fifty-seven. Freda's two tulku 'sons' died in tragic circumstances. The mercurial Trungpa Rinpoche died in hospital in Canada in 1987 while still in his forties. Akong Rinpoche, who ran the Samye Ling Buddhist centre in Scotland and established the Tibetan humanitarian charity Rokpa, met a violent death in October 2013 while visiting China.

Sister Palmo's guru, the 16th Karmapa Lama, Rangjung Rigpe Dorje, died in November 1981 in the small town of Zion in Illinois while on another Dharma tour. He was fifty-seven. The search for the new incarnation of the Karmapa occasioned one of the most unseemly disputes within Tibetan Buddhism. Ogyen Trinley Dorje, at the time a seven-year-old living in Tibet, was recognised by a search party as the new incarnation, and he was eventually accepted as such by the Dalai Lama. At the age of fourteen, the new Karmapa escaped from Tibet through Nepal into India. But the identity of the new Karmapa is contested. The other candidate is Trinley Thaye Dorje, accepted by some of the most senior lamas in the Kagyu lineage. He also as a youngster escaped from Tibet to India. Most of the lamas and tulkus who were close to Freda recognise the Karmapa accepted by the Dalai Lama. Anila Pema Zangmo, however, does not. She visited the supposed new incarnation in Tibet when he was a child and was immediately convinced that he was not the Karmapa. She is close to the other claimant. One of the saddest aspects of the controversy has been the tension and indeed punch-ups between rival camps of monks at Rumtek. Neither candidate has been enthroned there, and the monastery's role as the seat of the Kagyu tradition is in abeyance.

There is no simple answer as to whether, in the view of Tibetan Buddhists, Sister Palmo has been reborn. Two high lamas have suggested that their daughters are the new incarnation. The family says it awaits a decision by the 17th Karmapa. Tenzin Palmo, another English convert to Tibetan Buddhism, has commented: 'This may be the only occasion of a Westerner taking rebirth as a Tibetan tulku, as opposed to a Tibetan lama being reborn as a Westerner.'[10]

Freda Bedi—crossing borders to the last.

Notes

1. The Suicide Club

1. 'Birth and School', audio recording made by Freda Bedi c1976, Bedi Family Archive (BFA)
2. 'Birth and School', BFA
3. 'Birth and School', BFA
4. 'Oxford', audio recording made by Freda Bedi c1976, BFA
5. *Derby Daily Telegraph*, 18 December 1928
6. 'Oxford', BFA
7. Sheila Fugard, *Lady of Realisation: A Spiritual Memoir*, Bloomington, Indiana, 2012, p32
8. Audio recording of Freda Bedi's interview on the radio programme 'Frontiers of Consciousness', San Mateo, California, April 1974, BFA
9. Freda Houlston to Olive Chandler, 11 September 1931, BFA

2. The Gates of the World

1. 'Oxford' audio recording made by Freda Bedi c1976, Bedi Family Archive (BFA)
2. Tim Richardson, *Oxford College Gardens*, London, 2015, p236.
3. Laura Schwartz, *A Serious Endeavour: Gender, Education and Community at St Hugh's, 1886-2011*, London, 2011, pp147-153
4. Schwartz, *A Serious Endeavour*, p156
5. Barbara Castle, *Fighting All the Way*, London, 1992, p48
6. Olive Shapley, *Broadcasting a Life: The Autobiography of Olive Shapley*, London, 1996, p25

7. Castle, *Fighting All the Way*, pp46-7

8. Shapley, *Broadcasting a Life*, p23

9. Castle, *Fighting All the Way*, p49. There were twenty shillings to the Pound, so six shillings would be the equivalent of £0.30. Olive Shapley also recounts this episode and recalls that Barbara tested her friends on the book 'which was delightfully typical of her'—*Broadcasting a Life*, pp26-7

10. Anne Perkins, *Red Queen: The Authorised Biography of Barbara Castle*, London, 2003, pp21-2

11. Shapley, *Broadcasting a Life*, p24

12. *The Imp*, March 1930, St Hugh's College archive

13. 'Oxford' audio recording, BFA

14. Shapley, *Broadcasting a Life*, pp29, 25

15. Shapley, *Broadcasting a Life*, pp25-6

16. Freda Bedi handwritten notes apparently in preparation for making audio recordings about her life story, BFA

17. I am particularly grateful to Amanda Ingram, the archivist at St Hugh's College, for sending me copies of Freda's tutors' reports. In later life, Freda herself blamed her disappointing degree on an interruption in her studies occasioned by ill health, though she took some comfort that Nehru also got a third class honours degree. She wrote to her son Kabir, who faced a similar break in his college career: 'It isn't easy to get a good Division when you drop a year—rather like the kettle going off the boil. It happened in my case too: only I got a Royal Third as Panditji put it. (He also got the same!!)'

18. Freda Houlston, 'The Reality of Oxford', *Calcutta Review*, 1933, pp95-99. Established in 1844, the *Calcutta Review* was one of India's most venerated periodicals and between the wars it was an influential platform for Indian nationalism.

19. 'Oxford' audio recording, BFA

20. Castle, *Fighting All the Way*, p47

21. Shapley, *Broadcasting a Life*, p26. Her account is echoed—though without the reference to a mental hospital—in Castle, *Fighting All the Way*, p47

22. Sumita Mukherjee, *Nationalism, Education and Migrant Identities: The England-returned*, Abingdon, 2010, pp22-26. Shapley, *Broadcasting a*

Life, p26. Olive Shapley could have added that the Indian students at Oxford were overwhelmingly men—Freda appears not to have had any Indian student contemporaries at St Hugh's.

23. D.F. Karaka, *All My Yesterdays*, Bombay, 1944, pp8-9. The article appeared in the left-wing *Daily Herald* in 1934.

24. *Oxford Mail*, 22 January 1934

25. *United India*, June 1932

26. *Bharat*, January 1931

27. D.F. Karaka, *The Pulse of Oxford*, London, 1933, pp35-36

28. Castle, *Fighting All the Way*, p47

29. Shapley, *Broadcasting a Life*, p26

30. It is likely that Olive Shapley was in some measure a model for one of the characters in Zaheer's fiction. *A Night in London* is a novella, first published in Urdu in 1938 though written some years earlier, about Indian student life in London (where Zaheer studied law after his Oxford years). One of the most intriguing characters is Sheila Green, an intelligent and cultured Englishwoman with a fascination for India who falls in love with an Indian student to be forsaken by him for India and its national cause. Sajjad Zaheer, *A Night in London*, translated by Bilal Hashmi, Noida, 2011. This volume also includes a note by Carlo Coppola about Zaheer, and a translation of part of Zaheer's memoirs.

31. *Isis*, 1 June 1932

32. Shapley, *Broadcasting a Life*, pp28-9

33. Geoff Andrews, *The Shadow Man: At the Heart of the Cambridge Spy Circle*, London, 2015, pp36-41. Security service papers relating to Frank Strauss Meyer, KV2/3501, National Archive.

34. Francois Lafitte papers, US72: box 37, Cadbury Research Library, University of Birmingham. Lafitte's remarkable list of more than eighty names of fellow Oxford student communists and other documents and subsequent correspondence with MI5 are not available in the National Archive but are included in his personal papers. I am very grateful to Nicholas Deakin for permission to consult this normally 'closed' part of the Lafitte papers. Lafitte muddled many of the names of his former comrades. Freda Houlston is recorded as 'Freda Corbett'—the name of a right-wing Labour politician of the time—but there's no doubt which Freda he meant. Similarly, Zaheer's first name is given as 'Mumtaz'

rather than Sajjad. The other Indian communist mentioned is Gopal Kumaramangalam.

[35.] The Communist Party did, however, set up a student network, and from the mid-1930s—when international communism moved into its Popular Front period and abandoned sectarianism—was conspicuously successful in attracting student adherents, particularly at Oxford, Cambridge, the London School of Economics and University College, London.

[36.] V.K. Krishna Menon (ed.), *Young Oxford and War*, London, [1934], pp82-3.

[37.] Michael Foot, 'Oxford and Politics', *Cherwell*, 14 October 1933.

[38.] 'Oxford' audio recording, BFA

[39.] M.R. Masani, *The Communist Party of India: A Short History*, New York, 1954, p47.

[40.] B.P.L. Bedi interview transcript, Nehru Memorial Museum and Library (NMML), f31

[41.] A.G. Noorani, 'A Versatile Communist', *Frontline* (Chennai), 10 August 2012—an article consisting of extracts from an oral history interview with Sajjad Zaheer held at the Nehru Memorial Museum and Library in Delhi.

[42.] B.P.L. Bedi interview transcript, NMML, f52

[43.] B.P.L. Bedi interview transcript, NMML, f39

[44.] B.P.L. Bedi interview transcript, NMML, f285

[45.] Ganga Das, 'Indian Politics in London', *Hindustan*, December 1933.

[46.] India Office Records L/PJ/12/252, ff5-6. This file includes the only copy of *Bharat* located, for January 1931. It was subtitled 'A Journal of Indian students abroad', and consisted of 48 well produced pages with a striking graphic on the cover. This was superseded in 1932 by *New Bharat: Voice of India's Revolt!* which the authorities considered banning from India because of its determinedly rebellious language. It later changed name once more to *Indian Front*—several copies of which survive—while remaining explicitly communist in outlook.

[47.] B.P.L. Bedi, 'The Nation's Response', *United India*, January-February 1932

[48.] Freda Houlston, 'Women in the Limelight', *United India*, March 1932

[49.] Olive Shapley, 'Women in India', *United India*, March 1932.

[50.] *Derby Evening Telegraph*, 24 August 1932, 19 July 1932.

51. 'Berlin to Punjab 1934-39' audio recording made by Freda Bedi c1976, BFA

3. Everything That Was Good in Us

1. *Oxford Mail*, 10 February 1933
2. *Isis*, 25 January 1933. The *Times of India* (4 July 1933) also reported that the 'wedding was a sequel to their joint interest in the Oxford University October Club'.
3. Sir Alfred Zimmern papers, 32 ff209-210, Bodleian Library, Oxford
4. Freda M. Bedi, *Behind the Mud Walls*, Lahore, [1943], p1
5. *Oxford Mail*, 21 June 1933
6. *Derby Evening Telegraph*, 7 March 1933, 21 June 1933
7. India Office Records, L/PJ/8/714
8. *Answers*, 26 December 1936—cutting contained in India Office Records, L/PJ/8/714, f126
9. A.S. Lall, 'Mixed Marriages', *United India*, December 1933.
10. Freda Bedi, *Behind the Mud Walls*, pp1-2
11. Freda Bedi to Olive Chandler, 16-17 August [1933], Bedi Family Archive (BFA)
12. 'Berlin to Punjab 1934-39' audio recording made by Freda Bedi c1976, BFA
13. Freda Bedi to Bhabooji, 5 October 1933, BFA
14. Freda Bedi to Bhabooji, 9 November 1933, BFA
15. B.P.L. Bedi interview transcript, Nehru Memorial Museum and Library (NMML), f176
16. Freda M. Bedi and B.P.L. Bedi (eds), *India Analysed*, vol. 3, London, 1934, dust jacket
17. *Tribune*, 22 September 1933
18. Brij Narain, 'The Rupee and the Pound', *India Analysed*, vol. 3, pp94-125
19. K.T. Shah, 'The Public Debt of India', *India Analysed*, vol. 3, pp126-163
20. The records of Victor Gollancz's publishing house, with rudimentary details of titles published, are held at the Modern Records Centre, University of Warwick. The print run for the first volume of *India*

Analysed was 1,500; it was 1,000 for subsequent volumes. Each was priced at five shillings (£0.25).

21. *Times of India*, 23 November 1934
22. *Tribune*, 28 June 1934
23. Benjamin Zachariah, 'Indian Political Activities in Germany, 1914-1945', in Joanne Miyang Cho, Eric Kurlander and Douglas T. McGetchin (eds), *Transcultural Encounters between Germany and India: Kindred Spirits in the Nineteenth and Twentieth Centuries*, Abingdon, 2014, pp141-154. Joachim Oesterheld, 'Lohia as a Doctoral Student in Berlin', *Economic & Political Weekly*, 2010, 45/40, pp85-91.
24. Leonard A. Gordon, *Brothers Against the Raj: A Biography of Sarat and Subhas Chandra Bose*, New Delhi, 1990, p275
25. Subhas C. Bose, 'India Abroad', *Contemporary India*, 1935, 1/3, pp317-27. Freda and B.P.L. Bedi, 'Subhas Chandra Bose Is Not a Fascist! A Refutation of Some Unfounded Accusations', *Contemporary India*, 1936, 2/3, pp379-83.
26. B.P.L. Bedi, 'The Hitler Youth, a Note on Organization', *Contemporary India*, 1935, 1/3, pp416-8
27. Abram L. Harris, 'Sombart and German (National) Socialism', *Journal of Political Economy*, 50/6, 1942, pp805-835
28. Freda M. Bedi, 'Fascism and War', *Contemporary India*, 1935, 1/1, pp131-5
29. 'Berlin to Punjab 1934-39' audio recording, BFA
30. 'Oxford' audio recording, BFA
31. *Tribune*, 28 June 1934. The correspondent was probably Tarachand Roy, who was also the academic teaching Freda Hindi.
32. 'Berlin to Punjab 1934-39' audio recording, BFA
33. Freda Bedi, *Behind the Mud Walls*, p2
34. 'Berlin to Punjab 1934-39' audio recording, BFA
35. B.P.L. Bedi interview transcript, NMML, ff60-62

4. Your People Shall Be My People

1. Freda Bedi, *Behind the Mud Walls*, Lahore, [1943], p7
2. *Tribune*, 12 August 1935—the book under review was Lothrop Stoddard's *Clashing Tides of Colour*. By the 'Great War' she meant the First World War of 1914-18.

3. Book of Ruth, chapter 1, verses 16-17
4. Freda Bedi, *Behind the Mud Walls*, pp3-4
5. Freda Bedi, *Behind the Mud Walls*, p5
6. Freda Bedi, *Behind the Mud Walls*, p14
7. Freda Bedi, *Behind the Mud Walls*, pp10-11
8. Freda Bedi, *Behind the Mud Walls*, p5
9. 'Berlin to Punjab 1934-39' audio recording made by Freda Bedi c1976, Bedi Family Archive (BFA)
10. B.P.L. Bedi interview transcript, Nehru Memorial Museum and Library (NMML), ff18-19; this anecdote is repeated, f71.
11. *Tribune*, 19 September 1935
12. B.P.L. Bedi interview transcript, NMML, f64
13. Freda Bedi to Olive Chandler, 5 March 1936, BFA
14. At this time there were 64 pice in an Indian rupee. 1d is the pre-decimal British penny—there were twelve pennies in a shilling and twenty shillings in a pound.
15. Freda Bedi to Olive Chandler, 2 December 1936, BFA
16. 'Berlin to Punjab 1934-39' audio recording, BFA
17. Freda Bedi, *Behind the Mud Walls*, p6
18. B.P.L. Bedi interview transcript, NMML, f177
19. Subhas C. Bose, 'India Abroad', *Contemporary India*, 1935, 1/3, pp317-27
20. Freda and B.P.L. Bedi, 'Subhas Chandra Bose Is Not a Fascist! A Refutation of Some Unfounded Accusations', *Contemporary India*, 1936, 2/3, pp379-83
21. B.P.L. Bedi, 'The Congress Comes of Age: The Task Before Us', *Contemporary India*, 1936, 2/1, pp1-9.
22. Freda and B.P.L. Bedi, 'Indian Socialism Must Decide! The Psychological Moment', *Contemporary India*, 1936, 2/2, pp185-90
23. Freda Bedi to Olive Chandler, 2 December 1936, BFA
24. B.P.L. Bedi said many years later that the journal continued for four years and had to stop when the administration became impossible—interview transcript, NMML, f179. The run of copies in the Bodleian Library at Oxford ends with the ninth issue.
25. *Voltaire's Fragments on India* translated by Freda Bedi, Lahore, 1937
26. Karl Marx, *Letters on India*, edited by B.P.L. and Freda Bedi, Lahore,

1936. This was published in December 1936 and by the end of the following month was in its third impression. I am grateful to Spencer Leonard for sharing with me his as yet unpublished article about the publication history of Marx's letters on India. He says the Bedis were 'the first to publish a substantial selection of Marx's writings on India'.

5. The Huts beyond Model Town

1. Jawaharlal Nehru to Freda Bedi, 19 February 1947, Bedi Family Archive (BFA)

2. B.P.L. Bedi interview transcript, Nehru Memorial Museum and Library (NMML), ff68-70

3. 'Berlin to Punjab 1934-39' audio recording made by Freda Bedi c1976, BFA

4. Freda Bedi to Olive Chandler, 1 and 31 March 1940, BFA

5. *Tribune*, 25 March 1938

6. Som Anand, *Lahore: Portrait of a Lost City*, Lahore, 1998, pp14-16. Som Anand, 'Briton's Search for an Ideal in India', *Tribune*, 4 March 1979.

7. Som Anand, *Lahore: Portrait of a Lost City*, Lahore, 1998, p16

8. *Times of India*, 25 March 1959. The translation into Urdu was by the poet Shamim Karhani.

9. Freda Bedi, *Rhymes for Ranga*, Noida, 2010

10. 'Berlin to Punjab 1934-39' audio recording, BFA

11. Freda Bedi to Olive Chandler, 1 July 1939, BFA

12. 'Berlin to Punjab 1934-39' audio recording, BFA

13. Zia Siraj interviewed by Andrew Whitehead at Hampton near London, 12 October 2016

14. Kumari Jayawardena, *The White Woman's Other Burden: Western Women and South Asia during British Colonial Rule*, London, 1995, p225

15. Rajni Kumar to Ranga Bedi and Kabir Bedi, 30 October [1996], BFA. Rajni Kumar became a prominent educationist in Delhi after Partition.

16. Rajni Kumar (nee Nancie Jones) interviewed by Andrew Whitehead at Raynes Park, London, 15 June 2016

6.   A Martyr Awaiting Execution

[1.] Shalini Sharma, *Radical Politics in Colonial Punjab: Governance and Sedition*, London, 2010, p65

[2.] Ian Talbot and Tahir Kamran, *Lahore in the Time of the Raj*, London, 2016, p145

[3.] B.P.L. Bedi interview transcript, Nehru Memorial Museum and Library (NMML), f34

[4.] Freda Bedi to Olive Chandler, 2 December 1936, Bedi Family Archive (BFA)

[5.] *Tribune*, 20 February 1936

[6.] The hall, built in 1900 and still (just about) standing, was named after Charles Bradlaugh, a British radical, republican, freethinker and Parliamentarian who attended the 1889 session of the Indian National Congress in Bombay. Bradlaugh had been a close political partner of Annie Besant prior to her embrace of Theosophy.

[7.] 'Berlin to Punjab 1934-39' audio recording made by Freda Bedi c1976, BFA

[8.] *Tribune*, 11 November 1936

[9.] B.P.L. Bedi interview transcript, NMML, ff75-80

[10.] 'Berlin to Punjab 1934-39' audio recording, BFA

[11.] *Tribune*, 10 June 1937

[12.] *Tribune*, 13 April 1937

[13.] *Tribune*, 21 May 1937

[14.] Audio recording of Freda Bedi's interview on the radio programme 'Frontiers of Consciousness', San Mateo, California, April 1974, BFA

[15.] *Tribune*, 31 December 1938

[16.] 'Berlin to Punjab 1934-39' audio cassette recording, BFA

[17.] B.P.L. Bedi, *Harvest from the Desert: the life and work of Sir Ganga Ram*, Lahore, 1940

[18.] 'Berlin to Punjab 1934-39' audio recording, BFA

[19.] *Hindustan Times*, 12 September 2000

[20.] B.P.L. Bedi interview transcript, NMML, f180

[21.] Bhisham Sahni, *Balraj My Brother*, New Delhi, 1981, pp55-56

[22.] Shalini Sharma, *Radical Politics in Colonial Punjab*, p95

[23.] Freda Bedi to Olive Chandler, 1 July 1939, BFA

24. *Tribune*, 19 February 1941
25. Freda Bedi to Olive Chandler, 1 July 1939, BFA

7.   Behind the Mud Walls

1. Shalini Sharma, *Radical Politics in Colonial Punjab: Governance and Sedition*, London, 2010, p89
2. B.P.L. Bedi interview transcript, Nehru Memorial Museum and Library (NMML), f188
3. *Tribune*, 5 December 1940
4. B.P.L. Bedi interview transcript, NMML, ff190-2.
5. Freda Bedi, *Behind the Mud Walls*, Lahore, [1943], p92
6. *Tribune*, 7 December 1940
7. *Mud Walls*, p92
8. *Tribune*, 21 July 1937
9. 'Berlin to Punjab 1934-39' audio recording made by Freda Bedi c1976, Bedi Family Archive (BFA)
10. *Tribune*, 21 February, 19 February 1941
11. *Mud Walls*, pp93-4
12. *Mud Walls*, pp94-5
13. This is the central event depicted in a twenty-three page potted biography in Hindi for younger readers—Manorma Dewan, *Freda Marie Bedi*, New Delhi, 2008. Manorma was Binder's wife. Ranga Bedi has memories of his mother hiding under a podium to evade the police, and then being able to deliver her speech before the police struggled through the crowd to make the arrest.
14. *Mud Walls*, p97. A topee is the old fashioned sun helmet associated with colonial officials in India. Old Bill is both a nickname for the British police and the name of cartoon character from a century ago, an ageing British soldier with an abundant 'walrus' moustache.
15. *Mud Walls*, pp98-9
16. *Tribune*, 22 + 23 February 1941; *Derby Evening Telegraph*, 10 May 1941
17. *Tribune*, 4 June 1941. 'Convict No. 3613' appeared in *Mud Walls*, pp98-147
18. *Mud Walls*, pp101-2

19. *Mud Walls*, pp137-8
20. *Mud Walls*, pp113-4,128
21. *Mud Walls*, pp105-6
22. *Mud Walls*, pp129-30,144
23. *Mud Walls*, pp144-5
24. *Tribune*, 25 May 1941
25. *Tribune*, 2 June 1941
26. *Mud Walls*, p146. A darshan is a viewing of a holy person or image
27. *Tribune*, 29 June 1941
28. *Tribune*, 10 August, 17 August 1941
29. *Tribune*, 17 November 1941. For an account of the Deoli camp by a communist detainee, see Sohan Singh Josh, *My Tryst with Secularism: An Autobiography*, New Delhi, 1991, pp238-41
30. Sharma, *Radical Politics in Colonial Punjab*, p99
31. B.P.L. Bedi interview transcript, NMML, f201
32. *Tribune*, 1 + 2 December 1941
33. Victor G. Kiernan, 'The Communist Party of India and the Second World War', in Prakash Karat (ed.), *Across Time and Continents: A Tribute to Victor G. Kiernan*, New Delhi, 2003.
34. B.P.L. Bedi interview transcript, NMML, f308
35. *Tribune*, 18 January 1942
36. *Mud Walls*, pp153-5
37. B.P.L. Bedi interview transcript, NMML, ff108-111
38. *Tribune*, 9 May 1942
39. *Tribune*, 6 May 1942. Ten lakh is a million.

8.   From a Woman's Window

1. 'Berlin to Punjab 1934-39' audio recording made by Freda Bedi c1976, Bedi Family Archive (BFA)
2. *Tribune*, 27 March 1936
3. *Tribune*, 24 May 1936
4. *Tribune*, 26 June 1938
5. *Tribune*, 10 July 1938
6. H.L. Chowdhari—personal communication, 11 August 2017—has memories of *Modern Girl*. He believes the distinguished Urdu writer

Krishan Chander, a leftist, was also involved in its publication, and that it was in part financed by M.R. Duggal, who also enlisted the Bedis to write for his magazine *Careers* and for the digests he published to help candidates in competitive examinations.

7. *Tribune*, 31 July 1938. A much shorter and more favourable review appeared in the *Times of India*, 2 September 1938.
8. *Tribune*, 31 July 1938
9. Freda Bedi to Olive Chandler, 1 July 1939, BFA
10. Freda Bedi, *Behind the Mud Walls*, Lahore, [1943], pp62-3
11. *Tribune*, 28 February 1943
12. 'Berlin to Punjab 1934-39' audio recording, BFA
13. *Tribune*, 18 October 1942
14. *Tribune*, 10 January 1943. The sick bed was Ranga's who had suffered from typhoid.
15. *Tribune*, 31 January 1943
16. *Tribune*, 14 February 1943
17. *Tribune*, 21 February 1943
18. *Tribune*, 28 March 1943
19. *Tribune*, 24 January 1943
20. *Tribune*, 28 June 1943
21. *Tribune*, 7 March 1943
22. *Tribune*, 8 November 1943. Freda would probably have known John Donne's poetic reference in a sermon, likening the human body to mud walls which slowly crumble away. 'O Holy Ghost, whose temple I Am but of mud walls, and condensed dust'.

9. Bengal Lamenting

1. The most widely accepted figure for the number of deaths caused by famine in Bengal in 1943-4 is about two million.
2. *Tribune*, 28 December 1943. 'At one of the meetings', according to the *Tribune*, 'Mrs Bedi made an appeal in Punjabi and over R[upee]s. 125 was collected in coins and notes thrown into her "jholi".'
3. Freda Bedi to Olive Chandler, 10 September 1944, Bedi Family Archive (BFA)
4. Freda Bedi, *Bengal Lamenting*, Lahore, [1944], p70

5. *Bengal Lamenting*, pp39-40

6. *Bengal Lamenting*, p6. Another powerful account of the suffering, published at about the same time, is Ela Sen, *Darkening Days, being a narrative of famine-stricken Bengal*, which included remarkable drawings by Zainul Abedin.

7. *Bengal Lamenting*, pp102-3, 108

8. Freda Bedi to Kabir Bedi, 19 January 1965, BFA

9. Freda Bedi to Olive Chandler, 21 December 1944, BFA

10. According to these figures, the bulk of the CPI's membership was in South India and Bengal. The Kisan Sabha was much stronger in Punjab, with 106,000 members out of a national total of 754,000. Palme Dutt's notes are in the archives of the Communist Party of Great Britain at the People's History Museum in Manchester—CP/IND/DUTT/11/01

11. Jack Houlston to Freda Bedi, 3 January 1946, BFA

12. Gene D. Overstreet and Marshall Windmiller, *Communism in India*, Berkeley, 1959, pp236-7

13. Pran Chopra interviewed by Andrew Whitehead, Delhi, April 2007

14. Rajni Kumar (née Nancie Jones) interviewed by Andrew Whitehead, London, 15 June 2016

15. Som Anand, *Lahore: Portrait of a Lost City*, Lahore, 1998, pp31-32

16. *Tribune*, 16 January 1947

17. Freda Bedi to Kabir Bedi, 19 January 1965, BFA

18. Jawaharlal Nehru to Freda Bedi, 19 February 1947, BFA. V.K. Krishna Menon was the London-based secretary of the influential and pro-independence India League and became India's first high commissioner in London.

19. These figures are based on the tentative findings of research conducted as part of Harvard University's India Partition Project

20. Freda Bedi to Olive Chandler, [1 December 1947], BFA. Barbara Castle had been elected as the Labour Member of Parliament for Blackburn in north-west England in 1945 and by this time had begun her ascent up the greasy pole of national politics.

21. *Derby Daily Telegraph*, 25 October 1948

22. B.P.L. Bedi interview transcript, Nehru Memorial Museum and Library (NMML), ff225-6

23. Zia Siraj interviewed by Andrew Whitehead, Hampton near London, 12 October 2016

24. Anand, *Lahore*, pp69-70

25. Anand, *Lahore*, pp76-77

26. B.P.L. Bedi made a pilgrimage to Sikh shrines in Pakistan in 1957 and he combined this with visits to friends in Lahore and Karachi.

10. Kashmir in Disguise

1. *Tribune*, 25 January 1941

2. Among other inter-racial marriages, R.C. Kak, reputed to be the first Kashmiri to serve as the maharaja's prime minister, had an English wife. Sheikh Abdullah married into the Nedou family, hoteliers whose origins lay in what is now Croatia.

3. B.P.L. Bedi interview transcript, Nehru Memorial Museum and Library (NMML), ff202-3

4. B.P.L. Bedi interview transcript, NMML, ff203-4

5. *Tribune*, 18 April 1943. The Mangla Bridge was opened in 1967.

6. Freda Bedi, *Behind the Mud Walls*, Lahore, [1943], p166. The women's singing took place in the small town of Thanna, or Thanamandi, on the Old Mughal Road north of Rajouri. *Tribune*, 10 + 17 May 1943.

7. Bedi, *Mud Walls*, pp172-3

8. Andrew Whitehead, 'The Rise and Fall of New Kashmir' in Chitralekha Zutshi (ed.), *Kashmir: History, Politics, Representation*, Cambridge, 2018, pp70-88; Sumantra Bose, *Kashmir: Roots of Conflict, Paths to Peace*, Cambridge, Mass, p50. Sehar Iqbal heard from the descendant of a National Conference leader that Freda Bedi was directly responsible for the emphasis on gender in 'New Kashmir'—though Freda herself made no such claim.

9. Sheikh Mohammad Abdullah, *The Blazing Chinar: An Autobiography*, Srinagar, 2013, p217

10. B.P.L. Bedi interview transcript, NMML, f262

11. Pran Nath Jalali interviewed by Andrew Whitehead, Delhi, 30 March 2007

12. Sheikh Abdullah, *Blazing Chinar*, p218

13. C. Bilqees Taseer, *The Kashmir of Sheikh Muhammad Abdullah*, Lahore, 1986, pp141,175; Peer Giyas-ud-Din, *Jammu and Kashmir State and Society: Communist Movement in Kashmir*, Jammu, 1999, p53

14. Freda Bedi to Kabir Bedi, 19 January 1965, Bedi Family Archive (BFA)

15. *Tribune*, 21 June 1946

16. Palme Dutt papers in the archives of the Communist Party of Great Britain in Manchester, CP/IND/DUTT/11 06 and 11

17. R. Palme Dutt, 'Travel Notes No. 5', *Labour Monthly*, October 1946

18. Margaret Bourke-White, *Halfway to Freedom: A Report on the New India*, New York, 1949, pp200-1

19. Sajida Zameer Ahmed interviewed by Andrew Whitehead, Srinagar, 18 June 2007

20. Som Anand, *Lahore: Portrait of a Lost City*, Lahore, 1998, pp21-22

21. Sheikh Abdullah to Freda Bedi, 2 October 1946, BFA

22. The invasion and response to it is recounted in detail in Andrew Whitehead, *A Mission in Kashmir*, New Delhi, 2007

23. *Times of India*, 8 November 1947. Srinagar's main square continues to be known as Lal Chowk or Red Square.

24. Sheikh Abdullah to Freda Bedi, 5 November 1947, BFA

25. Margaret Bourke-White, *Portrait of Myself*, New York, 1963, p272

26. Sir George Cunningham, Diary, 4 November 1947, MSS Eur.D.607/6, India Office Records. The other journalist would have been Lee Eitingon, the reporter who accompanied Bourke-White on her second visit to India.

27. Bourke-White, *Halfway to Freedom*, pp207-8

28. Bourke-White, *Halfway to Freedom*, p194

29. Bourke-White, *Halfway to Freedom*, pp200-1,211

30. Bourke-White, *Halfway to Freedom*, p40.

31. Vicki Goldberg, *Margaret Bourke-White: A Biography*, New York, 1986, p306

32. B.P.L. Bedi to Margaret Bourke-White, 5 September 1949, Margaret Bourke-White (MB-W) papers, Syracuse University

33. Margaret Bourke-White to B.P.L. Bedi, 22 March 1956—in the possession of Saba Dewan

34. B.P.L. Bedi to Margaret Bourke-White, 25 March 1959, MB-W papers

35. Margaret Bourke-White to B.P.L. Bedi, 3 June 1960, MB-W papers

36. Margaret Bourke-White to Mary Ritter, Bollingen Foundation, 13 November 1964, MB-W papers. Bourke-White did not refer to Bedi

by name in her autobiography, referring to him—misleadingly—as 'an Indian newspaperman friend who could translate'. She also made no direct mention of Frank Moraes. The photographs that she must have taken in Srinagar have not come to light. Only one, a portrait of Sheikh Abdullah included in *Halfway to Freedom*, appears to have been published.

11. A New World

1. *Poems by Faiz*, translated by Victor Kiernan, Lahore, 1971, pp122-7
2. Freda Bedi to Margaret Bourke-White, 5 January 1948, Margaret Bourke-White papers, Syracuse University. A reredos is an altarpiece or a religious decoration placed behind a church altar.
3. H.E. Bates's novel *The Scarlet Sword* was published in 1950—Bates himself never visited Kashmir. The raid on the mission and its aftermath is recounted in Andrew Whitehead, *A Mission in Kashmir*, New Delhi, 2007.
4. Khwaja Ahmad Abbas, *I Am Not an Island: An Experiment in Autobiography*, New Delhi, 1977, pp304-6; Andrew Whitehead, 'The People's Militia: Communists and Kashmiri Nationalism in the 1940s', *Twentieth Century Communism*, 2, 2010, pp141-168
5. *People's Age*, 23 November, 7 December 1947
6. This 1'35" Pathe 1948 newsreel entitled 'Kashmir Celebrates Independence' is, at the time of writing, available on YouTube. Freda Bedi appears after 27 seconds.
7. 'Family Bedi Newsletter: Christmas 1951', cyclostyled, 4ff, Bedi Family Archive (BFA)
8. Freda Bedi to Olive Chandler, 19 January 1949, BFA
9. Freda Bedi to Olive Chandler, 19 May 1949, BFA
10. Gandhi Jayanti on 2nd October marks the anniversary of Gandhi's birth. This would have been the first such commemoration after Gandhi's assassination.
11. C. Bilqees Taseer, *The Kashmir of Sheikh Muhammad Abdullah*, Lahore, 1986, pp24-5; Josef Korbel, *Danger in Kashmir*, Princeton, 1954, p254
12. Freda Bedi to Olive Chandler, 19 May 1949, BFA

13. B.P.L. Bedi interview transcript, Nehru Memorial Museum and Library (NMML), f231

14. Shanti Swarup Ambardar, personal communication—he believes this meeting was around 1948-50

15. B.P.L. Bedi interview transcript, NMML, ff233-5

16. B.P.L. Bedi interview transcript, NMML, ff263-4

17. B.P.L. Bedi interview transcript, NMML, f268

18. Sheikh Mohammad Abdullah, *The Blazing Chinar: An Autobiography*, Srinagar, 2013, p413

19. Jawaharlal Nehru to Sheikh Abdullah, 30 May 1949—*Selected Works*, 2nd series, vol 11, pp143-4

20. Jawaharlal Nehru to Sheikh Abdullah, 4 June 1949—*Selected Works*, 2nd series, vol 11, pp149-151

21. B.P.L. Bedi and Freda Bedi, *Sheikh Abdullah: His Life and Ideals*, Srinagar, [c1948]

22. B.P.L. Bedi interview transcript, NMML, ff236, 243

23. 'Family Bedi Newsletter: Christmas 1951', BFA

24. 'Family Bedi Newsletter: Christmas 1951', BFA

25. Michael Brecher interviewed by Andrew Whitehead by phone to Canada, 2 May 2015

26. B.P.L. Bedi interview transcript, NMML, f238

27. B.P.L. Bedi interview transcript, NMML, f270

12. Buddha and Baba

1. *Tribune*, 11 June 1939, 12 November 1944

2. Audio recording of Sister Palmo (Freda Bedi) on the radio programme 'New Dimensions' broadcast on KQED-FM, 1976, held by the Graduate Theological Union, California.

3. Letter to Olive Chandler, undated, Bedi Family Archive (BFA)

4. Audio recording of an interview with Sister Palmo (Freda Bedi) conducted by Olive Shapley, Sikkim, 1968, in the possession of Olive's son, Nicholas Salt

5. Audio recording of Freda Bedi's interview on the radio programme 'Frontiers of Consciousness', San Mateo, California, April 1974, BFA

6. Indira Gandhi to Freda Bedi, 8 December 1953, BFA

7. Freda Bedi to Olive Chandler, [? December 1954], BFA

8. Freda Bedi to Olive Chandler, 20 November [1957], BFA

9. B.P.L. Bedi was a founder member of the Friends of New Kashmir Committee established by Mridula Sarabhai—Nehru to Syed Ahmad, 21 May 1953, *Selected Works of Jawaharlal Nehru*, 2nd Series, vol 23, pp47-8. He also met foreign diplomats to discuss the situation in Kashmir—Sten Widmalm, *Kashmir in Comparative Perspective: Democracy and Violent Separatism in India*, London, 2002, p167

10. B.P.L. Bedi interview transcript, Nehru Memorial Museum and Library (NMML), f274

11. B.P.L. Bedi interview transcript, NMML, f278

12. Ranbir Vohra, personal communication, 9 January 2018

13. 'Lady of the Lotus', unpublished film proposal, 1985, BFA

14. Manorma Dewan interviewed by Andrew Whitehead, Gurgaon, 23 March 2016

15. Sister Palmo on KQED-FM, 1976

16. *Social Welfare*, February 1958

17. Tara Ali Baig, *Portraits of an Era*, New Delhi, 1988, p122

18. Freda Bedi to Olive Chandler, 20 November [1957], BFA

19. This 40-minute film entitled 'H.H. Dalai Lama Visit to India 1956-57' is currently available on YouTube—Freda Bedi, with Guli and Kabir, appears after fourteen minutes.

13.   Brave and Wonderful People

1. 'A Long Postscript ... on the Tibetans', Bedi Family Archive (BFA). This was a single sheet duplicated addition to Freda's end of year newsletter to friends dated 28 November 1960. It was based on a letter Freda had sent three months earlier to American Theosophists seeking support for Tibetan refugees.

2. Freda Bedi to Olive Chandler, 27 June 1960, BFA

3. 'A Poignant Journey's End: Refugees from Tibet Struggle to Sanctuary in India', *Life*, 1 June 1959; *Times of India*, 12 May 1959.

4. Lama Yeshe Losal Rinpoche interviewed by Andrew Whitehead, Samye Ling, Scotland, 9 November 2017

5. Ayang Rinpoche interviewed by Andrew Whitehead, Delhi, 8 April

2017; Ringu Tulku Rinpoche interviewed by Andrew Whitehead, London, 2 July 2016. For more testimony about the poor conditions and oppressive heat at Misamari, see Birgit van de Wijer, *Tibet's Forgotten Heroes: The Story of Tibet's Armed Resistance Against China*, Stroud, 2010

6. 'A Long Postscript', BFA

7. To Subimal Dutt:Alleged Corruption at Missamari, 3 December 1959—*Selected Works of Jawaharlal Nehru*, 2nd series, vol 55, p366

8. *Times of India*, 4 February 1960

9. Freda Bedi, 'With the Tibetan Refugees: in Misamari', *Social Welfare*, October 1960, pp73-77

10. Tom Grunfeld, *The Making of Modern Tibet*, London, 1987, pp188-9

11. Grunfeld, *Modern Tibet*, p191

12. Freda Bedi to Jawaharlal Nehru, 3 March 1960—*Selected Works*, 2nd series, vol. 58, pp409-11

13. S. Dutt to Jawaharlal Nehru, 28 March 1960—*Selected Works*, 2nd series, vol. 58, pp411-2

14. Freda Bedi to Nehru, 3 March 1960—*Selected Works*

15. *Times of India*, 16 April 1960

16. To N.R. Pillai: Welfare of Tibetan Refugees, 24 June 1960—Nehru, *Selected Works*, 2nd series, vol 61, pp516-7

17. Jawaharlal Nehru to Freda Bedi, 22 March 1960—*Selected Works*, 2nd series, vol 58, p313

18. To N.R. Pillai, 24 June 1960—*Selected Works*

19. Tara Ali Baig, *Portraits of an Era*, New Delhi, 1989, p123

20. Baig, *Portraits of an Era*, p119

21. Freda Bedi to Nehru, 3 March 1960—*Selected Works*

22. To S. Dutt: Education for Tibetan Refugees, 28 March 1960—Nehru, *Selected Works*, 2nd Series, vol. 59, p338

23. Apa Pant, *A Moment in Time*, Bombay, 1974, p66. Sikkim was absorbed into India in 1975, much to China's displeasure. Bhutan remains an independent monarchy, closely aligned to India.

24. Audio recording of Sister Palmo (Freda Bedi) on the radio programme 'New Dimensions' broadcast on KQED-FM, 1976, held by the Graduate Theological Union, California

25. John Powers, *Introduction to Tibetan Buddhism*, Ithaca, NY, 2007, pp399-432

26. Chogyam Trungpa, *Born in Tibet*, Boulder, 1977, p251. This account of Trungpa Rinpoche's upbringing and turbulent flight from Tibet was first published in 1966. His story is also recounted in Grant MacLean, *From Lion's Jaws: Chogyam Trungpa's Epic Escape to the West*, Mountain, 2016

27. MacLean, *From Lion's Jaws*, pp273-4

28. MacLean, *From Lion's Jaws*, pp281-3

29. Freda Bedi to Olive Chandler, 26 November 1960, BFA. Freda added that she was also learning Tibetan, though 'slowly'.

30. Kabir Bedi in 'Akong: A Remarkable Life' a documentary film directed by Chico Dall'Inha and released in 2017

31. Baig, *Portraits of an Era*, p123

32. 'A Long Postscript', BFA. At the time Freda wrote this note, in August 1960, she estimated that in total there were 26,000 Tibetan refugees in India.

33. Cited in Muriel L. Lewis, 'A profile of the life of the late Freda Bedi', an 8ff duplicated article circulated to members of the Tibetan Friendship Group, BFA

34. Grunfeld, *Modern Tibet*, p195

35. 'A Long Postscript', BFA

14. The Young Lamas' Home School

1. Audio recording of an interview with Sister Palmo (Freda Bedi) conducted by Olive Shapley, Sikkim, 1968, in the possession of Olive's son, Nicholas Salt

2. John Powers, *Introduction to Tibetan Buddhism*, Ithaca, NY, 2007, pp204, 234

3. Audio recording of Sister Palmo (Freda Bedi) on the radio programme 'New Dimensions' broadcast on KQED-FM, 1976, held by the Graduate Theological Union, California

4. Chogyam Trungpa, *Born in Tibet*, Boulder, 1977, p251

5. Freda Bedi to Olive Chandler, [? December 1961], Bedi Family Archive (BFA)

6. Lama Yeshe Losal Rinpoche interviewed by Andrew Whitehead, Samye Ling, Scotland, 9 November 2017

7. Lois Lang-Sims, *Flower in a Teacup: Volume Two of an Autobiography*, London, 1973, p167

8. Lois Lang-Sims, *The Presence of Tibet*, London, 1963, pp119-120

9. Lang-Sims, *Presence of Tibet*, pp125-6

10. Lang-Sims, *Presence of Tibet*, p128

11. Lang-Sims, *Presence of Tibet*, p139

12. *New York Times*, 14 January 1962. Lama Yeshe recalls that at one stage he and two other youngsters were confined to bed at Green Park with chicken pox.

13. Anita Plattner (née Morris) interviewed by Andrew Whitehead, London, 10 August 2017

14. Freda Bedi to Olive Chandler, [c1962], BFA

15. Tenzin Palmo, 'Mummy-la: The Life and Accomplishments of Freda Bedi' in Karma Lekshe Tsomo (ed.) *Eminent Buddhist Women*, New York, 2014, pp211-8

16. *Social Welfare*, May 1962

17. Kabir Bedi to Margaret Bourke-White, 14 April 1963, Margaret Bourke-White papers, Syracuse University

18. Anne E. Owen, *Parkfields Cedars, True to the End: The History of Parkfield Cedars Girls' Grammar School, Derby, 1904-1975*, Derby, [1999], p107

19. Cherry Armstrong, 'My Recollections of Sister Palmo', typescript, 5ff, 2016

20. Cherry Armstrong personal communication, 17 June 2017

21. Cherry Armstrong set down her memories of the Young Lamas' Home School in an unpublished book, 'Tibetan Tapestry'. I am very grateful to her for sending me extracts and permission to quote from them.

22. Armstrong, 'Tibetan Tapestry'

23. Armstrong, 'Tibetan Tapestry'

24. Freda Bedi to Olive Chandler, January 1963, BFA

25. Anita Plattner interviewed in London, 10 August 2017

26. Diana J. Mukpo, *Dragon Thunder: My Life with Chogyam Trungpa*, Boston, 2008, p72

27. Armstrong, 'Tibetan Tapestry'

28. Lois Lang-Sims, *Flower in a Teacup: Volume Two of an Autobiography*, London, 1973, p167

29. *Current* (Bombay), 28 September 1963

30. Both Cherry Armstrong and Freda's daughter, Gulhima, recall that Freda held Sangharakshita culpable. Alethea Ato also remembers the disdain Freda harboured for her fellow convert.

31. Sangharakshita, personal communications, 11, 13 and 14 September 2017

32. Sangharakshita, *In the Sign of the Golden: Indian Memoirs of an English Buddhist*, Birmingham, 1996, p323

33. Cherry Armstrong, personal communications, 12 and 15 June 2017

15. A Nun's Life

1. Audio recording of an interview with Sister Palmo (Freda Bedi) conducted by Olive Shapley, Sikkim, 1968, in the possession of Olive's son, Nicholas Salt. Hanna Havnevik, *Tibetan Buddhist Nuns: History, Cultural Norms and Social Reality*, Oslo, 1989, p37 cites the most authoritative estimate available, that there were about 27,000 nuns in Tibet prior to 1959 (of which almost 5,000 were in the Kagyu school) and a further several thousand nuns in the Tibetan tradition based in India, Nepal, Sikkim and Bhutan.

2. Tenzin Palmo, 'Mummy-la: The Life and Accomplishments of Freda Bedi' in Karma Lekshe Tsomo (ed.) *Eminent Buddhist Women*, New York, 2014, pp211-8. Tenzin Palmo earlier took the name Diane Perry.

3. Cherry Armstrong, 'Tibetan Tapestry'

4. Armstrong, 'Tibetan Tapestry'

5. Armstrong, 'Tibetan Tapestry'

6. Vicki Mackenzie, *Cave in the Snow*, London, 1999, p36

7. Mackenzie, *Cave in the Snow*, pp27, 35

8. Tibetan Friendship Group, English Newsletter, June 1965, Bedi Family Archive (BFA)

9. Muriel L. Lewis, 'A Profile of the Life of the Late Freda Bedi', [1977], circulated to the Tibetan Friendship Group, 8ff, BFA

10. Ato Rinpoche and Alethea Ato (née Martineau) interviewed by Andrew Whitehead, Cambridge, 14 September 2017

11. Shenpen Hookham interviewed on the phone by Andrew Whitehead, 23 August 2017

12. Havnevik, *Tibetan Buddhist Nuns*, pp88-89. This book looks in detail at

the history and functioning of the Tilokpur nunnery, which even thirty years after the Dalai Lama's flight from Tibet was one of only four exile nunneries established in India.

13. Havnevik, *Tibetan Buddhist Nuns*, pp85-126, 192

14. Tenzin Palmo, personal communication, 26 February 2016.

15. Freda Bedi to Renee Webster, 6 August [1966]. I am grateful to Pat and Gordon Cant, friends of Renee and her husband, for sharing this correspondence with me.

16. Sister Palmo (Freda Bedi) to Renee Webster, 20/27 July [1970]

17. The privately printed prayer booklet was entitled 'In Praise of the Triple Gem', and the note she inscribed at the end was dated 21 October 1971—in the possession of Steve Watson

18. 'The Last Days of Sister Palmo by Anila Pema Zangmo', typescript, 5ff, BFA

19. Interview with Sister Palmo (Freda Bedi) conducted by Olive Shapley, 1968

20. Maxine Elvey to her parents, 29 October 1966. Maxine wrote the letter from her next stop, Srinagar. The letter survives only because Maxine's mother typed it out to show to relations. I am grateful to Maxine Elvey for sharing this with me. Milarepa is renowned as one of the greatest figures in Tibetan Buddhism and is associated with the Kagyu school. His guru, Marpa, was a disciple of Naropa who in turn was taught by Tilopa—such spiritual lineages are deeply important in Tibetan Buddhism.

16.   Seeding the West

1. Ayang Rinpoche interviewed by Andrew Whitehead, Delhi, 8 April 2017

2. Audio recording of Freda Bedi's interview on the radio programme 'Frontiers of Consciousness', San Mateo, California, April 1974, Bedi Family Archive (BFA)

3. Audio recording of Sister Palmo (Freda Bedi) on the radio programme 'New Dimensions' broadcast on KQED-FM, 1976, held by the Graduate Theological Union, California

4. Lama Yeshe Losal Rinpoche interviewed by Andrew Whitehead, Samye Ling, Scotland, 9 November 2017

5. Nancy Cooke de Herrera, *Beyond Gurus: A Woman of Many Worlds*, Nevada City, Calif, 1993, pp317-322

6. Cooke, *Beyond Gurus*, pp323-4

7. *A Garland of Morning Prayers: In the Tradition of Mahayana Buddhism*, Tilokpur, 1970

8. Shenpen Hookham interviewed by phone by Andrew Whitehead, 23 August 2017

9. H.H. Gyalwa Karmapa to Cyril Silberbauer, 2 September 1971—I am very grateful to Samten de Wet for providing me with the text of this and other documents relating to Sister Palmo's visit to South Africa

10. Sheila Fugard, *Lady of Realisation: A Spiritual Memoir*, Bloomington, Indiana, 2012. *Tribune*, 5 December 1972. Personal communications from Samten de Wet, Cape Town.

11. *Natal Mercury*, 11 April 1972—cutting in BFA

12. Darrel Wratten, 'Buddhism in South Africa: From Textual Imagination to Contextual Innovation', PhD thesis, University of Cape Town, 1995, pp212, 366-7

13. Hanna Havnevik, *Tibetan Buddhist Nuns: History, Cultural Norms and Social Reality*, Oslo, 1989, pp45, 199

14. 'Bedi / Sister Palmo's Journey / Rangoon - Bangkok - Ordination in Hong Kong', audio recording made by Sister Palmo (Freda Bedi) , 1972, BFA

15. Vicki Mackenzie, *Cave in the Snow*, London, 1999, p74

16. Judith Simmer-Brown, 'The Prospects for a Bhiksuni Sangha in Tibetan Buddhism', in Damien Keown (ed.), *Buddhist Studies from India to America: Essays in Honor of Charles S. Prebish*, London, 2006, pp56-70; Havnevik, *Tibetan Buddhist Nuns*, p100

17. 'Frontiers of Consciousness' radio interview with Sister Palmo (Freda Bedi), 1974, BFA

18. Stephen Batchelor, *The Awakening of the West: The Encounter of Buddhist and Western Culture*, London, 1994, p105

19. 'USA tour / NYC - Syracuse - Vermont / Boulder - Colorado / Sister Palmo' audio recording by Sister Palmo (Freda Bedi), 1974, BFA

20. *New York Times*, 21 September 1974

21. Batchelor, *Awakening of the West*, p101

22. Sister Palmo (Freda Bedi) to Baba Bedi, 9 June [no year given], BFA

23. Fugard, *Lady of Realisation*, p44

24. Chime Rinpoche interviewed by Andrew Whitehead, London, 12 July 2016

25. Steve Watson interviewed by Andrew Whitehead, Bristol, 28 May 2015

26. Fugard, *Lady of Realisation*, p70

27. Sister Palmo (Freda Bedi) to Baba Bedi, 26 October [1976], BFA

28. Sister Palmo (Freda Bedi) to Olive Chandler, 5 December 1976, BFA

17. Sister and Mother

1. Seerat Narindra interviewed by Andrew Whitehead, Delhi, 24 March 2016

2. Saba Dewan interviewed by Andrew Whitehead, Gurgaon, 23 March 2016

3. Audio recording of Sister Palmo (Freda Bedi) on the radio programme 'New Dimensions' broadcast on KQED-FM, 1976, held by the Graduate Theological Union, California

4. 'Letter to Family / Jan 1975' audio recording by Sister Palmo (Freda Bedi), 1975, Bedi Family Archive (BFA)

5. Sister Palmo (Freda Bedi) to Kabir Bedi, 10 November [? 1968], BFA

6. Sister Palmo (Freda Bedi) to Pauline and Steve Watson, 17 December [? 1969]—in the possession of Steve Watson

7. Sister Palmo (Freda Bedi) to Kabir Bedi, 27 June 1971, BFA

8. Sister Palmo (Freda Bedi) to Baba Bedi, 14/15 September [? 1974], BFA

9. Kabir Bedi, personal communication, 21 December 2017

10. Sister Palmo (Freda Bedi) to Kabir Bedi, [undated but c 1963-4], BFA

11. Anderson Bakewell interviewed by Andrew Whitehead, Oxfordshire, 13 July 2017

12. Jim Robinson interviewed by Andrew Whitehead, Oxfordshire, 13 July 2017. Richard Bach's novella *Jonathan Livingston Seagull*, first published in 1970, is the story of a seagull as it learns about life on the wing and is regarded as a spiritual classic.

13. Lama Shenpen Hookham interviewed on the phone by Andrew Whitehead, 23 August 2017

14. Lama Jampa Thaye interviewed in London by Andrew Whitehead, 10 January 2018

18. Postscript

1. Sister Palmo (Freda Bedi) to Baba Bedi, 8 February 1976, Bedi Family Archive (BFA)

2. Sheila Fugard, *Lady of Realisation: A Spiritual Memoir*, Bloomington, Indiana, 2012, p58

3. Sister Palmo (Freda Bedi) to Olive Chandler, 5 December 1976, BFA

4. Saba Dewan interviewed by Andrew Whitehead, Gurgaon, 27 March 2017

5. Tara Ali Baig, *Portraits of an Era*, New Delhi, 1988, p124

6. Nathan Katz, personal communication, February 2017

7. *Tribune*, 4 March 1979

8. 'The Last Days of Sister Palmo by Anila Pema Zangmo', typescript, 1996 (based on an account set down in 1978), 5ff, BFA

9. *Tribune*, 4 March 1979

10. Tenzin Palmo, 'Mummy-La: The Life and Accomplishments of Freda Bedi', in Karma Lekshe Tsmo (ed.), *Eminent Buddhist Women*, New York, 2014, pp211-8

Acknowledgements

The biographer, however courteously he seeks to pursue his craft, is an intruder—asking impertinent questions and barging into the most private corners of the lives not only of his subject but of those close to them. I am grateful to Freda's children, Ranga, Kabir and Gulhima, for the kindness and forbearance they have shown to this interloper. Ranga and Umi Bedi in Bangalore and Kabir Bedi and Parveen Dusanj-Bedi in Mumbai have welcomed me into their homes and allowed access to their family papers. Guli Scales has also been unfailingly helpful in sharing her memories. I am grateful for their permission to reproduce and quote from family documents and from their mother's writings.

I have also benefitted from the kindness of other members of the Bedis' extended family. Manorma Dewan, the widow of Berinder Dewan, spoke of her memories of Freda, as did Saba Dewan, their daughter. Saba Dewan and Rahul Roy also shared with me a trove of family letters and photographs. Seerat Narindra welcomed me to the home in south Delhi where she grew up and where Freda's husband also lived when she was a child. Steve Watson, whose late wife Pauline was Freda's niece, showed me his marvellous assembly of photographs, letters and documents.

Nicholas Salt is the son of one of Freda's closest friends at Oxford, Olive Shapley. He still has the reel-to-reel tapes his mother recorded while visiting Freda in Sikkim and took the trouble to copy them for me. Sunandita Mehrotra was a diligent and resourceful researcher, combing through the lengthy transcript of an oral history interview with B.P.L. Bedi in the Nehru Memorial Museum and Library in Delhi. She also went to Chandigarh and trawled through the newly digitised archives of the *Tribune*, which—when based in Lahore prior to Partition—published regular articles by Freda Bedi. I am indebted to Harish Khare, then editor of the *Tribune*, for allowing access to these holdings and to Roopinder Singh and Sakshi Kundra for the trouble they took in enabling this.

Cherry Armstrong worked as a volunteer with Freda Bedi at the Young Lamas' Home School and wrote 'Tibetan Tapestry', an as yet unpublished account of her time in Dalhousie and Delhi. I am grateful to her for sending me extracts from her writings and permission to quote from them. Anita Plattner and Alethea Ato also recounted memories of working with Freda at Dalhousie and showed me photos from that time. Shenpen Hookham, a volunteer at the Tilokpur nunnery, similarly spared the time to talk to me, as did Lama Jampa Thaye, who met Freda during her visits to Britain in the 1970s. It has been a real pleasure to meet high lamas in Tibetan Buddhism who knew Freda, notably Ringu Tulku Rinpoche, Lama Yeshe Losal Rinpoche, Ayang Rinpoche, Ato Rinpoche and Chime Rinpoche. Anderson Bakewell revered Freda as a spiritual teacher and has taken the trouble to share his memories. Samten de Wet in South Africa has pointed me towards sources of information I would otherwise have overlooked. Jangchub Mary Jane in Canada kindly sent me documents relating to the 16th Karmapa's pathbreaking visit to North America and Europe in 1974.

I have been taken aback by the number of people who have got in touch, or responded to queries, with memories of Freda Bedi as a Buddhist—and photographs too. The wealth of material tells a story in itself. My thanks to Barbara Barnett, Pooja Bedi, David Cull, Dickey Lama, Maxine Elvey, Sheila Fugard, John Hills, Nathan Katz, Tenzin Palmo, Sangharakshita, John Skrine, Isaac Sobol and

Lama Karma Thinley Rinpoche. I am grateful to Pat Murphy and Jane Samuels for their kindness in guiding me to the right people and in sharing their own sense of Freda Bedi's role and impact.

Freda Bedi left Lahore more than seventy years ago, but I have been fortunate in meeting or making contact with people who knew her in those pre-Partition days, notably the late Pran Chopra, H.L. Chowdhari, Rajni Kumar, Zia Siraj and Ranbir Vohra. From her years in Kashmir, I am grateful for the recollections of Farooq Abdullah, Sajjida Zameer Ahmed, Agha Ashraf Ali, Suraiya Abdullah Ali, the late Shanti Swarup Ambardar, Michael Brecher, the late Pran Nath Jalali, Neerja Mattoo, Krishna Misri and the late Mahmooda Ahmed Ali Shah. In Freda's home city of Derby, Pat and Gordon Cant provided valuable help and information. Derby People's History both encouraged my research and offered a platform to speak about it, and I am grateful in particular to Marcus James and Keith Venables. I still hope, as does the family, that Freda will one day be recognised by a civic plaque on her Derby birthplace.

In Oxford, I was helped by Amanda Ingram, archivist at St Hugh's College; Lucy Rutherford, assistant archivist at Hertford College; and Alice Millea, assistant keeper at the University Archives. Nicholas Deakin allowed me access to an otherwise closed file—an extraordinary record of Oxford student communism in the 1930s—in Francois Lafitte's papers at Birmingham. Sumita Mukherjee pointed me in the direction of files in the India Office Records about the political activities of Indian students in Britain. David J. Stiver, special collections library at the Graduate Theological Union in California, sent me the audio of a radio programme. The Asia Research Institute at the University of Nottingham, where I am an honorary professor, awarded me a travel grant to help meet the cost of conducting research in India. And my thanks too for the help and encouragement received from Mahir Ali, Rakesh Ankit, Gerd Bausch, Rahul Bedi, Shobhana Bhattacharji, Urvashi Butalia, Naomi Canton, Felix Driver, Andreas Gebauer, Seema Iftikhar, Sehar Iqbal,

Nyla Ali Khan, Spencer Leonard, Chris Lethbridge, Jaya Mehra, Joachim Oesterheld, David Page, Judith Simmer-Brown, Ramesh Tamiri and David Taylor.

This idea of this book grew out of a chance conversation with a friend and publisher, Ravi Singh, and I am delighted that his imprint Speaking Tiger has seen it into print. My thanks to Aruna Ghose for the care with which she has seen this book to publication. Jim Anderson, who knew Freda and whose own spiritual journey was shaped by her, not only shared his memories but also read this book in draft form and offered valuable advice. Two friends of long-standing, Martin Plaut and Yasmin Khan, also read many of the chapters—I am grateful to them. Anuradha Awasthi, my wife and sternest critic, has scoured this book at various stages in its gestation, has helped mould it and has nattered me to complete it. She has been stoically understanding in allowing another woman into my life. This book is dedicated to her, with my love.

Bibliography

PRIVATELY-HELD ARCHIVES

Bedi Family Archive (BFA): letters, documents, photographs and audio recordings pertaining to Freda and B.P.L. Bedi in the possession of Ranga Bedi in Bangalore (Bengaluru) and Kabir Bedi in Mumbai

Documents relating to the 16th Karmapa's visit to North America and Europe in 1974 in the archives of the Dharma Centre of Canada

PUBLIC ARCHIVES

Bodleian Library, Oxford: Sir Alfred Zimmern papers

British Library: India Office Records, notably files relating to 'marriages between Indian and British' (L/PJ/8/714), the proposed prosecution of *Bharat* (L/PJ/12/252), the Communist Party of Great Britain (L/PJ/12/383), the Indian Progressive Writers' Association (L/PJ/12/499) and Freda Bedi's passport (L/PJ/11/16/5057)

Cadbury Research Library, University of Birmingham: Francois Lafitte papers

Derby Local Studies and Local History Library: Parkfields Cedars school magazine

Graduate Theological Union, Berkeley, California: recording of Sister Palmo (Freda Bedi) on the radio programme 'New Dimensions' broadcast on KQED-FM in San Francisco, 1976

Modern Records Centre, University of Warwick: Victor Gollancz collection

National Archive, Kew: security service papers relating to Frank Strauss Meyer

Nehru Memorial Museum and Library (NMML), Delhi: Transcript of an interview with B.P.L. Bedi recorded by Dr Hari Dev Sharma on 5 September 1969, 311ff

People's History Museum, Manchester: papers of Rajani Palme Dutt in the archive of the Communist Party of Great Britain

St Hugh's College, University of Oxford: college and tutors' records; holdings of college magazines including *The Imp* and *The Cygnet*

Syracuse University, New York: Margaret Bourke-White papers

INTERVIEWS

Ato Rinpoche and Alethea Ato (née Martineau)—Cambridge, 14 September 2017

Ayang Rinpoche—Delhi, 8 April 2017

Bakewell, Anderson—Oxfordshire, 13 July 2017

Bedi, Kabir—London, 17 November 2015; Mumbai, 18-20 March 2016

Bedi, Ranga—Bangalore, 20-22 March 2016

Brecher, Michael by phone to Canada, 2 May 2015

Chime Rinpoche—London, 12 July 2016

Dewan, Manorma (née Das) and Saba Dewan—Gurgaon, 23 March 2016 and 27 March 2017

Hookham, Shenpen by phone to North Wales, 23 August 2017

Lama Jampa Thaye—London, 10 January 2018

Kumar, Rajni (née Nancie Jones)—London, 15 June 2016

Mattoo, Neerja (née Dhar)—Gurgaon, 27 March 2017

Narindra, Seerat—Delhi, 24 March 2016

Plattner, Anita (née Morris)—London, 10 August 2017

Ringu Tulku Rinpoche—London, 2 July 2016

Robinson, Jim—Oxfordshire, 13 July 2017

Scales, Gulhima (née Bedi) by phone to the United States, 2 November 2015 and 1 April 2016

Siraj, Zia—London, 12 October 2016

Watson, Steve—Bristol, 28 May 2015

Lama Yeshe Losal Rinpoche—Samye Ling, Scotland, 9 November 2017

BOOKS, CHAPTERS AND PAMPHLETS BY FREDA BEDI

(with B.P.L. Bedi, editors) *Gandhi: der heilege und der staatsmann*, Munich: Ernst Reinhardt, 1933

(with B.P.L. Bedi, editors) *India Analysed*, London: Victor Gollancz, three volumes, 1933-4

(with B.P.L. Bedi, editors) *Karl Marx: Letters on India*, Lahore: Contemporary India, 1937

(editor and translator) *Voltaire's Fragments on India*, Lahore: Contemporary India, 1937

Behind the Mud Walls, Lahore: Unity Publishers, [1943]

Bengal Lamenting, Lahore: Lion Press, [1944]

(with B.P.L. Bedi) *Sheikh Abdullah: His Life and Ideals*, Srinagar, [c1948]

'Problems of Hill People in the North Himalayan Region', in *Social Welfare in India*, New Delhi: Planning Commission, Government of India, 1955

'Voluntary Social Service' in *Women of India*, New Delhi: Ministry of Information and Broadcasting, 1958

A Garland of Morning Prayers in the Tradition of Mahayana Buddhism, Tilokpur, 1970

Rhymes for Ranga, illustrated by Anna Bhushan, Noida: Random House India, 2010

BOOKS AND PAMPHLETS

Abdullah, Sheikh Mohammad, *The Blazing Chinar: An Autobiography*, translated from the Urdu by Mohammad Amin, Srinagar: Gulshan, 2013

Anand, Som, *Lahore: Portrait of a Lost City*, Lahore: Vanguard, 1998

Andrews, Geoff, *The Shadow Man: At the Heart of the Cambridge Spy Circle*, London: I.B. Tauris, 2015

Baig, Tara Ali, *Portraits of an Era*, New Delhi: Roli Books, 1988

Batchelor, Stephen, *The Awakening of the West: The Encounter of Buddhism and Western Culture*, London: Aquarian, 1994

Bausch, Gerd, *Strahlendes Mitgefühl: Das Leben des 16 Gyalwa Karmapa Rangjung Rigpe Dordje*, Neuauflage Darmstadt, Edition Karuna, 2017

(to be published in English as *Radiant Compassion: The Life of the 16th Gyalwa Karmapa Rangjung Rigpe Dordje*)

Bazaz, Prem Nath, *Daughters of the Vitasta: A History of Kashmiri Women from Early Times to the Present Day*, New Delhi: Pamposh, 1959

Bazaz, Prem Nath, *The History of Struggle for Freedom in Kashmir, Cultural and Political*, Srinagar: Gulshan, 2003, first published c1953

Bedi, B.P.L., *Harvest from the Desert: The Life and Work of Sir Ganga Ram*, Lahore: Sir Ganga Ram Trust Society, 1940

Bedi, B.P.L. (ed.), *Muslims in U.S.S.R.*, Lahore: Indian Printing Works, 1947

Bongsar, Sremo Tsodi, *Nangchen Sremo: The Story of Sremo Tsodi Bongsar from Nangchen and a Brief Recent History of the Bongsar Family*, Kathmandu: Vajra Books, 2009

Bourke-White, Margaret, *Halfway to Freedom: A Report on the New India*, New York: Simon & Schuster, 1949

Brown, Mick, *The Dance of 17 Lives: The Incredible True Story of Tibet's 17th Karmapa*, London: Bloomsbury, 2004

Castle, Barbara, *Fighting All the Way*, London: Macmillan, 1993

Chogyam Trungpa, *Born in Tibet*, revised edition, Boulder: Shambhala, 1977

Cooke de Herrera, Nancy, *Beyond Gurus: A Woman of Many Worlds*, Nevada City, Calif: Blue Dolphin, 1992

De'Ath, Wilfred, *Barbara Castle: A Portrait from Life*, London: Clifton Books, 1970

Dewan, Manorma, *Freda Marie Bedi* [in Hindi], Delhi: National Book Trust, 2008

Dhar, S.N., *Kashmir: Eden of the East*, Allahabad: Kitab Mahal, [1945]

Dharma King: The Life of the 16th Gyalwang Karmapa in Images, Woodstock, NY: KTD Publications, 2014

Douglas, Nik and Meryl White, *Karmapa: The Black Hat Lama of Tibet*, London: Luzac & Co, 1976

Fazili, Manzoor A., *Socialist Ideas and Movements in Kashmir (1919-1947)*, New Delhi: Eureka Publications, 1980

Fields, Rick, *How the Swans Came to the Lake: A Narrative History of Buddhism in America*, Boulder: Shambhala, 1981

Fugard, Sheila, *Lady of Realisation: A Spiritual Memoir*, Bloomington, Indiana: Balboa Press, 2012

Goldberg, Vicki, *Margaret Bourke-White: A Biography*, New York: Harper & Row, 1986

Grunfeld, A. Tom, *The Making of Modern Tibet*, London: Zed, 1987

Haksar, Nandita, *The Many Faces of Kashmiri Nationalism: From the Cold War to the Present Day*, New Delhi: Speaking Tiger, 2015

Havnevik, Hanna, *Tibetan Buddhist Nuns: History, Cultural Norms and Social Reality*, Oslo: Norwegian University Press, 1989

Jan, Asifa, *Naya Kashmir: An Appraisal*, Srinagar: Zeba Publications, 2006

Jayawardena, Kumari, *The White Woman's Other Burden: Western Women and South Asia during British Colonial Rule*, London: Routledge, 1995

Josh, Sohan Singh, *My Tryst with Secularism: An Autobiography*, New Delhi: Patriot Publishers, 1991

Karaka, D.F., *All My Yesterdays*, Bombay: Thacker & Co, 1944

Karaka, D.F., *The Pulse of Oxford*, London: J.M. Dent, 1933

Karat, Prakash (ed.), *Across Time and Continents: A Tribute to Victor G. Kiernan*, New Delhi: Leftword Books, 2003

Khanna, Meera, *In a State of Violent Peace: Voices from the Kashmir Valley*, Noida: HarperCollins India, 2015

Korbel, Josef, *Danger in Kashmir*, Princeton: Princeton University Press, 1954

Lang-Sims, Lois, *Flower in a Teacup: Volume Two of an Autobiography*, London: Andre Deutsch, 1973

Lang-Sims, Lois, *The Presence of Tibet*, London: Cresset Press, 1963

Levine, Norma, *The Miraculous 16th Karmapa: Incredible Encounters with the Black Crown Buddha*, Merigar, Italy: Shang Shung, 2013

Levine, Norma, *The Spiritual Odyssey of Freda Bedi: England, India, Burma, Sikkim, and Beyond*, Merigar, Italy: Shang Shung, 2018

Mackenzie, Vicki, *Cave in the Snow*, London: Bloomsbury, 1998

Mackenzie, Vicki, *The Revolutionary Life of Freda Bedi: British Feminist, Indian Nationalist, Buddhist Nun*, Boulder: Shambhala, 2017

MacLean, Grant, *From Lion's Jaws: Chogyam Trungpa's Epic Escape to the West*, Mountain, 2016

Martineau, Lisa, *Politics & Power: Barbara Castle, A Biography*, London: Andre Deutsch, 2000

Masani, M.R., *The Communist Party of India: A Short History*, New York: Macmillan, 1954

Moraes, Frank, *Witness to an Era: India 1920 to the Present Day*, London: Weidenfeld and Nicolson, 1973

Mukherjee, Sumita, *Nationalism, Education and Migrant Identities: The England-returned*, Abingdon and New York: Routledge, 2010

Mukpo, Diana J., *Dragon Thunder: My Life with Chogyam Trungpa*, Boulder: Shambhala, 2008

Selected Works of Jawaharlal Nehru, multi-volume, 1972 onwards

Overstreet, Gene D. and Marshall Windmiller, *Communism in India*, Berkeley: University of California Press, 1959

Owen, Anne E., *Parkfields Cedars, True to the End: The History of Parkfields Cedars Girls' Grammar School, Derby, 1904-1975*, Derby: Derby Heritage Series, [1999]

Perkins, Anne, *Red Queen: The Authorised Biography of Barbara Castle*, London: Macmillan, 2003

Powers, John, *Introduction to Tibetan Buddhism*, Ithaca, NY: Snow Lion, 2007

Queen, Christopher S. (ed.), *Engaged Buddhism in the West*, Somerville, Mass: Wisdom Publications, 2000

Rawlinson, Andrew, *The Book of Enlightened Masters: Western Teachers in Eastern Traditions*, Chicago: Open Court, 1997

Sahni, Bhisham, *Balraj My Brother*, New Delhi: National Book Trust, 1981

Sangharakshita, *In the Sign of the Golden: Indian Memoirs of an English Buddhist*, Birmingham: Windhorse Publications, 1996

Saxena, H.L., *The Tragedy of Kashmir*, New Delhi: Nationalist Publishers, 1975

Schwartz, Laura, *A Serious Endeavour: Gender, Education and Community at St Hugh's, 1886-2011*, London: Profile, 2011

Shapley, Olive, *Broadcasting a Life: The Autobiography of Olive Shapley*, London: Scarlet Press, 1996

Sharma, Shalini, *Radical Politics in Colonial Punjab: Governance and Sedition*, London: Routledge, 2010

Sobhrajani, Manisha, *The Land I Dream of: The Story of Kashmir's Women*, Delhi: Hachette India, 2014

Talbot, Ian and Tahir Kamran, *Lahore in the Time of the Raj*, London: Hurst, 2016

Taseer, C. Bilqees, *The Kashmir of Sheikh Muhammad Abdullah*, Lahore: Ferozsons, 1986

Thinley, Karma, *The History of the Sixteenth Karmapa of Tibet*, Boulder: Prajna Press, 1980

Tsomo, Karma Lekshe (ed.), *Eminent Buddhist Women*, New York: SUNY Press, 2014

Whitehead, Andrew, *A Mission in Kashmir*, Delhi: Viking Penguin, 2007

Zaheer, Sajjad, *The Light: A History of the Movement for Progressive Literature in the Indo-Pakistan Sub-continent*, Karachi: Oxford University Press, 2006

Zangmo, Gelongma Tsultrim, *Where the Bees Are There the Honey Is: A Memoir*, Dzalendara Publishing, 2014

ARTICLES

Copland, Ian, 'The Abdullah Factor: Kashmiri Muslims and the Crisis of 1947' in D.A. Low (ed.), *The Political Inheritance of Pakistan*, London: Macmillan, 1991, pp218-54

Cox, Laurence, 'Researching Transnational Activist Lives: Irish Buddhists and the British Empire', *Interface: A Journal for and about Social Movements*, 2016, 8:2, pp171-183

Misri, Krishna, 'Kashmiri Women down the Ages: A Gender Perspective', *Himalayan and Central Asian Studies*, 6:34, 2002, pp3-27

Simmer-Brown, Judith, 'The Prospects for a Bhiksuni Sangha in Tibetan Buddhism', in Damien Keown (ed.), *Buddhist Studies from India to America: Essays in Honor of Charles S. Prebish*, London: Routledge, 2006, pp56-70

Whitehead, Andrew, 'The People's Militia: Communists and Kashmiri Nationalism in the 1940s', *Twentieth Century Communism: A Journal of International History*, 2, 2010, pp141-168

Whitehead, Andrew, 'The Rise and Fall of New Kashmir' in Chitralekha Zutshi (ed.), *Kashmir: History, Politics, Representation*, Cambridge: Cambridge University Press, 2018, pp70-88

Zachariah, Benjamin, 'Indian Political Activities in Germany, 1914-1945' in Joanna Miyang Cho, Eric Kurlander and Douglas T. McGetchin (eds), *Transcultural Encounters between Germany and India: Kindred Spirits in the Nineteenth and Twentieth Centuries*, Abingdon: Routledge, 2014, pp141-154

ONLINE ARTICLES (all articles accessed 13 November 2017)

Ambardar, Shanti Swarup, 'Kashmir 1947 - Communists, *Qabailis* and the *Salamati Fauj*', http://www.andrewwhitehead.net/shanti-ambardar-kashmir-1947.html

Dewan, Saba, 'I wish today to write about my father', Hillele, 2014 https://hillele.org/2014/06/16/i-wish-to-write-today-about-my-father-saba-dewan/

Harris, Vin, 'Choje Akong Tulku Rinpoche', Beshara online magazine, 2017 http://besharamagazine.org/metaphysics-spirituality/vin-harris-choje-akong-tulku-rinpoche/

Lopez, Donald, 'New Age Orientalism: The Case of Tibet', Tricycle Magazine, 1994 https://tricycle.org/magazine/new-age-orientalism-the-case-tibet/

Misri, Krishna, '1947: A Year of Change', http://www.andrewwhitehead.net/krishna-misri-1947-a-year-of-change.html

UNPUBLISHED THESES AND WRITINGS

Gaur, Meenu, 'Kashmir on Screen: Region, Religion and Secularism in Hindi Cinema', PhD thesis, School of Oriental and African Studies, University of London, 2009-10

Iqbal, Sehar, 'Social Impact of State Development Policy in Jammu and Kashmir: 1948 to 1988', PhD thesis, UNESCO Madanjeet Singh Institute of Kashmir Studies, University of Kashmir, 2018

Kanjwal, Hafsa, 'Building a New Kashmir: Bakshi Ghulam Mohammad and the Politics of State-Formation in a Disputed Territory (1953-1963)', PhD thesis, University of Michigan, 2017

Wratten, Darrel, 'Buddhism in South Africa: From Textual Imagination to Contextual Innovation', PhD thesis, University of Cape Town, 1995

Ambardar, Shanti Swarup, 'Days of Destiny: A Memoir'

Armstrong, Cherry, 'Tibetan Tapestry'
Leonard, Spencer, 'Treasure Still Buried: Marx's writings in the New York
    Tribune with particular reference to those on India'

NEWSPAPERS AND JOURNALS

Contemporary India, Lahore, quarterly, 1935-7
Derby Daily Telegraph / Derby Evening Telegraph, daily, 1925 onwards
Isis, Oxford, weekly, 1931-3
Oxford Mail, daily, 1931-4
Social Welfare, Delhi, monthly, 1954-64
Student Vanguard, London, monthly, 1932-4
The Tribune, Lahore (later Chandigarh), daily, 1933 onwards
United India, London (later Oxford), monthly, 1929-34

Index

A TIME TO DANCE, NO TIME TO WEEP

Rumer Godden

'Ms Godden has a magical skill in conjuring up with a few suggestive details a veritable panorama of Indian life.'—*The New York Times*

'Vivid and perceptive...lambent with the sense of atmosphere and mood which characterises her novels...Above all, the book is bursting with images of the sights, scents, sounds and landscapes.'—*Birmingham Post*

In this sensitive and superbly crafted memoir, one of the foremost English-language authors of modern times, Rumer Godden, chronicles her early life in India and England. She paints a vivid picture of her childhood, in the early 1900s—in Narayangunj, a village in undivided Bengal, where her father worked with the Brahmaputra Steam Navigation Company—and her early forays into writing. She movingly recounts the pain of being forced to return to England to complete her education, and the horrors of being bullied by teachers and older girls in a convent; but also her joy at finding a mentor who encouraged her writing.

After her return to India in 1925, life continued to be tumultuous—she faced social censure for allowing Anglo-Indian children in her dance school in Calcutta; and her marriage with a stockbroker, Laurence Foster, was an unhappy one. The unexpected success of Rumer's first novel, *Black Narcissus*, left Laurence insecure and he deserted her and their two daughters. Rumer's courage and resilience shine through as she writes about her decision to pay off her husband's debts and to move to Kashmir with her daughters; there they lived in a houseboat till Rumer bought an abandoned house, and began making a living by selling vegetables and medicinal herbs from her garden. But just as they were getting used to life in Kashmir despite hostility from the locals, a catastrophe forced them to return to London.

Bursting with vibrant imagery and a love for life, *A Time to Dance, No Time to Weep* is an unforgettable account of the unconventional life of a celebrated writer and also of India under British rule.

A HOUSE WITH FOUR ROOMS

Rumer Godden

'The miniature in her books [contains], by reflection, the vastness of the world. This is surely the reason why her work has given so much pleasure to generations in many lands, and continues to do so.'—Anita Desai

'A born storyteller, Godden continues... to parlay her memories, both personal and literary, into a saga that is at once winning and self-revealing.' —*The Washington Post*

'[*A House with Four Rooms*] is as elegantly structured, the characters as memorable, as if the memoir were actually a novel.' —*Los Angeles Times*

Rumer Godden's follow-up to *A Time to Dance, No Time to Weep*—the evocative story of her childhood and adolescence in early twentieth-century India—*A House with Four Rooms* begins with her return to postwar England. With characteristic honesty, wit and elegance, Rumer describes the London of the 1950s and trying to make a living as a writer along with raising a family. Through her unwavering commitment to the pen and steadily growing fame, she paints a fascinating picture of the literary and film world that came to fete her. She tells stories of her many houses, and her quest for a room of her own.

She also recounts her travels to America, her time in India during the filming of *The River* with French director Jean Renoir, noting the presence of a young Satyajit Ray and almost falling prey to a misguided mob; the origins of her novels and their reception; and her relationship with James Haynes-Dixon, her second husband.

The record of an extraordinarily rich life keenly observed and brilliantly recorded, this autobiography is one to treasure.